THE BOYS *of* BATH

THE BOYS
of BATH

The Civil War Diary of
Pvt. Charles Brother, USMC

CHRISTINE FRIESEL

BLOOMINGTON, INDIANA

ISBN: 978-1-7362087-0-0 (softcover)
ISBN: 978-1-7362087-1-7 (ebook)
ISBN: 978-1-7362087-2-4 (hard cover)

Library of Congress Control Number: 2020923272
Printed in the United States of America

Published by Charley Brother, LLC
Bloomington, Indiana

For general inquiries contact Charley Brother, LLC
PO Box 68, Smithville, IN 47458-0068
www.charleybrother.com

FRONT COVER IMAGE
Great Naval Victory in Mobile Bay, Aug. 5th 1864; New York: Published by Currier
& Ives, 152 Nassau St., [1864?] Library of Congress.

END SHEET IMAGE
USS *Vanderbilt* (1862-1873) Line engraving by G. Parsons, published in *Harper's
Weekly*, 1862, depicting the ship at sea. U.S. Naval History and Heritage Command
Photograph. NH 58744

BACK COVER IMAGE
The Miriam and Ira D. Wallach Division of Art, Prints and Photographs: Print
Collection, The New York Public Library. "Battle of Mobile Bay." New York Public
Library Digital Collections.

"*Difficulties are the things that show what men are. Henceforth, when some difficulty befalls you, remember that God, like a wrestling-master, has matched you with a rough young man.*"

—Epictetus (*Discourses*, I-XXIV)

Charles Brother (U.S. Navy)

Contents

List of Illustrations

Images courtesy of the Library of Congress (LOC), Steuben County Historical Society (SCHS) of Bath, New York, and Naval History and Heritage Command (NHHC) are noted below in parenthesis as are images held in private collections. Those without credit are in the author's collection.

1. Morris Street in Bath, NY, 1857 (LOC)
2. Brother Home in Bath, NY
3. Cornelia and Rebecca Brother (Marjorie Peterson)
4. Pratt Homestead in Prattsburgh, NY
5. Joseph P. Faulkner
6. William A. Hess, Navy cadet
7. William E. Howell
8. Pvt. "Dora" Harris, USMC (Adrienne Sachse)
9. Pvt. John Murdoch, USMC (Claudia Boggs)
10. Pvt. Vep Darling, USMC
11. Pvt. Josiah C. Gregg, USMC (Adrienne Sachse)
12. Cpl. Miles Oviatt, USMC (Adrienne Sachse)
13. USS *Vanderbilt* (NHHC, NH 58744)
14. Capt. John A. Winslow, USN (NHHC, NH 42384)
15. Lieut. Percival C. Pope, USMC (NHHC, NH 85788)
16. Pvt. George Bandfield, USMC (Troy Hillman)
17. George Washington stopped at Brother's Tavern (LOC)
18. Rear Adm. Theodorus Bailey, USN (NHHC, NH 56066)
19. Rear Adm. Hiram Paulding, USN (NHHC, NH 88387)
20. Valentine Brother (Marjorie Peterson)
21. Commodore Nutt, Minnie Warren, Giant, Tom Thumb (LOC)
22. Adm. Porter, USN, and Gen. Meade (LOC)
23. Fort Hamilton (LOC)

WHEN SHIPS COME IN

---

by Frances "Fannie" Brother Toyne

NEWS ITEM:

"Elderly Eccentric Disappears. Thought Drowned."

You say you're a Reporter,
And have called to ask me why
I'm telling everybody,
Your News Item, was a lie?

You never knew my Grandad,
So of course you cannot see,
That the Facts, as you have printed them,
Just aren't facts, to me.

For Granddad was strictly honest,
Still, I couldn't hardly see,
How I'd ever be rewarded,
Surely he could not help me.

Can't you see him sit and wonder,
How he'd ever get along,
If it wasn't for his grandchild?
All his life, things had gone wrong.

Can't you hear him ever saying,
"When you need a helping hand,
Why as long as God will spare me,
I am your child to command."

How he loved to sit and visit;
Even now I hear him say,
"I've a Ship, my little daughter,
And it's not so far away,

"When my Ship comes into harbor,
I'll be rich, and grand and free,
And it's then I will repay you,
For your goodness, dear, to me."

Still, I never thought that Granddad
Meant just all he ever said,
For he sometimes acted queerly,
And had trouble with his head,

And then the Doctor, when he'd come,
To comfort me would say,
"The old man's getting childish."
He was childish, in a way.

This Ship of his tho really came,
He met it at the shore,
And 'twas his Lord and Master,
He fell prostrate before.

I can't explain just how 'twas done,
This fact alone seems plain,
His Ship took Granddad past the vale,
Left me to mourn in vain.

And now, sometimes, when skies are dark,
There isn't any blue;
And in my utter loneliness,
I scare know what to do.

I pray and wish Granddad were here,
As in the days of old.
'Tis then he whispers in my ear,
Things that I have never told.

It seems as Granddad entered into Heaven,
Saint Peter stood within,
And said, "You get your dearest wish now,
Hurry up, begin."

And Sir, my Granddad spoke right up,
For once he wasn't slow,
And he said, "Make me an Angel, please,
And let me go below.

You see, I left a grandchild there,
Who'll grieve more than the rest,
So let me help to smooth her way.
And show her what is best.

He's paid his debt a thousand fold,
And I'd ungrateful be,
If I kept still about this thing,
Between Granddad and me.

I know now that he's living,
For he helps me some each day,
And he's happy; and my heart somehow,
Is lighter, in a way.

You still insist, there was no Ship?
Why Granddad saw it there,
And he was strictly honest,
So I don't need to care.

I've given you his story,
So Granddad would get fair play.
For he saw his Ship and met it;
And there's not much more to say.

And the reason he left
His hat and watch upon the shore,
Was this: he knew that Over There
They reckoned Time no more.

He saw his Ship approaching,
And God's banner floating high,
He doffed his hat and fell prostrate,
With, "Master, here am I."

So please print this Correction:
"An Old Man's Ship Comes In;
A Broken man; with luck so bad,
Death had to help him win."

Leave out the word, "Eccentric,"
I'll repay you if you do,
And when I get my dearest wish,
I'll minister to you.

Introduction

My great-grandmother Fannie was a private person, sharing little personal information, even with her own family. The only detail I knew about her childhood was that her earliest memory was of being thrown out a window—no further explanation about that either. In her poem, "When Ships Come In," she responded to the news headline that reported the death of her father, Civil War veteran Charles Brother, perhaps from the view of her own daughter. At the time of Brother's death at age seventy-three in 1917, he was living with Fannie and her family in Indiana. After Fannie's death in 1962, the poem was found by her daughter, Peg, among a small pile of writings. No one in the family knew what to make of it. Fannie had a regular outlet for her poetry in the early 1900s in a local newspaper under playful pseudonyms, however I found no evidence that this particular poem was ever published. My grandmother, Peg, knew so little about her mother's past that she was not even able to complete Fannie's death certificate, guessing incorrectly her city of birth, and writing "unknown" for Fannie's parents' names.

In 2009 my mother was moving out of the old family home. In a neglected part of the basement, she found Charles Brother's first Civil War diary. *Did I want it?*

I thought I'd struck gold. A librarian, I fired up my wheelhouse tools. I looked in museum and university archives. I discovered personal narratives, letters, photos, poetry, lists, newspaper articles, obituaries, pension records, and oral histories of those who served with Brother.

I had no idea that a ten-year process of further researching the life of my great-great-grandfather and "the boys" of Bath, New York, would not only reveal the remarkable experiences of Civil War Marines who had a firsthand role in American history, but would expose details that my great grandmother didn't want anyone to know. Surprising to me, in retrospect, was my own impulse to leave out Brother's references to "the feelings."

Charles Brother wrote often about the weather in his Civil War diaries, and I overlooked these ordinary reports at first. I focused instead on the prize: the famous people, the historical events, the war-time thrill in the pursuit of the enemy, the tragic end of Brother's life, and even the source citations. But disregarding the weather in a story about a Marine is missing the point. Proper respects must be paid to the man standing up in the punishing elements, his frozen beard, and his rheumatism. How on earth does a man rise daily to check the elements, document them, and then greet the ordinary, the unknown, the slaughter, the storms, the fog—and have a pleasant time of it, not bending to regret, emotion, or impressions, but standing guard for his brother, staying in his lane or bloody ditch?

Children of a vet with PTSD are in that ditch a lot. So when Fannie shoved the past under her bed, she was following the old regimen she learned as the daughter of a Marine and as a resident of an orphanage. She did what she was told, but reserved a few tricks too. She jerry-rigged her stuff and knew when her bunkmates had been in her business. When her loneliness got the best of her, she gave way to seasonal tears, and fell asleep on guard duty. Sometimes, *thank the Lord in Heaven who makes the rain, Jesus Holy Christ*, things got so wet that she wrote poetry. And every single day, she dressed up, made sure there was pie, and kept going.

In Fannie's poem about her father, she said that he was "strictly honest." Yet the more I learned about Charles Brother, the more I questioned my family's oral history. Fannie had a close relationship with her father. She managed his papers and dealt with his devastating end. But furious with the reporters on her porch, Fannie apparently cut off his story. So I begged the ghosts, *Tell me the truth about this person. Just give it to me. I can throw a punch and make a correction.*

But the Marine on my right and the poet to my left made it clear by their silence that I would have to learn the hard way. The art of debate about inclement weather or the horrors of the sea is still a rite of passage to earn a seat at that "liar's bench" where the old guys sat and told tales. I had to put in the time—a decade—to discern the actual details and prove I cared more about the truth than a glittery prize.

Charley Brother was someone to wrestle with, his real story hard to crack. I sought the advice of David M. Sullivan, an expert and author of several books on *The United States Marine Corps in the Civil War*. Sullivan generously showed me the ropes and introduced me to all "the boys," giving me access to more personal manuscripts written by Brother's shipmates. I began making annotations to Brother's diary and fell into the nineteenth century and all its minor moments. I reveled in the information. I thought I knew a thing or two about companionship, but I learned more about that getting to know "the boys" of Bath.

As a kid, Charley Brother liked to watch over things and run around, something he was known for in his hometown of Bath, New York. Being confined on a ship might cramp his legs, but sticking with his friends, the other boys in Steuben County, was his plan. He wanted to be with them when they intercepted and won a prize ship full of cotton. He wanted to be brave like his hero, George Washington. Brother loved to play with toy soldiers and hear about military history, but he hungered for the best parts: *the action*. When he was eight, Charley and the boys ran to watch the Bath Artillery Company. Led by former officers from the Mexican War, the company drilled with two brass cannons and a six-pounder field gun. Later in life one of Charley's childhood friends said that all the neighborhood boys planned on joining the company; they knew its marching cadences by heart.

On October 13, 1862, Charley Brother awoke early in a Brooklyn Hotel. I imagined the restless eighteen-year-old staring out his window, fixated on the downpour outside with his back to his unmade bed, still warm. As he watched an impromptu river form in the street below, his eyes followed its muddy line beyond the foggy city. Merchants, ships, and cargo were all coming and going. In his head was a sea of complicated feelings, comings and goings, as well—voices of his parents, two older brothers, four sisters, aunts, uncles, servants, Old Man Howell, and the boys in the neighborhood telling him what he should do. No doubt he rushed against the rain to the Brooklyn Navy Yards—excited and breathless. He was really going to do it. He was going to enlist. He was going to be a Marine.

On that day, he leapt toward adventure and into American history. Brother fought under Admiral Farragut at the Battle of Mobile Bay. He was there as Farragut started the battle with a column of confident ships.

Out in front were some ironclads, including the brand-spanking-new and long-awaited *Tecumseh*, followed by the steamer USS *Brooklyn*, which was followed by the flagship USS *Hartford*. The *Tecumseh* struck a torpedo mine, exploded, and sank. The USS *Brooklyn's* captain, in horror, ordered his ship to back up, delighting the enemy. Brother was there when Farragut was reported to have cried out, "Damn the torpedoes, full speed ahead!," ordering his flagship to the front. His men had to straighten out the twisted column of ships, having just witnessed the damage the torpedoes had done to their brothers, now with their blown-to-bit parts bobbing against the torrents.

Brother was there the day before with the sailors putting away miscellaneous gear and extra sails as if they were clearing the table for a strong-arm wrestling contest. They gave her deck a coating of sand so that the fighting men could get a grip against the running flesh (the deck would be wet with bloody gore that could compromise performance). In the stifling August humidity, the boys focused on holding their guns and helping their friends who might at any moment be decapitated by a flying bulwark, piece of deck floor, or a passing shell. They saw "windage," what happens when a man's skin is blown off, exposing internal organs, some still pumping, leaving only a bucket for a coffin. Brother described the scene as a slaughterhouse.

But the sailors were able to straighten out the line again, elongating the arrow of determination, and complete the plan that captured Fort Morgan and Fort Gaines. Those actions cut off the enemy's supplies, contributing to the end of the Civil War.

The night after the battle, Brother had trouble sleeping. He could not escape the stench. He was relieved when finally assigned to go ashore to inspect the burning fort. Having spent months on the ship, he found it hard to walk on the beach. A few weeks later, when time was allowed, he went for a swim and gave himself a thorough rinse.

Like the cavalry and infantry, sailors experienced the same limited supplies, annoying personalities of their bunkmates, poor training, death, and disease. However, the Marines and their shipmates had to do all this while wrestling with another adversary—the sea. Under confinement on the ship, loading and burning coal, breathing gun powder or the fumes of lead paint, and drinking questionable water, the boys bonded under pressure in more ways than one. The ship rolling and pitching in a hurricane, the boys clung to wet wood and spun around, never knowing if a storm or a shot would do them in.

Tightly packed, sleeping in hammocks, and standing close to their officers, the few Marine guards set in their tattoos a fierce loyalty and rigid culture of law and order. No one was going to rock the boat or waste supplies. There was no place to hide. This transparency, this authentic lifestyle, paved the way for trust that was essential to survive the coming melee: the ship would be disciplined; the country would have this correction.

After the war, Brother moved to Iowa to farm. He eventually sought and found work where he replicated these condensed and dangerous conditions as a railroad postal clerk. Hungry for the rocking and still immune to motion sickness, Brother returned to a system that would not stop for bad weather. He could deal with the weather. What he could not cope with was the stopping, the isolation, and not having something to watch over or study. He landed a highly competitive, plumb job working alongside veterans, including one who had been a prisoner of war. When not on the rail for his new boys, Brother was on the rail for home, steaming back to Bath. Ever restless, brisk, uncomfortable, and responsible, Brother was better with his kind. But he suffered difficulties, including his old adversary, "the feelings."

Brother and the boys of Bath preferred action: *Acta non verba*. (Actions not words)—the eventual motto for the United States Merchant Marine Academy. As I came to love the boys, I believed them to be sincere: men show us who they are by their actions, not words. As a writer I found it hard to accept the inadequacies of words, but I will be eternally grateful for the boys giving me a proper education. They wrote when nothing else was going on, but they wrote. Brother was a prolific, methodical correspondent.

Brother's words provide a portrait of a hero's journey. From his happy childhood, he leapt into adventure. He and his friends went through hell and out the other side, making sacrifices as required. Charley Brother, the boys, and their officers deliver an intimate, little-known version of the Civil War, and not all was fighting. During liberty hours, Brother became a tourist, walking great distances in New York's Five Points, Brooklyn, Manhattan, Boston, Yale College, and the tropics. He chased down Mary, his childhood sweetheart now living in the city, even frustratingly missing her because of the poor communication as she hurried to the barracks to see him.

My brother John asked if our ancestor was some sort of Forrest Gump. Our ancestor did touch the famous landmarks, events, theaters, and shirt tails of history-makers. Brother did, like Forrest, provide a tour of his country splitting apart and coming together. But it was when Brother introduced me to "the boys" that I became attached. Brother's story was about fraternity. And some of the boys did not get their proper taps.

Ingersoll died young with no offspring. Angus had no children and died penniless with the estate administrator instructing the courts that our pathetic Marine only owned a jackknife and the clothes on his back. Wilcox died in a mental ward, suffering from "nervous prostration." Johnson's family, especially the women, were embarrassed for his lack of business sense, even though he was a skilled writer and landscape artist. Drayton died with no heirs soon after the war ended, changing his will on his deathbed, leaving his fortune to his brother, a Confederate naval officer. Towle's shoes had to have a hole cut out for his big toe, which occasionally flared up from that time a shell dropped on it. Others were dismissed as eccentrics. Most were deaf. Some issued no sons to keep the military lore alive, but only daughters, who, while they may have preserved the letters and diaries, had no interest in the same here-we-go-again stories of the glory days, especially after debating the right to vote, temperance, or cigar ashes on the oriental rug. Many Marines died too young to have their heroic stories recorded and, if they were preserved, there was no appetite for battle scenes or war romancing. The world was busy with the Great Depression, the next war, new PTSD, protests. The audience had had enough of reality and were happy to have Disney or Hallmark.

But Brother and the boys had the prize all along, even up to the end—what a comfort to know what something real looks like. The love for freedom and your brothers makes you want to be the first to fight, makes you a good companion. Several moments of greatness occurred in the midst of that famous battle, including song, but nothing more shiny than watching Admiral Farragut climb up into the ropes above his men and the smoke, removing obstacles to see the devil more clearly, steering them into the path of the torpedoes, and holding steady to increase the light of God on the bloody truth that the obstacle is the way.

The Boys of Bath

When you can find your sea legs through the monotonous logs, you may be forever moved, as I was, to hold their glory days steady, in a right angle, upward, turning them, as a poor boy might do upon digging out a muddy coin or dented trinket embedded in the soil, allowing it with its apparently used-up time to have another pass under the sun. A little late, I know, but still a prize.

Service Chronology of Charles Brother, USMC

1862	Oct 13	Enlisted at Marine Barracks, Brooklyn Navy Yard
	Nov 4	Transferred to USS *Vanderbilt*
	Nov 6	Searched for CSS *Alabama*
1863	Jan 4	USS *Vanderbilt* touched at Havana, Cuba
	Jan 13	USS *Vanderbilt* at St. Thomas
	Feb 25	USS *Vanderbilt* took Steamer as prize, the *Peterhoff*
	Feb 26	Assigned to take *Peterhoff* (prize)
	Mar 28	Arrived with *Peterhoff* in New York
	Mar 31	Assigned to Brooklyn Navy Yard
	Jun 6	Transferred to the USRS *North Carolina* in New York Harbor
	Jul 25	Assigned to Brooklyn Navy Yard
	Aug 3	Returned to USRS *North Carolina*
	Dec 15	Transferred to USS *Hartford*
1864	Jan 5	USS *Hartford* departed from New York
	Jan 17	USS *Hartford* arrived in Pensacola, Florida
	Jan 19	USS *Hartford* sent off to tour to New Orleans
	Feb 9	USS *Hartford* sent back to Pensacola, Florida
	Dec 20	Assigned to Marine Barracks, Brooklyn New York
1865	Jan 22	Furloughed
	Feb 9	Assigned to Marine Barracks, Boston, Massachusetts
	Oct 21	Honorably discharged (furnished substitute)

A Note About the Diaries

Before Brother's first ship assignment, his father encouraged him to use a diary for entertainment, unaware that his boy was already keeping one. Charles Brother kept three known diaries during the Civil War. The first diary is available in original format, in my possession, with some erasures. The original second (middle) diary, covering the 1864 Battle of Mobile Bay, is at the University of South Alabama (Smith, 1964), and has some erasures and some blank pages. A third original diary remains lost. Typed fragments of the first and middle diaries were found in our family home and are in my possession. Though no name is added to confirm who created this record, the typing appears to match the type-written poetry written by Fannie, a writer of drive and discipline. I believe that Fannie made the effort to decipher and transcribe her father's handwriting in the three diaries that were once in her possession.

Two years after Fannie died, a young historian, C. Carter Smith, Jr., originally from Mobile, Alabama, was launching a publishing career in Chicago, and he included Brother's middle diary in his book, *Two Naval Journals 1864: The Journal of Mr. John C. O'Connell, CSN, on the C.S.S. Tennessee, and The Journal of Pvt. Charles Brother, USMC, on the U.S.S. Hartford at the Battle of Mobile Bay*, (Chicago: Wyvern Press of S.F.E., Inc. 1964). Smith's mother, who helped establish the Historic Mobile Preservation Society, was connected to this project, but I was unable to confirm how Brother's second diary ended up in Mobile.

In 1971 the U.S. Navy published that same text and photo used by Smith with the help of military historians who provided basic annotations. They flagged it significant because Brother's diary captured life as a guard on the USS *Hartford*. The editors must not have known of the other diaries, because they wrote, "During the cruise of more than 3,500 miles, perhaps the only incident he [Brother] would have found worthy of recording had he maintained a journal at this time would have been a minor collision with the British bark *Symmetry* on the 15th." (U.S. Navy, 1971)

When the Marine Corps published a diary in 1975 of Frank L. Church, USMC, they referenced Brother's diary, noting it as "the only acceptable writing, yet found, by a Marine Corps enlisted man of his Civil War experiences." (Church, 1975)

A transcript of all three diaries is held by Indiana University's Lilly Library, which also includes a revised transcript of the middle diary. I determined that Fannie created the transcript held by Indiana University when I found a similar typed version of the second diary in a box in the family home, which also contained Fannie's poems, letters, and short stories.

None of these versions match identically, but all have vague provenance. Some transcripts have added detail, suggesting changes for readability. In some cases, personal information was erased from the original, perhaps to protect privacy or reduce distractions for military historians. For example, the original diary reads, "Emma W," but the transcript says, "Emma Wilson." This indicates that someone typed the diaries and then erased personal information from the originals. Text was changed to modernized conventions ("&c" to "etc.") and parentheses were inserted about ships and surnames to individual officers mentioned originally only by rank. I believe that Fannie may have worked with her father to prepare the material for publication.

I have added further context with my own annotations in brackets, and every effort has been made to include the most accurate diary entries made by Brother from the versions in my own possession and the most complete transcript at Indiana University. Ninety percent of Brother's service days (about a thousand entries over three years) record his activities and performance, even if some are merely hash-mark days (or weather reports).

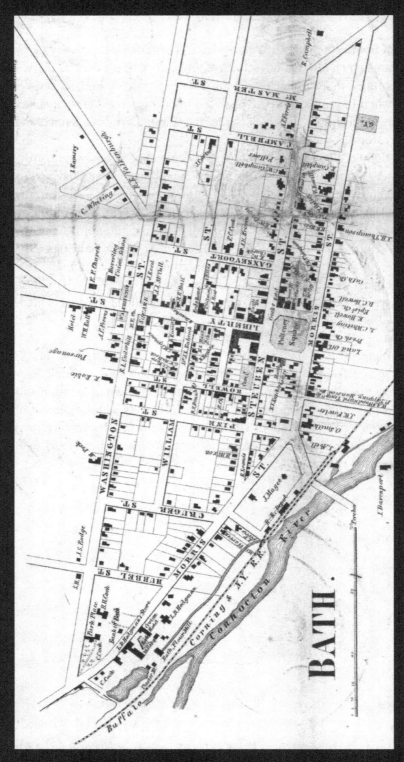

1. Morris Street in Bath, NY, 1857. Library of Congress

CHAPTER 1

The Brother Family

Charles Brother was born August 10, 1844 to Henry and Mary Ann Brother. The family called him Charley. The following June, he was baptized at St. Thomas Episcopal Church. His godfather was Hiram R. Hess, a clothing merchant, justice of the peace, and their neighbor on the south side of Morris Street.

The Brothers' ancestors arrived early in the Finger Lakes region of New York, surveying the lands and opening stores for the new residents who were excited to be the first to get the choice parcels and the traffic of hungry newcomers. Henry Brother was present when Bath, New York, incorporated. He was elected treasurer, and twice elected sheriff. He had several businesses, including grist mills and a general store, which delighted and supplied his children with toys, new gadgets, and (especially for the many women in his house) fabrics.

Young Charley was surrounded by many caregivers: his mother, servants, and four sisters who were busy dressmaking, tailoring, buttoning, measuring, cutting, and mistaking. Charley played under bolts and sheets of cotton.

When Charley was a toddler, his oldest sister (by sixteen years) Cordelia traveled to visit relatives for a wedding in July and visit Norwich and New Hartford, Connecticut. Staying industrious, she took along patterns and her sewing box. In a letter home to her sister Rebecca, she wrote, "Tell mother that I want her to make preparations for going to New York with Father this fall, to come this way and take me, as I am far on the road, and I have money enough with me to pay my passage there, and the folks would be delighted to see her and Father—she can

2. Brother home: 22 W. Morris St., Bath, NY

let the party along, and it could cost no more for her to go to NY than to make a party, and it would be much pleasanter for herself, tell her that she need not think of sending me any more work, supposing she had an opportunity, I have plenty on hand and am likely to have for a long time yet, both for myself and others . . . Last week Saturday I took my white dress . . . and made it all over—it sets very nicely now–I am going to see if by ripping my Bellarine [dress] to pieces I can make it look better than it does now—if you should happen to send my cashmere dress, I wish you would send the pieces like any Bellarine, though I may perhaps have fixed that dress so as not to need them by that time. . . Every time I go into the street, I am stared at by the old and young, the rich and the poor. You can't imagine of how much more consequence I feel than when I am at home."

The busy family entertained each other at home with political debate. With a houseful of children, church meetings, school, business, and theater, Charley would eventually become a writer, processing either his own adventures, those of his siblings, or those of his Revolutionary War patriots.

Heading into the 1846 election, Henry Brother weathered political attacks, including those printed in the *Steuben Courier* newspaper in Bath owned by his neighbor, Captain Smead. Benjamin Smead was a

3. Cornelia (L) and Rebecca (R) Brother, courtesy Marjorie Peterson

Freemason, printer, newspaper editor, and the son of a deacon in the
Presbyterian Church. He served in the War of 1812, and reached the rank
of lieutenant and was captain by 1813. An October 14, 1846 letter from
an Addison reader said: "Capt. Smead, Sir: The Whigs in this section
of the county are carping and harping. . . Will the aristocratic Whigs,
please inform us through their press whether their candidate for sheriff,
[Henry Brother] who was born and educated a federalist, reared in the
lap of wealth and luxurious ease, and who is now said to possess his
thousands, has ever confessed himself a defaulter and asked his creditors to forgive him a part of their debts—if so, will they please inform

us whether he has ever refunded from his abundant wealth, any of the debts which he compromised—if not, I trust we shall hear no more about Capt. Adams being a defaulter."

Criticism for Charley's father continued in the *Farmer's Advocate* on the same day, "In fact. . . Mr. Brother pursued a very selfish course when Sheriff, regarding only the interests of No 1, and that he should rest satisfied with the large amounts of money he has made out of the office, by which he has been enabled to establish himself in business, and is now interested in several stores in different parts of the county."

THE WHIG NOMINEE FOR SHERIFF

The nomination of Henry Brother will be hailed by the Whigs of the country as an omen of success. There was naturally a difference of opinion among the delegates as to the relative strength of the different candidates, but the vote on the informal ballot was, we trust, as satisfactory upon this point as it was decisive. Nine years ago Mr. Brother was elected Sheriff of this county, and performed the duties of his office faithfully and to general satisfaction—Prompt to attend to his official duties, and gentlemanly and courteous in their performance, he was deservedly a most popular Sheriff. He has the happy faculty which but few possess, of discharging the unpleasant duties of the office, without incurring censure for tardiness on the one hand, or causing complaint on account of a too rigid execution on the other.

—Steuben Courier, Oct 14, 1846

Six months after being sworn in, Sheriff Brother had to perform an execution.

SENTENCED TO DEATH

A colored man named Nero Grant, who was sentenced to death some months since in Steuben County, for a murder committed there by striking a man during some difficulty with an ax, but not carried into effect on the day appointed, owning to a bill of exceptions having been made, was brought before the Supreme Court this forenoon for sentence, the exceptions having been argued and overruled. Chief Justice Bronson addressed to him a few words and ordered that he be executed (in Steuben County) on Friday, 26th June.

— New York Tribune, May 20, 1847

Our excellent Sheriff then, with much feeling, read to him his death warrant, and asked him if he had anything more to say. He answered, nothing at all. He was then commanded to rise, and he did so without assistance. His arms were tied, his cap was drawn over his face, and the rope fastened about his neck. It was a solemn moment—not a word was spoken. The murderer did not even tremble, though standing over his own coffin. The Sheriff, with a quivering hand, cut the cord that fastened the poor man to life, and the work was done. He died without a pang. His pulse faintly for about 16 minutes, and then all was over.

— Steuben Courier, Jun 30, 1847

That fall, Rebecca graduated from a Normal School, advancing her education as a teacher. In October, the Eastern Assembly District of the Whig Party held their convention at Clifton Springs. They approved Captain Charles S. Brother, of Seneca, as their nominee for the state assembly. Captain Brother, Charley's uncle and namesake, would begin his term at the state assembly, representing Ontario County, stepping in the footsteps of his father, Valentine Brother.

When Charley's baby sister Anna died in February 1848, he became the youngest of the family. Days later, his grandmother, Henry's mother, died at the old homestead in Geneva. Henry continued to promote his business for his family's livelihood, advertising cloths, cassimere, satinells, and flannels, "complete order for business on a more extensive scale than heretofore, and business will be done at the shortest possible notice and at the lowest current prices."

Henry Brother frequently ran advertisements in the newspapers in Bath, New York, and neighboring villages.

REMOVAL: The subscriber informs his friends and the public, that he has removed his entire stock of Goods to the Yellow Store on Liberty Street, two doors north of the Clinton House, where he is prepared to give good bargains to all who will favor him with a call.

—*Steuben Courier*, Apr 28, 1846.

H. Brother & Co. At Painted Post are now offering for cash their large and valuable stock of merchandize at lower prices than have ever been named in this market, the proof of which will be furnished at their counter. They will also pay cash for good qualitied of lumber and shingles.

—*Steuben Farmer's Advocate*, Sep 9, 1846

Henry felt the responsibility and pride of a father of eight children. He was vestryman at St. Thomas Episcopal church and active in the Steuben County Agricultural Society. Always reading the newspapers, planning the next thing, Henry was soon thinking about the need for a dam across the Cohocton River. He appealed to the state house, securing the contract to get it done.

The young future Marine was settling into his practice as observer and reporter for the drama of his siblings. That spring and summer, he watched the workmen building the new school near their church and Sunday school, where the older Brother children would attend.

That spring the family showed up on the 1850 Census with two hired hands living with them: twenty-seven-year-old mulatto, Louis

Story, and twenty-one-year-old teamster, Calvin Fuller. Still peppering the family with robust political debate were their next-door neighbors, including newspaper editor, Captain Benjamin Smead, and the opinionated Mr. Gansevoort. (*Steuben Courier*, Feb 1, 1907)

Soon Mr. Gansevoort was excited to talk about the wedding at St. Thomas Church of Mary Gansevoort to Edward Howell, Jr. in 1850, joining two prominent families. The Howells attended St. Thomas Church with the Brother family and Mary was a Sunday School teacher there

In 1850, Charley was seven years old when his sister Rebecca left home to marry Robert Moses Lyon, a civil engineer and attorney attached to the Steuben County pioneer families who knew the Brother and the Pratt families. Later in life, Charley recalled good childhood times with men on Lyon's farm, shooting and firing cannon balls to fall into the nearby quarry.

When Charley was seven, his brother, Henry Brother, Jr., (called "H.H.") left home. Henry Brother had just purchased the Belfast Mill operation and hoped H.H. would work there. But H.H., turning eighteen in June, had another itch. Against his parents' wishes, he sailed for Australia to win his own prize: gold.

With H.H.'s sudden exit, Henry Brother Sr. was in a real bind. He asked for help from his former clerk, Reuben O. Smith, who was establishing a general store in Olean with his brother, Erastus H. Smith. The Brother family remained close to his friends in Olean. Just before the Civil War, Reuben Smith hired P.S. Towle to work his store in Olean. The boys of Olean knew and loved Towle. Nine years later, Willard Moon Smith, Miles Oviatt, and Charley Brother followed Towle when he joined the Marines to save the Union. (Ellis, 1879)

As Henry was steadying his new business, Cornelia became the third wife of their second cousin, Mr. William Beach Pratt of Prattsburgh. Pratt was a faithful democrat, which rubbed Henry Sr.. Henry was still feeling rejected by H.H. but happy to have Cornelia close by, settled on the familiar hilltop dairy farm, established by great-grandfather Capt. Joel Pratt.

Brother turned eight on August 10, 1852. With a few of his older siblings out of the house, he occupied himself with the newly formed Bath Artillery Company. Located on Buel Street with parade grounds in the front, the company provided great theater for the boys of Bath. Colonel

4. Pratt Homestead in Prattsburgh, NY

Levi C. Whiting erected the building, which later was converted into the Congress Hall, a hotel. *The Farmer's Advocate* on October 6, 1852 reported Col. Whiting's call for the Bath Artillery to organize in the fall.

When the artillery was not performing, the boys watched the construction of the Erie Railroad. The father of Charley's friend Will Dutcher, William A. Dutcher, Sr., was the chief contractor who built the Erie Railroad through Bath in 1853. Two years later, these boys watched the stores burn on Liberty Street—the worst catastrophe the village had ever experienced, and it left a strong impression of the boys. (After the war, the same boys established the Bath fire department.)

DESTRUCTIVE FIRE

One Half of the Business Portion of Bath in Ashes. Yesterday morning about 5 o'clock a fire broke out in the rear part of the Clinton House, and before the alarm was fairly given, the whole building was enveloped in flames; spreading thence north, it rapidly consumed the entire range of stores on Liberty street, between Pulteney Square and Orchard street, where it was finally subdued after destroying Congress Hall and barns, and the armory of the Bath Artillery company. . .

—Bath Advocate, Mar 14, 1855

By 1855 the Brother home included their forty-five-year-old black servant, Jane Kug. At the dinner table, they talked about Mr. Brother's recent purchase of 400 acres in Grundy County, Iowa. The state census enumerator reported H.H., age twenty-one, lived there, but he was in Australia. Val, about age twenty-eight in 1855, was not listed. The US Department of the Interior Bureau of Land Management. General Land Office Records showed the Brother family had seven parcels in Iowa, all located in section three and four of Fairfield Township.

When Charley was about twelve, he met Mary Becker. He said he remembered the details of this day for his entire life, but some things are so shiny and beautiful, they remain private. (In other words, I could not find her.)

The Brother family knew a Becker family in Geneva, those attached to land speculator and lumber manufacturer, Martinus Vroman Becker, whose relatives from Schoharie County were in the state legislature with Mr. Henry Brother's father (Valentine Brother), and his sibling, Charles S. Brother. In the late 1840s, M. Vroman Becker sold his estate and businesses. By 1856 he was harvesting the forests of Michigan and purchased a ship to move his product. Some Beckers were working with the politicians in Albany, and some Beckers were starting a picture framing shop in New York City, recruiting their German relatives to bring their gilding and carpentry skills to America. Charley Brother would stay with the New York City Beckers during the Civil War.

When Brother met Miss Becker, he enjoyed visiting his pals at the drug store run by Alexander Hess, the father of another childhood friend, William Hess. Brother's schoolmate and friend John Sutherland, now fifteen, had just started working for Mr. Hess. The Hess family also attended St. Thomas Church with the Brother family, but the Sutherlands were Presbyterians.

Taking a glance at events in Bath in 1856, see the topics at the "liar's bench" as described by Steuben County Attorney James S. Drake's in his profile of Bath on December 29, 1956, in the *Steuben Advocate*:

. . .about the political theater,

> The political parties "Know Nothings" and Democrats were campaigning hard. They "put on the big rallies with hired

bands, refreshments, speeches, group singing, poetry recita-
tions, torch light parades, and bonfires. . ." some lasting days.
Those who were against slavery, the Republicans, were going
quietly "door to door, farm to farm, and group to group."

. . .about the progressives,

"We had at least five organizations of women in Bath, Canisteo,
Corning, Hornell, and promoting the cause of women's rights
and equal suffrage. . . Let the newspapers publish speeches
and letters poking fun at the very thought of adding more
rights to those of dictating what poor man can eat three times
a day, what he can wear, how he must spend the weekly wages
and the work to be done around the house on his days off. Let
Postmaster-General Kendall send in men to check on how the
merchant and tavern postmasters and owners of stagecoach
mall carriers were standing up for the party furnishing their
jobs."

. . . and about the jail,

After learning of the six escapes over a period of a year and the
jail "not large enough to accommodate the average number
of prisoners," a special committee was formed to "purchase
the land from Steuben Street back to East Morris with enough
room to erect a new jail, fence in an exercise yard, and erect a
new barn for the sheriff and his deputies with a hay mow and
enough stables and buggy room."

At age fourteen, Charley attended the county fair, organized by the
Steuben County Agricultural Society. The Brother family was attached
to the fair board and judging. Even years later, Charley made it a practice to return to Bath about this time. The fair prides itself as being the
longest-running county fairs in America, run consecutively since 1819.
    In 1861, Charley enjoyed watching the drills of the 60th New York
State militia in July. Under the direction of Col. Levi C. Whiting, the

officers included Merlin Graham, drum major, and Julius C. Smead, trumpet major.

Leading up to the war, the Brother family enjoyed an order of things with their regular dramas. Even with the heartbreak of H.H. in Australia, the family started off the next decade looking steady. In the home with his folks, Charley, sixteen, lived with Ellen, now twenty-two, and Mary, twenty. With their seventeen-year-old white-girl servant C. Stewart (so named in the 1860 Census), they planned Ellie's wedding to an accountant, James Young, who was an old family friend.

Charley's paternal side brought the hardwires for adventure: calculation, strategy, construction, technology, speculation, surveying, scouting, and retelling stories of bulletproof General Washington, who knew Brother's ancestors in the raw elements. His paternal ancestors took Freemason oaths for loyal connection and immortality seriously, organizing horse races, and drinking beer with the boys, those pal legislators, militia, and police in their "wet goods" taverns. (Jeffrey, 1991)

Charley Brother's maternal side contributed to character development and refinement of temperament from words and books. Having established the Franklin Academy and contributing to the development of Geneva College and Hobart College, the Pratts focused on their religious tradition, preferring the rhythm of the academic, the sabbath, and agricultural life. Having lost her parents at a young age, Charley's mother, Mary Ann, had learned as an orphan how to build a network of friends, especially Mrs. Metcalf but including the Beckers. All were virtuous and loyal to the scriptures. From his mother, Charley was warned, maybe even lectured, that God has his own agenda. The boy had to be ready for disaster to strike in his home or those of his friends. He had to be a good companion "for times like these."

Holding the *Common Book of Prayer*, the family sought comfort in St. Thomas Episcopal Church, which was growing in members. They were now planning a bigger place of worship. But that had to wait. With the bombardment of Fort Sumter in April 1861, the Brother family mined the newspapers and expressed their opinions. They looked to the boys at the Freemason lodge and the mills. Who would sign up?

In September 1861, Gilbert Ingersoll and Frank Smead headed to Elmira to sign up for 1st Artillery Regiment (Light) Battery E.

5. Joseph P. Faulkner

On November 19, 1861, Charley went to work for the British tailor, James Sutherland. Mr. Sutherland had come to Bath in 1848, about the time Henry Brother was running his fabric store. He brought with him a young family, including sons John and James, Jr., who became Charley's playmates. But now Charley was needed to help out an old friend in the store when the Sutherland boys enlisted.

In July 1862 President Lincoln called for 300,000 volunteers. Their friend Robert Bruce Van Valkenburg was just beginning his term in the 37th Congress and would serve as colonel for the 107th, New York Volunteer Infantry. He prepared to open a recruiting center in Elmira, New York. Van Valkenburg had little time to get the boys ready. Only two weeks later they were sent, wholly unprepared, into The Battle at Antietam. (New York (State), Adjutant General's Office 1864). The 107th NY Volunteers went on to fight at Antietam, then Chancellorsville, Gettysburg, James Crossroads, Atlanta Campaign (May 3–Sept 2, 1862,) and again in Atlanta (Jul 21–Aug 26). During the Civil War, Steuben provided twenty-nine regiments. (Hakes and Adrich, 1896)

This made an impression on Charley Brother, he wanted to join Van Valkenburg. When Charley turned eighteen, he watched his classmates leave for Elmira: George W. Fuller, John Sutherland, Frank Smead, and even the previously injured Joe Faulkner. Faulkner, age eighteen, was the son of Daniel and Caroline Faulkner and the grandson of Maj. Daniel, founder of Dansville, 30 miles west of Bath. Faulkner was just three or four years old when his father died in 1846, leaving his mother to raise seven children. Mrs. Faulkner leaned on the Presbyterian Church in Bath, where Charles Brother's maternal grandmother, Rebecca Turner Pratt, attended. Joe Faulkner worked as printer before the war and had fallen 30 feet out of a building, causing significant injuries, showering him with well-wishers, including Charley.

Joseph P. Faulkner enlisted on August 15, 1862. He wrote in 1878, "Almost all my old chums were enlisting. Seized with the ailment, as it then showed itself like a contagious disease among the patriots, I too resolved to don the suit of blue and to go for a soldier. And as soon as sufficiently whole I volunteered, passed the surgical examination necessary and became enrolled as 'food for powder,' and one of my country's 'stays in duty and hour of danger' in the 107th Regiment NYSV."

Charley Brother's eye caught up with group of older boys who were more confident, and better dressed more like his older brothers. Some of the guys were sweet on Charley's sister Mary. Some were taking off for the Brooklyn Navy Yards. Gregg, Harris, and Towle (who Mary later wed) were enlisted as Marines on August 23, 1862, by Captain Heywood. Will Ingersoll enlisted a week later.

Charley Brother was soon to follow.

CHAPTER 2

Brooklyn Navy Yard in 1862

Wed Oct 1, 1862

Left Bath for New York on the 10:15 pm train. Mother gave me
a prayer book and Father gave me much good advice. They all
went down to the depot with me. There I found nearly all the
boys. Dutcher and Hess gave me a dozen cigars. Fred Towner of
Corning was at Bath and went down on the same train. When
we arrived at Corning we went over to Dutcher's and had something to eat. Left Corning about half past eleven. Got into a seat
with a couple of strange looking chaps. Did not like them very
well so on arriving at Elmira took another seat in a front car and
went to sleep.

[The book given to Charles by his mother is now a worn-out *Common
Book of Prayer* in my possession; in the back flap and inside cover is a list
of names of Marines with references to dates, hometowns, and ships.
Will Dutcher, age fifteen here, was the grandson of Ruhl Dutcher, a civil
engineer who built the Erie Railroad through Bath. William A. Hess was
in the Naval Academy, the son of the druggist Alexander Hess, who at
one time kept the Clinton House hotel and later became the county treasurer. While sheriff, Henry Brother auctioned off foreclosed properties
at the Clinton House.]

Thu Oct 2, 1862

Woke up about five o'clock, raining quite hard. Arrived at Port
Jervis (?) shortly after. There the train stopped half an hour be-

6. William A. Hess, Navy cadet

fore breakfast. Arrived at Jersey City about Noon. Took a ferry boat to New York. Went over to Brooklyn to the Marine Barracks but could not get in. Went back to New York and had something to eat. While walking down Broadway met Will Ingersoll. He went with me to the Belmont Hotel in Fulton St. where I engaged a room for a week. Went to Barnum's (?) museum in the evening. Bills were posted up all over the building "Beware of Pickpockets" so I held onto my money. Wrote a letter to Father.

[Port Jervis, New York. IU Lilly transcription: (?) appears in the typed manuscript after the word "Jerins." In the original version, the word is clearly "Jervis." For this book, all the (?) marks are included and belong to what I believe is the first and only attempt to transcribe the entire three diaries by Fannie. In his 1889 pension records, Will's mother reported her address was 47 Morris Street in Bath. Before the war, he worked for a shoemaker for H.R. Bushwell. Ingersoll, age eighteen, lived on Morris Street down the street from the Brothers. He was the son of Nancy and Gilbert Ingersoll. Will's father had been injured in June, struck by lightning while serving with the 1st Independent Battery Light Artillery. Gilbert entered the war in September 1861 as Full Quarter Master Sergeant at the age of thirty-eight.]

Fri Oct 3, 1862
Went to call on Mary Becker in the morning. Got into a 42nd Street stage at the museum to ride to 41st. Got there at last and inquired where they lived. Was told that a family by that name lived in the 4th story of a large brick building corner of the 41st and 3rd Ave. Went up there but could not find anyone. Went back down town again.

[Mary was living with picture framers and guilders. These Beckers would enjoy access to great lumber pricing through M. V. Becker, who was an old friend of Brother's father and grandfather and who, when Mr. Brother was buying land in Iowa, was heading north with his ships to mine forests. (Burhans, 1894) (S.J. Clarke Publishing Company 1898).]

About noon went up to East Broadway to see Ed Howell. He was not in. Called again in the afternoon and saw him. He said that I was foolish to think of going into the Navy, told me to come up the next morning at 10 o'clock and he would go over to the Navy Yard with me. Went down town again. Went to Niblo's Theatre in the evening.

[Ed Howell, age seventy, was the father of Brother's friend, William E. Howell. Ed's father was a sea captain, captured in the Revolutionary War and held prisoner in Jamaica and confined on a prison ship. Ed made voyages with his father and became a teacher, lawyer, and congressman. The Howells attended St. Thomas Church with the Brother family. Ed's brother William had a son, John A. Howell, who was a graduate of the Naval Academy, who treated Brother kindly, encouraging him in his in-

7. William E. Howell

terest in the sea. John later invented the Howell Torpedo. (*Steuben Advocate*, Dec 29, 1956. *Steuben Farmers' Advocate*, Dec 8, 1915.)

Sat Oct 4, 1862
Went to see Ed Howell in the morning. He was not well enough to go to the Navy Yard with me. Told me to come again on Monday. Went down town again. Went to Central Park in the afternoon and to the Christie's Minstrels in the evening.

[The Christie's Minstrels were a blackface performance group.]

Sun Oct 5, 1862
Went to Trinity Church in the forenoon. A Bishop preached
the sermon. Went to 36th Street in the afternoon, then walked
down 5th Avenue. Saw a good many nicely dressed ladies. Went
over to Merchant's Hotel in the evening and saw Mr. John T. Allen of Bath. He walked around town with me some time. Went
through the famous "Five Points." Saw George Fuller of Corning but did not recognize him at first so did not speak to him.
Wrote a letter to Mother and one to Will Dutcher.

[John T. Allen was the son of William W. Allen, a banker and treasurer
of St. Thomas Church, the Harverling Academy, and other clubs and
organizations. The Allen family lived down from Brother's friend Ed
Church. Brother's niece Helen grew up and married an Allen boy.]

Mon Oct 6, 1862
Went up to Earl's Hotel in Canal Street in the morning and saw
Geo Fuller. Says he came down to buy goods. Went to see Ed
Howell but he was not in. Went up again in the afternoon and
he went over to the Navy Yard with me. We went on board the
North Carolina. Saw some pretty rough looking sailors on board
of her. Ed says that if I will come up again on Tuesday he will
take me to a shipping master of his acquaintance who will do
well by me. Rec'd a letter from Father in the afternoon, one
from Mary and one from Reding Harris. Reding says that the
boys are getting sick of soldiering and would gladly get home
again if they could. Went to the Old Bowery Theatre in the evening with Mr. Allen. Wrote a letter to Mary.

[Theodore "Dora" Redding Harris, age twenty, was the son of Morris
Harris. Dora had four brothers: Rodney, age eighteen, Marcus, the twins:
Myron and Frank Murphy. Rodney signed up with the 107th Co. A.]

8. Pvt. "Dora" Harris, USMC, courtesy Adrienne Sachse

Tue Oct 7, 1862

Went to see Ed Howell in the morning but he did not feel inclined to take me to see the shipping master just then. Talked a
long time about the horrors of a sailor's life and c. Saying that
some time when he felt like it he would go with me to see the
shipping master. I then went over to the Marine Barracks in
Brooklyn. Got admitted without any difficulty, and saw all the
boys. They want me to enlist there with them. Don't know but I
will, they have very pleasant quarters.

9. Pvt. John Murdoch, USMC, was from Ithaca, NY, courtesy
Claudia Boggs

[Howell was an experienced seaman. He understood that the horrors
would include the containment and spread of brutality, diseases, ro-
dents, lice, scurvy, drowning by shot or by storm, nausea, starvation,
loss of coal, claustrophobia, etc. Howell married into the prominent
Gansevoort family (a Sunday school teacher at St. Thomas Church, Mary
Gansevoort Howell, who, as a widow in 1862 married Henry Brother's
good friend, Hiram R. Hess, Charley's godfather.). Herman Melville's
mother was a Gansevoort. I wondered if the boys of Bath, including Ed
Howell, read *Moby Dick*, which was published in 1852.]

Thu Oct 9, 1862
Just a week since I arrived in New York. Was going up to see Ed
Howell in the morning when I met him coming down. He says

if I will come up Friday morning he will take me to see the shipping master he has talked so much about. Went up to the Bulls Head Hotel and saw Mr. George Metcalf. Saw Mr. Randall in St.

[Jacob D. Randall was the father of Brother's friend Jim or "Jimmy" Benjamin Franklin Randall. Mr. Randall was the former sheriff of Orange County. Note also that on Oct 9, 1862, after the slaughter of the Battle of Antietam, Congressman and Colonel of the 107th regiment Robert Bruce Van Valkenburgh was discharged October 9, 1862, returning to his House seat, which he kept until 1865.]

Fri Oct 10, 1862
Went over to the Brooklyn Navy Yard. Saw a good many sailors but none of them very decent looking. Mr. Allen went up town to see a store in the evening and I went with him.

Sat Oct 11, 1862
Wrote a letter to Mother. Saw Will Ingersoll in the evening and played a game of billiards with him. He wants me to enlist in the Marine Corps and I don't know but I will.

[Will Ingersoll could have been trying to get a bonus or finder's fee for recruiting more Marines. Gideon Welles approved the extension of this incentive until the end of 1862. (Sullivan, 1997)]

Sun Oct 12, 1862
Went over to see Mr. Allen in the morning. He was feeling rather unwell. Stayed with him some time. Went up to Greenwood Cemetery in the afternoon. A very nice place. Saw Wood Howell and wife there. They asked me to call and see them. It is a very easy matter to get into Greenwood, but a harder one to get out again. I wandered about some time trying to find my way out but could not. Asked a man to show me and found that he too was trying to get out. Took a fresh start and succeeded in finding the gate. Met Mr. Fellows today in Fulton St. He did not have his basket with him. Weather very cool.

[Wood Howell might be the assemblyman from Schuyler County and Seneca, NY or, possibly, Edwin W. Howell, who later became the sheriff of Chemung County in Elmira, elected 1864. Mr. Fellows might be Joseph Fellows who is buried in Grove Cemetery in Bath and was a land agent from Pulteney Estates in partnership with Benjamin Franklin Young (1822–1898). The Youngs were a prominent family with the St. Thomas Episcopal Church; Charles' sister married James Young in 1860.]

Mon Oct 13, 1862

Rained very hard this morning. Made up my mind to enlist in the Marine Corps and went over to the Barracks. A Sergeant took me over to the Navy Yard to be examined by the Surgeon. He was not there. Took me then on board the North Carolina to see the Surgeon there but he would have nothing to do with me so went back to the Barracks. I was then sent over to No. 18 – Bowery New York where the Marine recruiting office is. There I was examined by a surgeon and sworn in the four years unless sooner discharged. Went back to barracks and was given a bunk in room No. 3.

[Records show Brother was enlisted by Capt. Brevoorst. Brother reports it was Maj. Garland.]

Tue Oct 14, 1862

Wrote a letter to Father this morning telling him of my whereabouts. In the afternoon received my clothing as follows. 1 blue fatigue coat, 1 pair light blue platoons, 1 leather stock, 1 fatigue cap, 1 blanket, 1 knapsack, 1 pair shoes, 1 white shirt, 2 blue shirts, 2 pair woolen socks, 2 pairs cotton drawers. Towards evening the drill Sergeant took me in hand and put me through a few motions. Says I am competent to go into a squad he has been drilling some two or three weeks. Wrote a letter to Dutcher in the evening.

Wed Oct 15, 1862

Drilled a short time with the squad in the morning. Got along very well for a green hand. In the afternoon wore our muskets and belts and told to clean them up ready for drill tomorrow morning. Wrote a letter to Val, one to Will Birchard, one to Eliakim Field and one to Mr. Sutherland.

[Eliakim Field, age seventeen, was son of Major Almeron Field, who named the boy after his brother, Maj. Eliakim Field. Both older brothers were prominent owners of hotels, including the Dickenson House in Corning. Mr. Sutherland was Brother's old boss, an English tailor. His son John Sutherland, age twenty, went to the Haverling Union School until he turned fifteen, when he went to work for Will Hess' father as a clerk at Hess's drug store. John enlisted in the Army. His skills in the drug store would later keep him close to the makeshift hospitals to care for his wounded friends.]

Thu Oct 16, 1862
Drilled a short time with muskets in the morning. Find it rather hard work. Makes my arm ache. The boys tell me I will get used to it after a while.

Fri Oct 17, 1862
Weather quite warm. Drilled twice with muskets today. They seem heavier than ever. Made my arm so lame that I can hardly raise it.

Sat Oct 18, 1862
Commodore Hudson of the US Navy was buried in the afternoon, and all marines had to turn out at the funeral. So they put us recruits on guard. It came pretty hard on me and I was glad to go to bed when we were relieved.

Sun Oct 19, 1862
Was on the "liberty list" today but did not go out. Received a letter and a paper from Father, and wrote to him. Wrote also to Fred Towner, Azel Gould, and Jim Cranen.

Liberty was authorized leave, often forty-eight hours and with rules on how far a sailor could travel. (Noel and Beach, 1988). Brother's friend A.

R. Gould, Jr., age twenty-one, lived down the street from Brother's boss, English tailor James Sutherland and near the merchant Jonathan Robie. He was the son of A.R. Gould, Sr. (1808–1886), who ran the Clinton House Hotel and was in the room with Brother's father when the original boys of Bath incorporated the village. Azel's father, like Brother's father, had been with Bath's sheriff with the Whig Party and Freemasons. The Whig Party nominated Gould's father for sheriff in October 1843. Gould, Jr. was a sutler (civilian merchant) with the 161st N.Y. Volunteers. Brother followed any news about Azel Jr.'s younger brother James William Gould, who was with 78th NY Regiment, but then later joined the 102, Company F; ranking to corporal. (Johnston, 1900). Azel moved to Michigan after the war with other Bath boys.]

Mon Oct 20, 1862
Weather very pleasant. Drilled twice today. Am beginning to get used to it now. The muskets do not tire my arm as much as they did at first.

Wed Oct 22, 1862
Weather very pleasant. Drilled but once today. Rec'd a letter from Fred Towner. Wrote a letter to Mother. A Sergeant, two musicians and three privates from Washington. They are going on board the *Vanderbilt* when she goes into commission.

Thu Oct 23, 1862
Drilled twice today. Sergeant Jones says we will be turned over for duty before many days. Weather quite cool. All the Sentries are wearing their watch coats.

Fri Oct 24, 1862
Weather quite cool. Drilled but once today. Received a letter from Mother and one from Ella W. Mother gave me much good advice.

[Brother's original diary shows a line after the surname, so it appears as "Ella W——." Could this be Ella W. Willson, who lives two houses down from Ed Smead and who is nearly the same age as Charles? John A. Wil-

10. Pvt. Vep Darling, USMC

_____

son and wife Rebecca Minott had ten children, including Warren W.,
who married Susan Metcalf, and Ella, who married Alonzo Hadley after
the Civil War.]

Sat Oct 25, 1862
Did not drill any today. Cleaned out our room this morning. At
noon Harris, Kelsey, Towle, Darling, and I went over to New
York. Went on board the steamer *Vanderbilt*. She is a very nice
vessel, most too nice for a man of war. Went to the Belmont ho-

tel and had something to eat, and then went to the Post Office. Saw W.W. Wilson of Bath at Earl's Hotel. When I got back to Barracks found two boxes of goodies from home. They tasted pretty nice.

[George W. Kelsey (1840–1917) was twenty-one and a carpenter who enlisted August 19, 1862. Miles Oviatt was also from Olean. Phineas S. Towle was from Bath but worked in Olean. Towle enlisted on August 23, 1862. Thomas Velpeau "Vep" Darling, age twenty-two, enlisted as private by Major Garland. He grew up, but in Lawrenceville, Pennsylvania, about 25 miles south of Bath, but had worked in both Bath and Olean where other Marines were recruited.]

Sun Oct 26, 1862
Weather rather cool. Received a letter from Mary. Wrote one to Val, one to Ella W., one to Tom Seymour and one to Mary. Ate so many good things yesterday that I am nearly sick today.

[Tom, age eighteen, was the son of Orange S. Seymour, the sheriff.]

Mon Oct 27, 1862
Weather pleasant. Drilled but once today. Jones our drill Sergeant tells us that we will be turned over for duty in a few days.

Wed Oct 29, 1862
Drilled a short time this morning and then drew on full uniform coats, hats and c. Spent the afternoon fixing them up. Jones went to Philadelphia in the afternoon.

Thu Oct 30, 1862
Received a comforter from home in the morning and a short note from sister Mary. Applied for liberty and got it. Asked officer of the day (Lieut. Kidd) for permission to wear uniform coat and got that too. Went out for dinner. Went to Navy Yard with Gregg. He went to the sail loft and got several clothes bags, some canvas to make a ditty bag of twine, needles, bees wax and c. The men in the loft were very obliging and seemed anx-

11. Pvt. Josiah C. Gregg, USMC, courtesy Adrienne Sachse

ious to do all they could for us. Charged us nothing for what we got. Went over to New York and had my photograph taken in full uniform at a place in Chatham Street. Went down to south Ferry and had something to eat. Then back to barracks.

[Josiah Collins Gregg, age twenty, signed on for four years by Captain Heywood. A schoolteacher and clerk. He was the son of Hobart and Jane Elder Gregg with siblings Joanna, Mary, Margaret "Maggie," Sarah, Euphemia or Orphelia (who was the same age as Charles Brother), Julia and George.]

Fri Oct 31, 1862
Got up in the morning with a sore throat and violent headache. Did not go out to second roll call, and made Serg't Jones mad and he sent after me. Told to report myself to the doctor. Did so and was put on the sick list. Had a high fever in the night with a slight touch of my old complaint, "the feelings."

[The doctor's diagnosis was tonsillitis.]

Sun Nov 2, 1862
Fever all gone but throat still very sore. Am afraid that I cannot go away on the *Vanderbilt* with the rest of the boys on account of the sickness.

CHAPTER 3

USS *Vanderbilt*

Tue Nov 4, 1862

Came off the sick list this morning. At about eleven o'clock AM we were ordered to pack our bags and get ready for sea, to go on board the steamer *Vanderbilt*. Marched from Barracks about one o'clock PM. After we got on board ship we stacked arms on the quarter deck and I was left in charge of them while the rest of the boys went to get our baggage on board. We then went below and put our muskets in the rack. I went on post at 4 o'clock on the gangway. Came off at six and had for supper coffee and hard biscuit. When the Bath boys enlisted, Major Garland in command at the Barracks promised to send them away together, and I enlisted upon his promise to send me with them, and he has kept his word by sending all of us on the *Vanderbilt*.

[Addison Garland was about fifty years old at the time. Hard biscuit or hard tack is a cracker, made of flour and water without yeast, that would not spoil.]

12. Cpl. Miles Oviatt, USMC, courtesy Adrienne Sachse

[Oviatt wrote when he joined USS *Vanderbilt*: "The whole scene was rather imposing & Solemn. The whole company took off their hats." —Nov 4, 1862 (Oviatt, 1998)]

13. USS *Vanderbilt*, NHC NH 58744

[Brother's father wrote to him the day he joined the *Vanderbilt*.]

I write this in the expectation it will be the last letter you will receive from home before you leave on your cruise.

As you may well suppose this is an occasion of deep concern to us and will cause in us a lively interest in the movements of your ship. I am afraid you are not well prepared for a voyage and enclose you here four dollars for the purpose of enabling you to procure such little comforts as you may want & wanting and in that way use up all your earnings

You must at any rate, curb and control your appetite for superfluities and you will soon learn to live on the rations furnished you with comfort.

It would be well to provide a little memo book in which to write out a journal of your cruise which will be interesting to look over afterwards.

You should have some reading for your voyage and if yourself and messmates should each purchase a different book the whole would afford an amt. of reading sufficient to while away the hours which otherwise might hang heavy on your hands.

I know not whether there is any chance for preferment in your department of the service, but if there is, it can only be obtained by merit & proficiency in your duties. So it behooves you to exert yourself to the upmost & be prompt and punctual in the discharge of your duties. Remembering your duty first of all to your God. Read your Bible and peruse your prayer Book daily and let your motto, while in the service, be God & your Country.

We learned yesterday of the death of Maria Goodspeed which leaves Aunt Rice quite alone.

I am obliged to close in order to send this by and by the young ladies who go down to see you & their more particular friends off. Goodby, God Bless you.

Yours Affectionately, H. Brother. (Smith, 1964)

[Maria was Anna Pratt Rice's caretaker. Mrs. Anna Pratt Rice was Charley's aunt. Anna married Burrage Rice, the uncle of Captain Burrage Rice with the 189th NY Regiment. Anna and Mr. Rice adopted young Burrage when his parents died.]

Wed Nov 5, 1862
Slept on deck last night as I had no hammock claws. An attempt was made to get our ship out into the stream in the afternoon but she was stuck in the mud and could not be got off. Got her off about nine o'clock in the evening and going down the river came to anchor off the Battery. On post in the Brigg today.

Fri Nov 7, 1862
Weather very cold and wind blowing a gale. The bay is so rough that we cannot take our powder on board. In the morning a sloop loaded with hay drifted against us.

Sat Nov 8, 1862
Weather more mild. Bay not so rough as yesterday. Took our powder on board today. Stood post in the brig in the morning

from 4 to 6, and again in the evening from 4 to 6. Drum beat to quarters at two o'clock for the first time. We marines went to the after pivot gun and were stationed. Drilled a little under the direction of a masters mate. Had bean soup for dinner and I managed to eat a little for the first time in my life. Nothing like rough weather to give a fellow an appetite.

Sun Nov 9, 1862
Got up this morning at 4 o'clock to go on post at the starboard gang-way. Was relieved by Vep Darling. Weather quite cold. Wind blows and it rains and snows all the time. Ship very uncomfortable. Lieut. Parker our Marine officer came on board in the morning. Wrote a letter to Mother.

Mon Nov 10, 1862
Under way at last. Got up anchor about half past twelve, arrived off Shady Hook about 2 o'clock. Sent a letter for mother on board by the Pilot. Don't know where we are going, but everyone seems to think that we will go first to the West Indies. Drilled at the Pivot gun about two hours in the afternoon. Lieut. Parker and the ships first Lieut. Mr. Daniels say that we handled it splendidly for men who have had no more experience than we have.

[Joseph D. Daniels was Act 1st Lieut. Ex. Officer for USS *Vanderbilt*. He died of tuberculosis in 1865. (Benson, et al., 1923) Daniels was born in Baltimore, the son of a commodore in the Colombian Navy. When appointed to the Navy in 1841, he was attending the St. Mary's Seminary. He served in the Mexican War but resigned in "a moment of impulsiveness" in 1861 while in Baltimore before returning for duty. (Porter, 1886)]

Tue Nov 11, 1862
Out at sea. We are heading E by SE. Some of the boys are beginning to get sea sick. I am not sick but a little dizzy, expect my turn will come soon. Drilled at the gun twice today, and at boarding and repelling boarders. Stood post at the Scutter [scuttle] Butt in the evening.

[Scuttlebutt refers to the drinking fountain or water barrel or butt.]

Wed Nov 12, 1862
Weather very pleasant. In the afternoon a ship hove in sight and hoisted American colors. The drum beat to quarters and we drilled a little.

Thu Nov 13, 1862
Weather cloudy but not unpleasant. In the morning a small schooner hove in sight and hoisted English colors. As she had no name on her stern which was considered rather suspicious, a boat was sent from us to board her, but she was found to be all right. Nearly all the boys are sea-sick, and say that if they ever get on shore again they will stay there. I have not been sick yet but don't like the service over much. Drilled at the big gun and fired her once. Made my ears ring for half an hour. On post in the Brigg once and once as Captain's Orderly.

Fri Nov 14, 1862
Weather damp and cloudy but not very cool. In the morning a sail hove in sight which we immediately made for. She hoisted the English Ensign. Proved to be the British Brigg *Diane* of South Hampton, from St. George to Plymouth.

Sat Nov 15, 1862
Weather damp and cloudy. Towards evening the wind set in strong from the NE and before midnight was blowing a gale.

Sun Nov 16, 1862
Wind blowing a gale. Nearly all the boys are heaving up at a tremendous rate. I am not at all sick. In the morning the look out aloft reported a sail ahead but we could see nothing of it from the deck. All hands were mustered aft on the gun deck and the first lieut read the articles of war. Ship rolled so badly that no one could stand still and all staggered about like drunken men.

Mon Nov 17, 1862

This morning the sea was quite smooth again. We drilled a short time by Ser'gt Morgan who instructed us in light infantry tactics, loading and firing on our knees and c. After drill had target exercise. Kelsey and McKee made the best shots. I fired twice, missed the first time and hit the second time within five inches of the bull's eye. Drilled a short time at the pivot gun. A barrel was sent adrift and our gun, the forward pivot gun, and three of the broadside gun were fired at it, but none came very near it. The sea was so rough that the target could hardly be seen.

[Patrick Morgan, Orderly Sergeant]

Tue Nov 18, 1862

Weather rather cool. Sun came out bright and warm in the afternoon, but soon hid itself again. Just two weeks today since we came on board. It seems more like two months. Towards night the look out at the mast-head reported four vessels in sight. We put on all steam but at dark but one could be seen from the deck. On post in the Brigg from 8:00 to 10:00 in the evening.

Wed Nov 19, 1862

Just a year ago today went to work for Mr. Sutherland. This morning a sail was seen on our starboard bow, probably the same one we saw last night. We made for her and hoisted our colors, she showed the English ensign, we hove to and told her to do the same but she kept on her course and ran into us. She struck us on our starboard wheel house, slightly damaging the wheel but not enough to amount to anything.

Thu Nov 20, 1862

Expect to see land before long. Weather very pleasant. Drilled once at the pivot gun in the morning. A small fishing boat hove in sight and hoisted English colors. We sent a boat off to her but don't know what they made out. Suppose she was all right as they let her go.

Fri Nov 21, 1862

Weather quite warm and very pleasant, just such weather as we have in spring in New York. About noon land was discovered on our port bow. Proved to be Bermuda. Was a very welcome sight for me and all the others being the first land we have seen since leaving New York. About three o'clock we were boarded by a black Pilot and anchored about a mile from shore at dark.

Sat Nov 22, 1862

Sentry (?) go on the forecastle this morning from 4:00 to 6:00. Have a good view of the island from where we are. On our right is the town of St. George, in front of us a few houses build apparently of white stone, on our left a large fort and another directly above it on the hill. The hills are covered with vegetation, with here and there small groves of trees very much resembling our pines and cedars. Weighed anchor about ten o'clock AM and steamed part way around the island, as we went around more forts came in sight and we could see the red-coats on parade. There are about five thousand British soldiers on the island and the British flag waves from all the fortifications. After we got away from the island a sail was discovered which was half down [unintelligible]. She showed American colors so we did not board her. She stood in toward the island. Another sail was then seen which appeared to be standing away from us. She had all sail set and was going very fast. We made directly for her and soon proved that she was no match for the *Vanderbilt* for we came up with her in a short time. She hoisted the English flag and hove to, a boat was sent to board her. Suppose she was all right as she was permitted to go on.

Sun Nov 23, 1862

Not much like Sunday at home. At half past nine in the forenoon we marines had to turn out for inspection, and a glorious time we had too. The ship rolled so heavily that we could hardly keep on our feet. Our shoes were white with salt from the water and our muskets red with rust. Lieut. Parker swore that we must clean them, and we swore that we could not, nor could we. We tried in every way but it was of no use. The stains would not come off. Expect we will all be put in the brig next if [unintelligible] we appear on inspection. Saw a sail on our port beam this AM and immediately gave chase, but after coming nearer and seeing nothing suspicious about her gave up the chase and resumed our course. The *Vanderbilt* beats anything we have seen yet. In the night about eleven o'clock a bright light was seen on our starboard beam, looked like a steamers light, was visible only a few minutes when it suddenly disappeared. Weather rather cooler than for some days past but not uncomfortable. Sea rather rough. Just enough to be nice.

Mon Nov 24, 1862
Drilled at the pivot gun in the forenoon and at boarding and repelling boarders. About eleven o'clock a small schooner hove in sight and hoisted English colors. Our captain told her to heave to which she did, and a boat was sent to board her. It soon returned and she was permitted to go on. In the afternoon a sail was seen which we made for. She showed American colors and we sent a boat to her. She proved to be the Bark *Revolution* of Boston bound for the West Indies. She said that yesterday during a heavy storm she was chased and fired at by a vessel which she supposed to be the 290, but got away from her after a run of four hours. At ten o'clock at night, as the starboard watch were sound asleep, the drum beat to quarters. Such a lashing up of hammocks I never saw before. The boys all flew around as if the ship was on fire, and some of them thought we had come across the 290 sure. We stowed our hammocks, put on our belts, took our muskets and made for the after pivot gun. The order to cast loose and provide was given and our gun was the second one ready. Went thought the exercise of loading and firing once, when the retreat was beat and we turned in again. Weather rather cool. Pork and beans for dinner.

[A bark is "usually a three-masted sailing ship with the first two masts square-rigged and the third fore-and-aft rigged." The 290 is the *Alabama*. "The bark *Revolution* and the schooner *D. Dewolf*, hence for *New-Orleans*, were brought back today by the revenue cutter. They are supposed to have contraband goods on board." (*The New York Times*, Nov 15, 1862) Duff was a type of pudding or dumpling.]

Tue Nov 25, 1862
Weather rather cool. General quarters at 10:00 AM. Drilled about one hour at the big gun at boarding and c. A target was sent adrift and the port and starboard batteries and forward pivot gun fired at it. None came very near it. The best shot was made by No. 3 gun. We did not fire at it as the order to fire was not given until we were out of range. The "First Lieut."(?) says he thinks we need a little extra drill. Duff for dinner.

Wed Nov 26, 1862
Weather cloudy and damp. Fine sail in sight from the mast-head in the morning. We came up with one about 10 o'clock. She was a Bark from Providence bound for San Francisco, and showed the stars and stripes. The next was a Brig and she also showed our colors. The third and last one we overhauled was a Brig and showed a flag of two red stripes and one white. Bean soup for dinner.

Thu Nov 27, 1862
I suppose this is Thanksgiving day. Shall spend it very differently from what I did a year ago. Weather quite rough. Did not drill any at the big gun. Murdoch, Darling, Oviatt and I were late in getting up our hammocks and were reported by Masters Mate Pierce. Each got 4 hours extra duty. In the evening Vep Darling fell asleep on post at the scuttle butt and was given extra duty of two hours on and two off until further orders. Beef soup for dinner.

Fri Nov 28, 1862
The starboard watch scrubbed hammocks this morning, but as I was on post from 4:00 to 6:00 could not scrub mine. Saw a sail on our port bow this PM but we did not overhaul her. Drilled a

short time at the big gun in the forenoon. Expect we will be in New York soon.

Sat Nov 29, 1862
Weather rather cool. In the morning spoke [?] a small schooner from Philadelphia. Drilled a short time at the pivot gun in the forenoon. Pork and beans for dinner.

Sun Nov 30, 1862
Weather pleasant but cool. Steamed up the narrows and into New York harbors this AM. Wrote a letter to Father. Guard in uniform at inspection. Bean soup for dinner.

Mon Dec 1, 1862
Weather quite mild for this time of the year but cold enough for a watch coat to feel comfortable.

[The Navy reported about this on December 6, 1862, "The USS Vanderbilt resumed search for CSS Alabama and to take Capt. John Winslow and two other officers to Fayal, Spain. After taking on coal on Spanish harbor, crossed Atlantic to look for CSS Alabama, refueling at Hampton Roads, VA." (U.S. Navy, 1971)]

Wed Dec 10, 1862
Sailed from New York this AM. Have been at anchor off the battery since Nov 30th. Weather so cold did not feel much like writing. Rec'd several letters from home. Purdy rec'd an appointment as Ass't Paymaster in the Navy and left us. All very sorry to have him go but glad of his good fortune. Think we will live better this time out. Our mess now has a scouse Kettle, five barrels of potatoes, and of onions. Don't know where we are going. Mr. Parker says we are bound for the Mediterranean Sea and I think we are as everyone else seems to think so. Rec'd some good things from home a few days ago. Among them was a box marked in sister Mary's handwriting, "Sealed orders for Messers Brother and Johnson, not to be opened until two days out." The box is in Johnson's mess chest and will be inspected accordingly.

Remington and Cameron were sent on shore sick, and three new men came from Barracks to fill their places and Purdy's. They are two brothers named Kimmerle (?) and a man named Loomis. I go on the Cabin door as orderly today in place of Harris who will do regular duty in the Guard. Beef soup for dinner.

[Johnson knew Charley: his sister married Charley's uncle Schuyler.]

Thu Dec 11, 1862
Weather much warmer than at New York. Drilled at the pivot gun a short time this PM. Several ships in sight but we did not chase any of them. Beef soup for dinner. We have on board as passengers, Captain Winslow, Lieut. Commander Thornton, and a Young Lieutenant. They are going somewhere with us.

Fri Dec 12, 1862
Weather much warmer. Drilled a short time at the pivot gun in the afternoon. In the evening a bright light was seen on our starboard beam. Appeared to be bearing down for us. We hove to and it soon went out of sight. One of the Negro landsmen was found to have more lice than he could take care of and was scrubbed accordingly. Duff for dinner.

Sat Dec 13, 1862
Two months today since I enlisted. Two months of hard living. Only forty six month more before I am entitled to a discharge. Weather cooler. Beef soup for dinner.

Sun Dec 14, 1862
Weather quite cool and sea rather rough. In the morning about six o'clock a sail was discovered on our part beam. Proved to be a large ship bound to Westward. Our colors were hoisted but I could not see whether she showed hers or not. All hands mustered aft in the afternoon and the rules of the service in general and of this ship in particular were read by the first Lieut. Beef soup for dinner.

14. Capt. John A. Winslow, USN, NHHC NH 42384

Mon Dec 15, 1862
Weather pleasant but sea quite rough. Drilled about two hours
at the pivot gun. Ship rolled so badly we could hardly work it.
While at quarters a ship hove in sight and hoisted US colors.
The first Lieut. hailed her and ordered her to heave to, but as

she did not seem inclined to so our after pivot gun was brought to bear on her. We sent an officer in boat to board her. Don't know what he made out but suppose she was all right as she was permitted to go on. A target was sent adrift and the two pivot guns and starboard guns fired at it. Our gun was made the best shot. Beef soup for dinner.

Tue Dec 16, 1862
Weather quite pleasant. A sail hove in sight in the forenoon and hoisted the English flag. As we passed we dipped our colors and she did the same. We did not board her. Drilled a short time at the pivot gun, in the forenoon. Duff for dinner.

[Dipping colors was the act of lowering the ship's national flag part way and then raise them as a salute to a passing warship.]

Wed Dec 17, 1862
Weather quite pleasant. A sail was discovered in the morning on our port bow. Was in sight all day, but we did not chase her. Beef soup and dandy funk for dinner.

[Dandy funk was a pudding made using crumbled hardtack, fat, and molasses.]

Thu Dec 18, 1862
Weather pleasant, not a sail in sight today. Drilled a short time at the pivot gun in the forenoon. Beef soup for dinner.

Fri Dec 19, 1862
Sea quite rough. Gen'l quarters at the usual hour. Duff for dinner.

Sat Dec 20, 1862
Wind high and sea very rough. The hardest storm we have had yet. Ship rolls heavily. The Captain says he thinks there has been a heavy storm about here and we are getting the last end of it. Bean soup for dinner.

Sun Dec 21, 1862

Weather quite warm and very pleasant. Sea gradually getting quiet. Quarters for inspection at 10:00 AM. Marines in fatigue coats, new trousers, and cross belts, cap covers off, chin straps down, boots black and gloves white. A Negro stood at the main mast with a fools cap on his head with the inscription, "I am one of the thieves." He is put there in punishment for stealing Vep Darling's blanket. He says he will write to Abe Lincoln and tell him how he is abused. Boiled rice for dinner.

Mon Dec 22, 1862

Weather damp and cloudy. Land in sight from the master head. Not visible from deck. Bean soup for dinner.

Tue Dec 23, 1862

Very high land in sight in the morning. Came near the first, the island of Corvo (?) about ten o'clock. We were not near enough to tell much about it. There are a few white houses at one end. We next passed the island of Flores. It appears to be more fertile than the other and has quite a town at the foot of the mountain. As we approached nearer we saw three ships, one apparently at anchor near the shore, and the other two standing in toward the island. We hoisted our colors and they all showed the English flag. We sent out a boat and boarded one of them. As our boat was returning a boat was seen putting out for us from shore with the Portuguese flag flying. She soon came alongside and contained several Portuguese and one Englishman. Capt Baldwin asked the Englishman to come on board but he declined. After asking some questions about the war and other matters he returned to the island and we stood away on our course. He said that the *Alabama* was here last September when she destroyed two whalers. Had heard nothing of her since. We passed out of sight of land about two PM. Duff for dinner. In the night a bright light was seen on our port beam. Made it out to be a large ship. Soon left [unintelligible].

Wed Dec 24, 1862

Came in sight of land again early this morning. Proved to be the island "Fagel" one of the "Azores." Said to contain about five thousand inhabitants. The houses seem to be nearly all large and white. In the evening one of the churches was illuminated and at twelve o'clock a display of fireworks was sent off. In the afternoon some bum (?) boats came alongside with eggs, oranges and c. to sell. The oranges are rather sour but very juicy. Bean soup for dinner. Christmas Eve. Did not hang up my stocking.

[Faial-Azores was the island. Gregg's diary mentions the show.]

Fri Dec 26, 1862

Weather pleasant. The American ship *Typhoon* came in today and hoisted the quarantine flag. She has been leaking badly and all her men are worn out. Has lost seven men and one mate from over work. Duff for dinner.

[Oviatt wrote in his diary for this day and refers to a yellow flag.]

Sat Dec 27, 1862

Weather damp and rainy. A French Bark and English Brigantine arrived in port to day. Fresh grub for dinner.

Sun Dec 28, 1862

Weather very pleasant. Marines at inspection in full uniform. The American brig *Azore* arrived today, having been thirteen days out from Boston. She brought some war news which is not very encouraging for us. Wrote a letter to Ed Church. Fresh grub for dinner.

[Edwin L. Church, age nineteen, was a dear friend. Brother wrote to him after important events.]

Mon Dec 29, 1862

An iron screw steamer flying the Spanish flag came in port to-day. Resembles the 290 very much. Fresh grub for dinner.

Wed Dec 31, 1862

Last day of '62. Weighed anchor at 11 o'clock AM and bid adieu to Fagal. We passed the Spanish steamer we dipped our colors but she did not return the salute. General quarters at 2:00 pm. Also at eleven PM. The first gun fired was No. 3 on the port side. So Peter Dick her captain is entitled to the barrel of slush. Fresh grub for dinner.

Thu Jan 1, 1863

New Year's Day. Left home three months ago today. In the morning about three bells the fire rung and away we went to fire quarters. Stayed there about twenty minutes when retreat was beat and we went below again. Had hardly got our belts off when the drum beat to quarters and away we went to the pivot gun. Drilled about an hour at the gun and half an hour with small arms, for the purpose I suppose of celebrating New Year's Day. In the afternoon two ships hove in sight which we have down for. The first one boarded her was French Whaling Bark. The other was an English Bark. After our boat returned we changed our course and headed North East. Marines worked all the forenoon cleaning bright work at the pivot gun. Wish it was [unintelligible]. Duff for dinner.

Fri Jan 2, 1863

Weather somewhat cooler. Drilled a short time at the pivot gun and then with small arms. Mr. Parker thinks we don't do very well. In the afternoon fired at a target with muskets. Gregg made the best shot. About forty bullets hit the target. Bean soup.

Sat Jan 3, 1863

No quarters in the morning. Last night while on watch at the cabin door I fell asleep and was discovered by Ensign Jones. Suppose he will report me. Discovered a sail on our starboard bow this PM and gave chase. Came up with her in a short time. She showed the English flag. We did not board her. Duff for dinner.

Sun Jan 4, 1863

Mr. Parker told me this morning that I had been reported for sleeping on post. Says that the next man who is caught at it will be made to walk the deck with a loaded knapsack for four days. Told me to go below and he would attend to my case. About an hour after Sergeant Morgan told me that Potts would take my place as orderly, while I would do regular guard duty, suppose this is my punishment for sleeping on post. Not very severe as I will now have less duty to do than before. All hands mustered after on the gun deck in the forenoon, and the articles of war were read by the first Lieut. Capt. Baldwin. Spoke to Mr. Parker about my old pantaloons looking badly. Not a sail in sight to-day. Boiled rice for dinner.

Mon Jan 5, 1863

Weather rather rough wind quite high. No quarters in the fore-noon. Towards evening the wind blew strong from the North East and by midnight blew a gale. The hardest blow we have had as yet. Bean soup for dinner.

Tue Jan 6, 1863

Weather very stormy. Sea very rough, the hardest storm we have had yet. The ship rolls heavily and things are flying about very promiscuously. We are in the Western Ocean said to be the most stormy in the world and we seem to be getting the full benefit of it. Duff for dinner.

Wed Jan 7, 1863

This morning sea quite smooth, compared to what it was yes-terday. Towards night the wind began to blow again and we pitched as badly as ever. Don't like this western Ocean very much. It is altogether too stormy to suit me. Don't know where we are bound but think we will put into New York again before long. Beef soup for dinner.

Thu Jan 8, 1863
Sea rather smooth again but the air cold and damp. Bob Langly says we are off the grand banks of Newfoundland. In the morning a sail was seen on our port bow which we bore down for. When we came up with her the first Lieut. ordered her to heave to which she did and we went a boat to her. She proved to be a packet ship eleven days out from New York. Gave us some papers containing news of General Burnside's defeat. Bullion beef for dinner.

Fri Jan 9, 1863
Weather very cold. Hope we may not go to New York this winter as the papers say they are having very cold weather there now. Quarters in the forenoon at the usual hour though the weather was so cold we could hardly work the gun. Duff for dinner.

Sat Jan 10, 1863
Weather rather cool but quite pleasant. The fore and main top-gallant yards were got up this morning all sail. Ship scrubbed from stem to stern and everything cleaned up bright. In the PM cleaned belts muskets and c. for Sunday inspection.

Sun Jan 11, 1863
The very roughest day we have had yet. Wind is blowing a hurricane and waves rolling mountains high. Ship rolls and pitches tremendously and sea washing over her continually. Still she carries herself nobly and all the sailors say she is a splendid sea-boat. At one time when a heavy sea struck us the wheel slipped from the hands of the wheelmen and spun around a few times but was soon secured. Boiled rice for dinner.

Mon Jan 12, 1863
Sea smooth this morning compared with yesterday. Still the ship rolls heavily and occasionally the sea washes over her. One of the sailors told me that he never knew the wind to blow so hard for so long a time as it did yesterday. Three ships in sight

today but we did not interfere with them. The sea was so rough that it was impossible to board them. Bean soup for dinner.

Tue Jan 13, 1863
Weather quite pleasant. Not a sail in sight today. General quarters at the usual hour and a short drill with muskets. Did not drill any with the pivot gun. Duff for dinner but it did not go very well as we have no molasses.

Wed Jan 14, 1863
Weather quite warm and very pleasant. Marines laid aside fatigue coats and wear jumpers. At half past one PM we fell under arms for drill on the quarter deck. Drilled about an hour. Was reported by Sergeant Pope for allowing Kimberly 2nd to go forward of the galley while it was his watch on deck. Gave me four hours extra duty. Bean soup for dinner.

[Percival Clarendon Pope, age twenty-three, was First Lieutenant. Born in Boston, Massachusetts, the son of a naval officer. Pope was promoted to Brevet Captain for action at Ft. Sumter, South Carolina. (D. Sullivan, 2019)]

Thu Jan 15, 1863
Weather warm and pleasant. In the forenoon a sail hove in sight which the officer of the deck reported to resemble the 290. Of course all hands came on deck to have a look at her. After coming nearer made her out to be a sailing frigate. Passed within about six miles of her. She did not show her colors. We had ours bent on but did not hoist them. Soon another sail hove in sight and hoisted the Breman flag. We hailed her and ordered her to heave to but she did not obey. A blank charge was then fired from one of our broadside guns but she paid no attention to that. The forward pivot gun then sent a shot across her bow (?) which brought her to in short order. We then lowered a boat and boarded her. She said she did not know what we wanted or she would have hove to sooner. Bean soup for dinner.

15. Lieut. Percival C. Pope, USMC, c. 1863, NHHC NH 85788

[The warning shot was ordained by sea law to force a ship to show nationality or colors to determine threat or purpose as ordained by the sea law.]

Fri Jan 16, 1863

Another very stormy day. The sea as rough as it was on Sunday. At one time it broke completely over the hurricane deck. I suppose we are off Cape Hatteras. The general belief on board is that we will see land in a few days. Hope it won't be New York. Duff for dinner.

Sat Jan 17, 1863

Weather cold. About 3pm came in sight of land, and came to anchor under the guns of Ft. Monroe at Clark.

Sun Jan 18, 1863

Weather very cold and coming as we do from a warm climate we feel it very keenly. Three schooners came alongside in the morning and all bands commenced coaling ship. Wrote a letter to Mother. Fortress Monroe is exactly what I expected to see. Still it looks very formidable and could no doubt sink any ship that proved the fire from its guns. The harbor here is filled with shipping of every description. The most conspicuous among them is the old Frigate *Brandywine*. She was in the war of 1812 and brought Lafayette to this country when he made his last visit here. Our boatswain's mate Welsh says he was on her when she made her last cruise. She is now a dismantled hulk and is used to store ship here. It looks too bad to see these noble old ships thrown aside as useless, when smaller and seemingly inferior ones used in their stead. Still these little non-clads do good service, and one of them could sink a dozen old ships of the line. Boiled rice for dinner.

Mon Jan 19, 1863

Weather somewhat warmer. All hands at work coaling ship. Bean soup for dinner.

Tue Jan 20, 1863

Weather colder than yesterday. Wind blows and lags (?) is quite rough. There is probably a heavy storm outside. Wrote a letter to Father in the afternoon. Mr. Parker said several other officers went to Norfolk today. Fresh grub for dinner.

Wed Jan 21, 1863

Weather warm and very pleasant. All hands still at work coaling ship. Johnson, Gregg, Harris and Towle went on shore for four hours. They went all through the fort and say it is a [unintelligible] thing. Beef soup for dinner.

Thu Jan 22, 1863

Weather rather cool. The gun-boat *Iroquois* came in this PM. Also one of our new iron-clads built on the monitor plan. Fresh grub for dinner.

Fri Jan 23, 1863

Last night the new Rebel iron-clad the *Merrimac No 2* was expected down the river and in the night the Monitor and Iroquois steamed up to Norfolk, Everything on board of us was got ready for a fight but she did not bother us. Wrote to Ella W. Duff for dinner. About eleven o'clock at night after we had all turned in, the fire bell rang and all hands turned out and commenced lashing up hammocks. Just as we were ready to stow them the First Lieut. came along and began cursing us for not getting them up sooner. Said he would have the hose turned on us the next time. Hammocks were then piped down. There was no good reason for his blowing us for none of the sailors had their hammocks stowed. Some of the men were sleeping on deck and in the hurry of dressing Johnson and Towle both got the same pair of pantaloons and each got one leg in before they discovered the mistake, finding that one pair would not cover four legs one of them surrendered the pants to the other.

Sat Jan 24, 1863

Weather quite warm. In the afternoon the steamer Mt. *Washington* came alongside with some wood for us and we marines were set to work to unload it. Worked until supper time. In the evening Vep Darling fell asleep on post again. He has been put on extra duty of four hours on and two off. Bean soup for dinner.

Sun Jan 25, 1863

Felt very unwell upon turning out in the morning. But as the Orderly Sergeant could not or would not excuse me without my seeing the Doctor, I had to do duty as usual. Worked all morning passing wood. Saw the doctor in the afternoon and was put on the sick list. Gregg took my hammock into the sick bay for me and I turned in early. This is one of the times when a fellow thinks about home. Boiled rice for dinner.

Fri Jan 30, 1863

Came off the sick list this morning. The boys were very kind to me during my sickness, Gregg and Towle in particular. Last Wednesday night we weighed anchor and dropped a little way down the bay and anchored again. Next morning we again got up anchor and went to sea. Don't know where we are bound, but everyone seems to think we are bound for Havana. Duff for dinner.

Sat Jan 31, 1863

Weather very pleasant. All hands scrubbed hammocks on the gun deck in the forenoon. No quarters until after supper. Drilled a short time at the pivot gun and at boarding and repelling boarders. Bean soup for dinner.

Sun Feb 1, 1863

Four months since I left home. Suppose I have got to stick through the four years now. All hands mustered aft on the gundeck in the forenoon and First Lieut. read about the court-martial of some bad marine, for our benefit I suppose. Boiled rice for dinner. Came in sight of land about noon. Proved to be the island "Aleaco" or "hole in the wall." One of the Bahamas. A light house was the only building we could see.

Mon Feb 2, 1863
Weather very pleasant. Bean soup for dinner. About noon a screw steamer making black smoke was discovered ahead of us. On our coming up with her she showed English and French colors. The drum beat to quarters and marines loaded muskets with ball cartridge. We sent a shot across her bows which brought her to and Mr. Alexander boarded her. She proved to be a French transport with troops bound for Mexico. We had hardly got out of sight of her before another steamer was reported ahead. We hove down for her and beat to quarters, we did not appear to gain on her much so the retreat was beat but guns were left cast loose in readiness for use. I lay down on the quarter deck near the break of the poop and went to sleep. About nine o'clock Loomis woke me up and said that the steamer was right alongside. The (our) crew were already going to quarters. I hurried below, got my belts and musket and went to my station. The steamer lay about three fourths of a mile off our port quarter. Was a long low bark ridge propeller and seemed to answer the description of the 290. We could see that she had ports and all of us expected to have a fight, or at least that we would keep in sight of her until morning, but instead and without hailing her at all we passed by and soon left her astern. The retreat was beat, hammocks piped down and the starboard watch turned in. We were all disappointed at not finding out what the steamer was. She looked suspicious at all events, and should have been overhauled. The boys seem to think that there is not much danger of our getting into a fight, and that our Captain is not much of a fighter.

[Robert J. Alexander enlisted as a private at the Marine Barracks in New York on February 24, 1832.]

Tue Feb 3, 1863

Weather warm and pleasant. Land in sight early in the morning, proved to be the island of Cuba. Steamed into the harbor of Havana and anchored about noon. I was on post in the after cock-pit at the time and could not enjoy the view of the shore we passed going in which the boys say was very nice. As we lay at present we seem to be completely surrounded by land and cannot see out to sea at all. The harbor is filled with shipping of every description. Close to us lays an English man of war a two decker, and a French three decker. Both are splendid looking vessels. There are ferry boats and horse cars here in regular New York style. Weather very warm. Thermometer at 80 today. Duff for dinner.

Wed Feb 4, 1863

Three months today since the *Vanderbilt* went into commission. A great many bum-boats around us but greenbacks will pass only at a great discount. The American Counsel for this port came on board in the forenoon. Bean soup for dinner. About four o'clock in the afternoon we weighed anchor and once more stood away to sea. In going out we passed the famous "Mora Costa." It is used as a fort and prison. A good many guns are mounted on the walls but they do not look to be very effective. Sea quite rough but weather warm. Think we are bound for Key West.

Thu Feb 5, 1863

Weather warm and pleasant in the morning but rained in the afternoon. Gave my musket a good cleaning but suppose it will be as rusty as ever in the morning. This forenoon two sails were discovered which we bore down for. One showed American colors and the other hoisted the Hamburg flag. The American did not seem inclined to heave to so a shot was fired across her bows which brought her to in short order. We sent out two boats and boarded both of them. The Hamburg ship says that the *Alabama* is off Kingston Jamaica undergoing repairs, that she lay outside the harbor as the authorities will not let her in. I suppose we will go there and see about it. In the afternoon we boarded another American ship, don't know what she was nor where from. Boiled rice for dinner.

Fri Feb 6, 1863
Weather damp and rainy. One of the most disagreeable days we have had yet. Duff for dinner.

Sat Feb 7, 1863
Weather pleasant. Cleaned our muskets and other traps in the afternoon for Sunday's inspection. My musket not very clean. Bean soup for dinner.

Sun Feb 8, 1863
Came in sight of land about two o'clock AM. Proved to be the island of Jamaica. Arrived off Port Royal about eleven o'clock and hove to for a pilot. A black pilot soon came alongside, came on board and took us in. We stayed in the harbor of Port Royal but a short time, then went around the bar to Kingston, and came to anchor. At Port Royal a bum-boat came alongside and Hooper bought four dozen oranges for a fifty cent note. Several British men of war were laying there (at Port Royal). One two decker and two three deckers. We were boarded by an officer from one of them. As we entered the harbor we passed a buoy with a cross on it said to mark the place where a church sank when the old town of Port Royal was destroyed by an earthquake. Several vessels lay at Kingston. Among them the English steamer *Clyde* of London, famous as being the vessel from which Mason and Slydell were taken by Commodore Wilkes.

Kingston is said to have thirty five thousand inhabitants, but from what we can see of the town, it does not seem to have half that number. A gentleman came on board who says that the 290 has been here but left two days ago. She was allowed to stay here as long as she chose for coal and repairs. Greenbacks don't pass here, are not worth a cent. Marines at inspection in jumpers, cross belts, white gloves, and cap covers off. My musket passed all right though I feared it would not. Boiled rice for dinner. Thermometer 87.

[George H. Hooper. Brother refers to him later as "Music Hooper." Greenbacks are paper currency printed during the Civil War.]

Mon Feb 9, 1863
Steamed out of Kingston this morning at seven o'clock. The report is that the British authorities would not let us stay there. Suppose we are now going to St. Thomas, will have to coal somewhere soon. Bean soup for dinner.

Thu Feb 10, 1863
Weather warm and pleasant, quarters at the usual hours. Land in sight nearly all day. Suppose it was St. Domingo. Passed within about seven miles of some very highland just before dark. Boarded a Spanish bark. Duff for dinner.

Wed Feb 11, 1863
Weather warm and pleasant. Thermometer at 80, no quarters in the morning. Bean soup for dinner.

Fri Feb 13, 1863
Four months since I enlisted. Came in sight of land early in the morning and in the afternoon put into St. Thomas. The US Gunboat *Alabama* is here. We will probably remain here a week or ten days. We are going to take in coal and give the ship a new coat of paint. Duff for dinner.

Sat Feb 14, 1863
All hands commenced coaling ship except the painters who are painting the ship black. Marines commenced scraping the pivot gun. It will be painted black.

We hoisted the Danish flag at our foremast and fired a salute of twenty-one guns which was returned by the fort. The town here is called St. Thomas, the same as the island. It is built on three hills, on the center hill near the top is the residence of Santa Anna the old Mexican General. On the other hills are the so called "Black Beard" and "Blue Beard" castles, said to have belonged to two old pirates of that name. Bean soup for dinner.

Sun Feb 15, 1863

Weather still very warm. Inspection in the morning but I escaped it being on post on the forecastle. All the crew were dressed in white throughout and looked very nicely. In the afternoon Serg't Pop, Music Hooper and Streaper, Privates Smith, Carberry, Kelsey, Kimmerle 2, and I went on shore. Went first to Black Beard's castle, a very old building. The steps leading to the top were rotten. After staying there a while we went over to the other hill to Blue Beards Castle. It has been re-built during the past year by the Frenchman who lives near. The shops open here in the afternoon on Sunday. As soon as they were open we went down into the town and had some refreshments.

[Charles Carberry (1835–1902) enlisted as private at Philadelphia on December 3, 1860, and joined the USS *Vanderbilt* with the other boys of Bath on November 4, 1862.]

Mon Feb 16, 1863

Carberry (?) and Pope came on board this morning. The sailors have been coming on board all day, most of them pretty drunk. Serg't Morgan, Corpl McCandles, Ed McKee, Bandfield [George H. Bandfield], Angus, Oviatt, and Potts went on shore in the PM. In the evening Angus was brought on board in a shore boat. He had lost his blouse and was soaking wet, having jumped overboard in coming from shore.

[George N. Angus was from Ithaca, New York, and a neighbor to Johnson, Murdoch, and was acquainted with the telegraph innovator and wealthy Ezra Cornell, later living next door to him.]

Tue Feb 17, 1863

A brig loaded with coal came alongside this morning, and all hands, except those on liberty commenced coaling ship. Corporal Kane, Darling, Devlin, Kimmerle 1, Loomis and Ingersoll went on shore in the afternoon. Fresh grub for dinner.

16. Pvt. George Bandfield, USMC, was from Hinsdale, NY, courtesy Troy Hillman

Wed Feb 18, 1863

Darling, Kimberly 1, Ingersoll and Loomis came on board this morning about nine o'clock. Vep had a bottle in pocket but the ships Corporal found it and broke it. The boys say that Kane and Devlin are in the lock up on shore. Hope they may stay there a while. The orderly Serg't from the *Alabama* was on board this afternoon. Gregg and Harris went on shore at half past six PM. Bean soup for dinner.

Thu Feb 19, 1863

Weather very warm. Gregg came on board this AM at ten o'clock and was immediately put in the brig by orders of the first Lieut. It seems that this morning while the boat was at the wharf, Gregg and Harris were on the beach picking up shells, when Mr. Conner and Mr. Jones came along and told them to go on board immediately. Gregg told them that he had liberty for twenty-four hours and that the time had not yet expired. Mr. Conner said that that made no difference, that Mr. Daniels ordered him to bring them on board. Gregg told him that Mr. Parker gave them their liberty and that he had often told them to take no orders from any one unless they came through him. Conner said that Mr. Parker was under the command of the First Lieut. Luff the same as anyone else. Gregg and Harris then got into the boat. Harris got out to get some bread and while he was gone the boat shoved off. As soon as they came on board Connor reported Gregg to the first luff who had him put into the brig without irons. I hope the time will come when we will have a chance to get even with some of these officers. Kane and Duvlin came on board this morning. Have been in the fort since Tuesday night. Devlin's face is pretty well pounded. He got into a fight with some of the sailors and as they are all down on him he was soundly threshed. Harris came on board about eleven o'clock AM. In the afternoon Towle, Johnson, and Murdoch went on shore. The last batch of the marines is now on liberty and I am glad of it for we have been doing duty at the rate of two on and four off since Monday. A steamer arrived in port today bringing in the captain and crew of the *Jacob Bell* an American merchant vessel which was captured and burned by the privateer *Florida*. For dinner today we had the regular old original bullion soup. It didn't taste as good as usual. Boacher has forgotten how to make it, or else does not care.

[Luff is name for the executive officer.]

Fri Feb 20, 1863

Towle, Johnson, and Murdoch came on board this forenoon. Duff for dinner. At seven o'clock in the evening we got up anchor and steamed out of St. Thomas. We have a pilot on board who is acquainted with every nook and corner of the West Indies, and he promises to find the 290 for us. Captain Baldwin offer him five thousand dollars if he will lay us alongside of her on the high seas. This same pilot found the sumpter for the *Iroquois* when she was cruising after her. The US Steamer *Alabama* left St. Thomas early this morning. She also is in search of rebel privateers. Don't know where we are going, some say to Martinique.

Sat Feb 21, 1863

Land in sight all day. Bean soup for dinner. In the evening about nine o'clock all hands were called to quarters. The report is that a steamer was seen bearing down for us. I was on post in the brig at the time and thought we were going to have a fight sure as we commenced getting up shell from the shell rooms. After remaining at quarters about fifteen minutes the retreat was beat and port watch turned in.

Sun Feb 22, 1863

The birthday of those two good men, George Washington and Henry Brother. The latter is sixty-two years old.

This morning early we came in sight of Martinique. As we were running along the coast a steamer came out from under cover of the land and hailed us. She was the USS *Alabama*. We hove to and sent a boat to her. We were at that time off the town of St. Prince. The *Alabama* went in to the harbor to see if she could hear anything about privateers, while we lay outside and waited for her. After a while she came out and we both stood and waited for her. After a while she came out and we both stood away along the coast. She proved to be no match for us in speed for we soon left her astern and lost sight of her. Martinique as we saw it from the deck was the most beautiful sight of the kind that I ever saw.

The land is hilly and covered with vegetation. We passed out of sight of it and at sundown came to anchor off the town of Point-a-Pitre on the island of Guadeloupe. This is one of the prettiest places we have seen. It is owned by France and nearly all the vessels in the harbor float the French flag. Some of the people came on board to have a look at our ship: She excites a great deal of attention. We are surrounded by boats from the town. So large a ship was ever here before. They say our money will pass here. Oranges are sold three for a cent, and bananas two for a cent, so one of the darkies told us. We have not as yet had a chance to buy any. Boiled rice for dinner.

[Brother's father Henry served two terms as sheriff. His grandfather Valentine was sheriff too, but also quartermaster, state senator, land surveyor, and tavern owner. His great grandfather leaped to his adventure from Germany and boarded a ship to America to be sold on her shore to the highest bidder. He did his time as an indentured servant and then married his matron, produced more children, and modernized a tavern in the right spot at the right time so that George Washington, John Adams, and their men stopped to refuel, reload, and burst into song. (Towle, n.d.)]

Mon Feb 23, 1863
Steamed out of Point-a-Pitre this morning at seven o'clock. About noon a steamer was discovered ahead. Proved to be the *Alabama* laying to and waiting for us. We soon came up to her, hove to and sent a boat to her. The boat soon returned and she steamed away and was soon out of sight. We lay to until eight o'clock in the evening. In the afternoon a shark was seen around our bows and a hook baited with a piece of pork was put overboard to catch him. He was caught and pulled clear out of the water but fell off the hook before he could be got on board. He was five or six feet long. Some dolphins were also seen, and Cornel the Armorers mate harpooned one of them. They were very pretty fish. Bean soup for dinner.

17. George Washington stopped at Brother's Tavern. Library of Congress

Tue Feb 24, 1863
Duff for dinner. In the afternoon came to a small sandy island called "Bird Key." Sent a boat and got a few bags of sand. Some of the sailors brought off some very pretty shells and some sponges. Five negroes live on the island to tend a light kept there. In the evening about nine o'clock a large ship was discovered near us and apparently bearing down for us. All hands flew to quarters, but as usual we passed her without hailing.

CHAPTER 4

The *Peterhoff*

Wed Feb 25, 1863

Came in sight of the island of St. Thomas about 10:00 AM. Arrived off the same port we were in before at one PM. Saw three US men-o-war inside. We hoisted our colors and number and they did the same. They were ship *Shepard Knapp* and Steamers *Oneida* and *Wachusett*. The latter is Commodore Wilke's flag ship. As were coming around the point before we were in sight of the ship of the town a two masted screw steamer came out and stood away to sea. She showed the English flag. We hove to and sent a boat into the harbor. It was met by a boat from [unintelligible] with instructions for us to overhaul the steamer that had just gone out. Our boat returned and we immediately got under way and bore down for the Englishman. It is said that when she was going out she passed directly under the stem of the flag ship and someone on board of her sung out "her's a prize catch us if you can." They did not know that the *Vanderbilt*, the fastest ship afloat was coming around the point. We soon overtook her and sent a boat to her. Our officer (Mr. Kiser) reported that her papers were not right so we sent an armed crew to take possession of her. We then put into St. Thomas and came to anchor. Weighed anchor about seven o'clock and stood away from the steamer. While we were getting up anchor Sergeant Morgan came to me and told me to get ready to go on board the prize and go to Key West with her. Darling, Deuling, Kimmerle 1st and Corp'l McCandles were also detailed to go.

We went on board about eleven o'clock at night. I was the first one for post duty. Was stationed at the cabin door with orders to allow no one to go in or out without permission from the officer on deck. We marines were put into the 2nd cabin, the filthy hole I ever slept in. All the sailors and firemen and most of the officers of the prize were sent on board the *Vanderbilt*. The captain and Mate and several men claiming to be passengers left with us. They are a hard looking set and we may have trouble before we are rid of them. The prize is the English steamer *Peterhoff*. I will be glad to get on board the *Vanderbilt* again. Several sailors and firemen from the *Vanderbilt*, and Act'g Master Leims, Masters Mate Jones and an Ass't Engineer, complete the prize crew.

[These parentheses indicating that the officer was Mr. Kinser were part of the Lilly transcript. Possibly William Kisner? Deulin could be Devlin.]

Thu Feb 26, 1863
At four o'clock this morning the Paymaster came on board and we all signed our accounts. We got under way at seven o'clock. As we stood out to sea the *Vanderbilt* stood away apparently for St. Thomas. Our engine gave out about eleven o'clock and we set all sail but made very little headway. For dinner we had some corned beef that we had stolen somewhere about the ship, and some hard bread. Kimmerle and Darling got a box of raisins somewhere so we got along very well.

Fri Feb 27, 1863
Cleaned out our state room this morning. Got the engine to work again about eight O'clock. About 10:00 AM a steamer hove in sight and bore down for us. Proved to be the US steamer *Alabama*. She hailed us, asked us when we left St. Thomas, where the *Vanderbilt* was and c. and c. She did not board us. Land in sight all day. Have made very good progress. Sea in the afternoon quite rough. Ship rolled heavily and let in considerable water over her bows.

Sat Feb 28, 1863
Weather pleasant. In the afternoon passed a brig, bound west.

Sun Mar 1, 1863
Weather very warm. The English captain and passengers held service in the cabin in the forenoon. Five months since I left home.

Mon Mar 2, 1863
Weather very pleasant. Vep Darling got some flour and made a cake for dinner, such cake.

Tue Mar 3, 1863
Weather warm and pleasant. Ate some fried pork for the first time in my life.

Wed Mar 4, 1863
Four months since the *Vanderbilt* went into commission. Nothing new on board the *Peterhoff*.

Thu Mar 5, 1863
Passed Cape St. Antonio light house this morning at four o'clock, expect we will make Key West tomorrow or next day. Hope so, am getting tired of this prize.

Fri Mar 6, 1863
The post on the cabin door was taken off this morning. We marines now stand watch and watch with bluejackets.

Sat Mar 7, 1863
Came in sight of Cedar Keys this morning. Came to anchor off Key West about four o'clock PM. The flag ship St. *Lawrence* steam frigate *Colorado* and other US vessels are here. The *Colorado* is the first ship I have seen except *Vanderbilt*.

18. Rear Admiral Theodorus Bailey, USN, NHHC NH 56066

Mon Mar **9, 1863**
Admiral Bailey came on board this afternoon and we marines
turned out to receive him. Don't know what he will do with the
Peterhoff. Sent a letter to Father.

[Theodorus Bailey (1805–1877) was from upstate New York, becoming a
midshipman at age thirteen.]

Tue Mar 10, 1863
Orders were received from the Admiral today to take our prize to Boston. Am afraid we will never see the *Vanderbilt* again. Hope we may get back to her sometime. McCandles went on shore and brought some soft tack, two hams, some sugar, salt and cheese. Cost us each a dollar. Everything is very high on shore, we will live a little better for a while.

Wed Mar 11, 1863
Capt. Temple came on board this morning and took the captain's little dog on board the flagship. Ten negroes were sent on board of us from shore. And commenced getting the coal out of the fore-hold and filling up the bunkers.

Sun Mar 15, 1863
All quiet on board the *Peterhoff*. In the forenoon four of our passengers went on board a British bark. She is bound for Mexico.

Mon Mar 16, 1863
The darkies came on board again this morning and went on with the coaling. One of them brought off some very nice shells and Vep Darling and I bought them off him.

Thu Mar 19, 1863
Weighed anchor about five PM and bit adieu to Key West. We are bound for either New York or Boston. We have another Engineer on board who is going North with us. Also a gentleman passenger. Passed a steamer about nine o'clock in the evening. Between ten and eleven o'clock Mr. Wright our Engineer had one of this fingers cut off by the machinery, and another so badly crushed that it will have to be cut off as soon as we come across a surgeon.

Fri Mar 20, 1863
Weather in the morning cloudy and damp. In the afternoon the wind freshened up and by six o'clock blew a gale. The ship rolled badly. Cannot weather a storm as well as the *Vanderbilt*.

Sat Mar 21, 1863
The storm continued all night, but wind has gone down and sea quite smooth today.

Sun Mar 22, 1863
Came in sight of the fleet off Port Royal at two PM. Were boarded by a boat from a side wheel steamer. A Surgeon came on board and looked at Mr. Wright's hand but did not like to do anything to it. He is a young looking chap and doesn't seem to understand his business very well. The captain of the steamer came on board also. After they left us we stood in for Port Royal. Were boarded by a pilot who took us in and anchored us near the frigate *Wabash*. She is flag ship at this station. The old line of battle ship *Vermont* is also here. There are several monitors here, the fleet here is expecting a fight soon. In the evening Mr. Wright went on board the *Wabash*.

Mon Mar 23, 1863
We got some fresh water from the *Vermont* today. Weighed anchor about eleven o'clock, but after going out a little way came to anchor again because of the fog being so heavy. After a little while we got up anchor again, but dropped it again after going a short distance. After the fog cleared away I found that instead of going out towards sea we had only gone over nearer the north shore. Mr. Wright returned from the flag-ship. The surgeon there declined to do anything for his hand unless he stayed on board of her. Am afraid he will lose his hand.

Tue Mar 24, 1863
Weighed anchor at seven o'clock this AM and put out to sea. Expect we will be in New York in five or six days. Weather damp and rainy.

Sat Mar 28, 1863

Came in sight of Egg Harbor light house last week. Were boarded by a New York pilot at three o'clock this morning. Steamed up the bay and came to anchor off Brooklyn Navy Yard about 8:00 AM. Weather here is quite cold and feels very severe after our being in warm climate. In the afternoon we had a hard rain and during my watch on deck I got wet through. Don't know what will be done with us marines but we will probably be sent to the barracks before long. Hope to get off this boat soon as we are all heartily sick of her.

Sun Mar 29, 1863

The prize steamer *Nicholas 1st* came in today and anchored alongside of us. She was captured while trying to run the blockade by the gun boat *Victoria*. She is loaded with arms and ammunition. Weather today quite cold. Mr. Lanis (?) and Mr. Jones both on shore.

Tue Mar 31, 1863

Weather cold, rained and snowed all day. All of us got wet through again. About four o'clock PM two tug boats came alongside. We shipped our cable and they took us down the river and into the Atlantic docks. There we bid adieu to the *Peterhoff*, took our baggage on board one of the tugs and were taken to the receiving ship *North Carolina*. There we got off. The sailors and Firemen went on board the *North* and we, leaving our bags there marched up to the barracks. Were put into room No. 4. Sent out and bought some soft tack, butter and cheese and had a good supper. Cameron is here doing duty. Says he likes it first rate.

CHAPTER 5

Brooklyn Navy Yard in 1863

Wed Apr 1, 1863
Scrubbed out our room this morning. Had the best breakfast that I have had from some time. The grub is better than when we were here before. We now have potatoes scouse and soft tack, and all the coffee we can drink, first rate soup for dinner and all we want of it. Lots of good bread and coffee for supper. Major Zeilen is in command here and the boys all like him so well they call him "Billy Zeilen."

Thu Apr 2, 1863
Cameron went to the Naval Lyceum last night and got a letter for me and two for Vep Darling. They said at the Lyceum that they had sent the Vanderbilt's mail to Key West only a few days ago. Kimmerle and I went to the Major in the morning and asked for liberty and he gave all the *Peterhoff*'s guard liberty until Friday morning at 8 o'clock. We went out at 10 o'clock. Crossed over to New York at Cath St. Ferry. Went down to the Belmont Hotel where Kimerle left us promising to be back at two o'clock. Darling and I had dinner there and then walked about until two o'clock when we went back to the Belmont. About half past two Kimerle came along and we all went to Union Square. In the evening took supper at the Belmont and went to the New Bowery theatre. Got to barracks shortly after midnight.

Fri Apr 3, 1863
Good Friday. Nothing to do today. Am on for guard tomorrow.

Sat Apr 4, 1863
On guard at barracks, post No. 5–1st relief countersign "Colonel" weather cold and damp. Rained and strong wind from North West.

Sun Apr 5, 1863
Easter Sunday. On liberty, did not go out until evening. Went to Cath street ferry and over to New York. Got back to barracks at half past nine.

Mon Apr 6, 1863
On guard at barracks. Post No. 21st relief, countersign "Squadron." Received a letter and two papers from Father and a letter from Mary. Father sent me a five dollar bill and Mary some postage stamps and paper and envelopes. All were acceptable.

Tue Apr 7, 1863
On liberty not feeling well, have a bad cold. In the evening went over to the Belmont and had something to eat. Got back at eight o'clock.

Wed Apr 8, 1863
On guard at barracks, 3rd relief post No. 6, Countersign "Ship."

Thu Apr 9, 1863
On liberty, went over to New York in the afternoon, got very tired walking so much and came back to barracks at 8 o'clock so lame I could barely walk. Wrote to Father.

Fri Apr 10, 1863
Supernumerary (?) today to the barracks guard. Sear'gt Conner passed me out in the evening, went over to New York. Got back at twelve o'clock. Wrote to Mary.

Sat Apr 11, 1863

On guard at barracks, post No 6, 3rd relief. Countersign "Hunter." Lieut. Bishop inspected us in the morning and ordered me out because my gloves were black and shoes white, when they should have been visa versa.

[Henry Jeremiah Bishop, about age twenty-five here, was born in New Haven, Connecticut, and commissioned as second Lieutenant of Marines in September 1861. He would not go out to sea until his detachment on USS *Sabine* two weeks later, on April 25th. (D. Sullivan, 2019)]

Sat Apr 12, 1863

On liberty, in the evening went to the Belmont and had a good supper. Got back to barracks about half past eight. Rec'd a letter from Mary. Wrote to her and to Fred Towner.

Mon Apr 13, 1863

On guard at barracks. Post No. 2 2nd relief Countersign "Ironsides." Weather pleasant. Rec'd a letter from Mrs. Ingersoll to send to Will. Rec'd a paper from Father.

Tue Apr 14, 1863

On Liberty. All hands in barracks paid off. We of the *Peterhoffs* guard do not get our pay as our accounts did not come in time. Went over to New York in the evening, went to the old Bowery Theatre, got back about one o'clock.

Wed Apr 15, 1863

For a wonder I am left off today. Nothing to do. Guard went on in full uniform. I had to wear Vep Darling's uniform coat as I left mine on the *Vanderbilt*. Old Baker leaves the canteen today. The orderly Sergeant is going to run it hereafter.

Thu Apr 16, 1863

On guard at Navy Yard. Post No 5 (Dry Dock) 2nd relief. Lieut. Powell officer of the day. Countersign "Storm." And very appropriate too as the weather was cold and it rained nearly all day and night. The officer of the day visited me twice on post. Rec'd a letter from Mary and one from Fred Towner. Mary writes that Mr. J.T. Allen is coming to New York.

Fri Apr 17, 1863
On Liberty. Went over to New York in the evening. Went to the Merchants hotel and saw Mr. Allen. Also saw Charley Hagadorn of Elmira. It seems good to see someone from home. We all went to Barnum's Museum in the evening. Saw Commodore Nutt and Minnie Warren. Also some Indian Chiefs. Got back to barracks at eleven o'clock.

Sat Apr 18, 1863
On guard at barracks. Post No. 5, 2nd relief. Worst relief of all. Countersign "Norfolk."

Sun Apr 19, 1863
On liberty. Wrote a letter to Mary, one to Fred Towner and one to Val [Valentine Brother]. Went over to New York in the evening. Went to Merchants Hotel but did not see any one I knew. Got back about eleven o'clock.

Mon Apr 20, 1863
On guard at Navy Yard. Post No 5 (Dry Dock) Countersign "Troy." Lieut. Stillman officer of the day.

Tue Apr 21, 1863
On liberty, went over to New York in the evening and saw Mr. Allen and Charley Mather. Got back about eleven o'clock.

Wed Apr 22, 1863
Left off today. Was sent with the carpenter and another man to Major Doughty's house in Brooklyn to help his wife move. Got back about noon. After dinner layed down and went to sleep. Did not wake up for roll call. Came near being put in "the brig."

[The 1860 Census shows Isaac T. Doughty (1799–1890) as ship master and his wife was Eliza or Elizabeth. (D. Sullivan, 2019)]

Thu Apr 23, 1863
On guard at Navy Yard. 1st relief, post No 5 (Dry Dock) Countersign "West." Lieut. Stillman officer of the day. Did not take my fatigue cap with me for which omission I got a blessing from the officer of the day.

Fri Apr 24, 1863
On liberty. Charley Mather came over to barracks and Darling and I went down to the Navy Yard with him. In the evening Vep and I went over to New York. Went to the Belmont Hotel and had supper. Found Charley Mather there. He went over to Brooklyn. Got back to barracks at half past one. Rec'd a letter from Mary in the morning with five dollars from Father.

Sat Apr 25, 1863
On guard at barracks. Post No. 6 (Officers quarters) Counter sign "Mackinaw." Lieut. Meeker officer of the day. Weather warm and pleasant.

[Edward Percy Meeker, age twenty-six, was born in Brooklyn, NY. He entered the Navy when he was twenty-two in 1859, starting his career as a captain's clerk. His great grandfather, Jonathan Meeker, was captain of the Essex County Troop in the Revolutionary War. He eventually ranked up captain with his last duty as Commanding Marine Guard, USS *Chicago* Jun 1892–Mar 1893.]

Sun Apr 26, 1863
On liberty. In the morning rec'd a letter from Fred Towner. In the afternoon Darling and I went over to New York. Got into a 3rd Avenue car at the City Hall to go to Central Park but missed the park and went up to Harlam. Stayed there a short time then went down town again. Had supper at the Belmont, got back about one o'clock.

Mon Apr 27, 1863
On guard at Navy Yard. Post No 8 (Ironclad *Roanoke*). Countersign "River." Lieut. Powell officer of the day. Weather warm and pleasant.

Tue Apr 28, 1863
On liberty. Went to the Merchants hotel to see Mr. Allen but he was not in. Went to Baum's [Barnam's Museum] to see his dog show. It didn't amount to much. Got back at twelve o'clock.

Wed Apr 29, 1863
Ready man today for a wonder, and a greater wonder still no police work to do. In the evening about half past seven a fire broke out in the soap factory opposite the barracks. It burned some time before the engines could get to work, but when they got started they soon put it out. It was all out by nine o'clock. No tattoo in the morning.

Thu Apr 30, 1863
On guard at Navy Yard. Post No. 8 3rd relief. Countersign "Fast." Lieut. Stillman officer of the day. On account of this being a national fast day, all work is suspended in the yard. Rec'd a *Steuben Courier* from home.

Fri May 1, 1863
On liberty. Went to merchants hotel to see Mr. Allen but he had gone home.

Sat May 2, 1863
On guard at barracks. Post No. 3. 1st relief. Countersign "Saxon." Weather quite warm.

Sun May 3, 1863
On liberty. In the afternoon went down by the Naval Hospital and took a stroll in Williamsburg. In the evening Kimberle and I went over to New York. Got back about half post twelve.

Mon May 4, 1863
Ready man today. Weather damp and rainy. Therefore no police work to do. Rec'd a letter and paper from Mary.

Tue May 5, 1863
On guard at Navy Yard. Post No. 5. Countersign "Stoneman." Lieut. Mead officer of the day. Erastus Farr of Bath and a friend of his came to the yard to see me. Got them passed down into the yard. Weather very unpleasant. Cold and rainy.

[J. S. Farr had a watch, clock, and jewelry store in Bath since 1842. By 1866, if not earlier, they were advertising sewing machines. Erastus B. Farr, age twenty-two, was also a jeweler, watchmaker, and inventor. When E.B.'s son John died in 1936, his friends wrote the following: "He had served as Bath village treasurer. He was long active in the Bath Fire Department, a former president of the Rescue Hook and Ladder Company. He was a member of the St. Thomas Episcopal Church. . . He loved Bath, its institutions and its people and his life was but one after another service, gladly rendered in their interests and frequently at his personal sacrifice." E.B. was a Freemason, like Brother, but rose with the Cryptic Masons, serving as officer alongside our Marine's older brother Valentine Brother and Charles Dudley. E.B. liked fishing. After the war, E.B. and their friend James Sutherland took serious efforts to restock Lake Salubria with choice fish varieties. (*Steuben Advocate*, Dec 11, 1936) E.B. was a celebrated inventor at the age of fifteen, winning the county fair's special mention for his miniature steam engine. (List of Premiums. Awarded at the 4th annual Fair of the Steuben Co. Agricultural Society, held at Bath, on the 8th and 9th of Oct 1856 under "Farming Implements")]

Wed May 6, 1863
On liberty but did not go out. Promised to go over and see Erastus Farr, but did not go on account of rain and cold.

Thu May 7, 1863
Weather very unpleasant. No police work to do. Have so far been very lucky in that respect. Wrote to Mary.

Fri May 8, 1863
On guard at Navy Yard. Post No 7, 3rd relief. Lieut. Stillman officer of the day. Countersign "Putnam." Weather very pleasant. Rec'd a letter from Mother.

Sat May 9, 1863
On liberty. In the afternoon went over to New York. Went up to 32nd Street to see Mary Becker. Found her after hunting around some time. She knew me once at once though it is six years since we had met. Spent the afternoon very pleasantly, stayed there to supper. In the evening went with her to see a friend of hers on 3rd Ave, Miss Maggie Cooper, got back to barracks at twelve o'clock.

[Brother met Mary Becker about 1858. In the Bath newspaper The Advocate on October 7, 1891, Brother's name appears on a register of names of persons who attended the 1858 fair, which may have been an extra special event to print a list of attendees. It was an appropriate place to mingle with girls outside of church and school. Vroman Becker's large estate sale in 1858 in Geneva was an event too. Mary Becker and Maggie Cooper both graduated from the Female Department of the high school, fitted to be primary grade teachers under the instruction of Frances E. A. Gutch, who was in charge of the department for school No. 49, located at 239 E. 37th Street, just a few steps from the Becker family. Mary and Maggie Cooper were schoolteachers with the Ward School No. 49, in the 21st Ward. School No. 49 was on 37th Street, near 2nd Ave.]

Sun May 10, 1863
Ready man today and being Sunday no police work to do. Wrote to Mother. Weather warm and pleasant.

Mon May 11, 1863
On guard at Navy Yard. Post No 7. Was detailed for No 1 but changes with Dogherty. 3rd relief. Countersign "Grand." Lieut. Mead officer of the day. Weather warm and very pleasant.

Tue May 12, 1863
On liberty. In the forenoon a guard of 12 privates, 2 corporals and a Sergeant were sent on board the gunboat *Ticonderoga*. Charley Kimberle with them, we were very sorry to have him go but that made no difference, he had to go. In the afternoon Darling and I went down to the Navy Yard. Tried to get on board the *Ticonderoga* but could not. We then went to the Lyceum and over to New York. We saw the 1st Reg't New York Volunteers come home. They were as brown as Negros. The NY City 6th and 7th Regiments turned out to receive them. They all marched through the park in front of City Hall. We had supper at the Belmont Hotel. In the evening went to hear Woods Minstrels. Got back to barracks at half past eleven.

Wed May 13, 1863
Seven months since I enlisted. Rec'd a paper from Mary. On guard at barracks, post No 2 (Major's quarters) countersign "Court." Weather warm in the morning but cool in afternoon and evening.

Thu May 14, 1863
On liberty. In the forenoon a draft of 21 privates was sent on board the *San Jacinto*, Vep Darling was sent with them. I am now the only one left of the *Peterhoff*'s guard. Very sorry to part with Darling and he didn't not want to go without me but it could not be helped. In the afternoon about 40 men came to barracks from the *Susquehanna*. She has just gone out of commission. They are fine looking men. In the evening went over to New York. Had supper at the Belmont. Then walked up to 35th street and rode down in the 3rd Avenue Car. Got back to barrack's about half past eleven.

Fri May 15, 1863
In the cook room. In the evening went out by permission of Serg't Deemer. Walked about Brooklyn a while and then back to barracks.

Sat May 16, 1863
On guard at Navy Yard, past No 7, 3rd relief. Countersign "Gileson." Lieut. Powell officer of the day.

Sun May 17, 1863
On liberty, did not go out. Wrote to Mary.

Mon May 18, 1863
On guard at Navy Yard, post No 1 2nd relief. Countersign "Porter." Lieut. Meeker O.D.

Tues May 19, 1863
On liberty in the evening went over to New York, got into a stage and rode to 36th St. Rode down in a 3rd Ave. car. Got to barracks about eleven o'clock.

Wed May 20, 1863
Very much surprised by receiving a visit from Father and Mary in the afternoon. Was on duty with the prisoners when Barger came and relieved me saying that he guessed my father and sister had come to seem me. Was of course glad to see them but sorry that Mother did not come too. Took them around the barracks and showed them the rooms. They seemed very much pleased with them, promised to come over next morning at 10 o'clock. On guard at barracks, post No 6. 2nd relief.

Thu May 21, 1863
On liberty. Father and Mary came to barracks about eleven o'clock. We all went over to the Navy Yard. Went around the yard and through the Lyceum. Went over to New York to the Merchants Hotel to dinner about half past one o'clock. Stayed there all afternoon. In the evening all went to Niblo's Theatre. Saw Miss Bateman in the play of *Leah the Forsaken*. A fine play and drew tears from many in the audience. Went back to the Merchants Hotel with Father and Mary. Then back to barracks with a box full of eatables brought from home.

Fri May 22, 1863

Was detailed for Navy Yard guard but Ser't Deemer let me off and gave me a pass to go out until twelve o'clock PM. Father and Mary came over about 10:00 AM. From the barracks we went to Fulton Ferry there took a car for Greenwood Cemetery. Stayed there about an hour. They were very much pleased with it. Came back on the South Ferry car, crossed over to New York. Went to Wall Street. Saw the Merchants exchange and US Treasury buildings. Went to the Merchants Hotel for dinner. In the afternoon went up to Central Park with Mr. and Mrs. Geo Knight who also were at the Merchants. We drove out and all around the park. Got back to the hotel about half past four o'clock. Then went over to Jersey City where Mary and Father took the car for home. Went back to New York and up to see Mary Becker. Got back to Barracks about twelve o'clock.

Sat May 23, 1863

On guard at Navy Yard, post No. 5, 2nd relief, countersign "Vicksburg." Captain Heywood officer of the day. The warmest day we have had this season.

Sun May 24, 1863

On liberty. Not feeling well did not go out. Weather cold. Wrote to Val.

Mon May 25, 1863

On guard at Navy Yard. Post No 1., 2nd relief. Countersign "Victory" Lieut. Bishop Officer of the day. Rec'd a letter and *Courier* from Mary.

Tue May 26, 1863

On liberty. Darling came over to barracks in the afternoon and we went to New York. Had supper at the Belmont. While in New York we met the English steward of the *Peterhoff*. He says she is not a lawful prize. Went to Niblo's theatre. Saw Miss Bateman in *The Hunchback*. Got back to barracks at one o'clock.

Wed May 27, 1863
On guard at barracks. Post No 6. 1st relief. Countersign "Cabinet." Weather very warm.

Thu May 28, 1863
On liberty, went to New York after supper. Went to Niblo's theatre. Saw Miss Bateman in the play of *Geraldine*. Like her better every time. Got back to 12 o'clock.

Fri May 29, 1863
On guard at barracks. Post No 6–3rd relief. Countersign "North." Two privates sent on board the *Circassian*.

Sat May 30, 1863
On liberty but did not go out.

Sun May 31, 1863
In the cook room. Went over to New York in the evening. Went to St. Paul's Church.

Mon Jun 1, 1863
On guard at Navy Yard. Post No 1 2nd relief. Countersign "Champion." Lieut. Bishop officer of the day. Rec'd a letter and paper from Mary.

Tue Jun 2, 1863
On liberty, did not go out until evening. Went to Myrtle Ave and bought some white lead and zinc. Got back before tattoo.

Wed June 3, 1863
On guard at Navy Yard. Post No 1. 1st relief. Lieut. Meeker officer of the day. Countersign "Mexico."

Thu Jun 4, 1863
On liberty, did not go out until evening. Then took a walk up to Myrtle Avenue.

Fri Jun 5, 1863

Ready man today. Rec'd a letter from Father saying that he had sent a blanket for me by Mr. W.W. Wilson of Bath and that he will leave it at 326 Broadway New York. Went to the Major and he gave me special liberty. Went over to 326 Broadway but did not get the blanket. Was told that Mr. Wilson had probably left it with the man who sold to him and that the man was not in. Saw the 6, 7, 8, 23, 69, and several other New York Regiments on parade. Saw General T. F. Meagher. Wrote to Father in the evening.

[Thomas Francis Meagher was Army Brigadier General of the 69th or Irish Brigade.]

Sat Jun 6, 1863

In the morning rec'd orders to pack my duds and get ready to board the *North Carolina*. Did not want to go and tried to get out of it but there was no use in talking, had to go. Only two of us were sent. Fleming and I. Got on board about 10:00 AM. Was not put on post until ten at night. Don't like this ship very well and will get out of her soon if it is possible. Rec'd a paper from home.

[Fleming was about twenty-five years old here, from the New York Finger Lakes region.]

Sun Jun 7, 1863

Weather warm and pleasant. In the forenoon Admiral Paulding came on board. Marines in full uniform and white pants. The admiral inspected the men, shook hands with some of the old sailors and left after staying on board about an hour. Rec'd a letter from Mary.

Mon Jun 8, 1863

Weather warm. In the morning early a draft of sailors left for Philadelphia to go on the sloop of war *Tuscarora*. In the afternoon another draft went on board the *Seminole*. She went into commission today.

19. Rear Admiral Hiram Paulding, NHHC NH 88387

Tue Jun 9, 1863
Weather warm, rained in the PM. A draft of sailors went on board the steamer *Adelia*. Wrote to Mary. In the afternoon cleaned muskets, belts and c.

Wed Jun 10, 1863
In the forenoon at 9 o'clock, marines in full uniform went over into the yard and were drilled about an hour by Serg't Alexander. Weather warm. Wrote to Val.

[Robert J. Alexander, age forty-six here, enlisted in 1832. Had been attached to the USRS *North Carolina* since 1849.]

Thu Jun 11, 1863
A draft of sailors left the ship for the *Adelia*. On liberty. Went out about noon. Went over to New York and bought a pair of boots in Fulton Street for four dollars. Went to 326 Broadway and got my blanket. Went to the Belmont Hotel and got something to eat. Went over to Brooklyn to the barracks and had supper there. Went over to New York again. Went to Niblo's theatre. The play was *The Dukes Motto*. After the theatre went over to the Navy Yard. As it was too late to get on board the *North* spent the night at the guard house.

Fri Jun 12, 1863
Got on board about six o'clock in the morning. Darling came on board for a short time. Drew a pair of shoes and three pairs white pantaloons.

Sat Jun 13, 1863
Damp and rainy. Cleaned belts on the [unintelligible] deck.

Sun Jun 14, 1863
Weather very warm. In the morning all hands mustered on the spar deck and Captain Mead read the articles of war. Rec'd letters from Val and Mary. Wrote to Mary.

20. Valentine Brother, Charley's oldest sibling, courtesy Marjorie Peterson

Mon Jun 15, 1863
In the morning had knapsack inspection on the berth deck.
Then went over into the yard and drilled an hour and a half.

Tue Jun 16, 1863
On liberty, went over to New York after dinner. Went over to
Fulton St. and to the City Hall park. Had supper at the Belmont

Hotel. Took a car and rode up to 45th St. Went over to Madison Avenue and came down in a stage. Saw Jim Randall in Fulton St. Got on board about 9 o'clock.

[James or "Jim" was a classmate from Bath and the son of Sheriff Jacob Randall, whose occupation was "a gentleman." This meeting must have been after the Battle at Chancellorsville (April 30–May 6, 1863) with the 24th NY Cavalry. He was at Chancellorsville and later paymaster with McClellan's staff. According to his 1893 obituary, "At Chancellorsville he received a shot through the groin which paralyzed his lower limbs. He managed to crawl into a nearby cornfield where he buried his lower parts in the soft dirt and staunched the flow of blood which kept him from bleeding to death. . . His war wounds continued to cause pain all his life and he became addicted to narcotics." (*Middletown Daily Times*, Nov 27, 1893)]

Wed Jun 17, 1863
Weather very warm. Some gentlemen came on board who I suppose were important personages as the guard was called out in full uniform to receive them. A salute of eighteen guns was fired from the Cole [coal] Deck battery, when they came on board and when they left the ship.

Thu Jun 18, 1863
Corporal Chas Brown was today reduced to the ranks by order of Captain Mead for allowing a boy to escape from him. Private Wood received a worthless discharge for overstaying his liberty and c.

[Charles Brown enlisted as a private June 5, 1858, Brooklyn, New York and re-enlisted on June 5, 1862. Brown was aboard USS North Carolina and discharged on February 6, 1866. (D. Sullivan, 1997)]

Fri Jun 19, 1863
The sloop of war *Savannah* pulled out into the stream today. It is said she is going to sea.

Sat Jun 20, 1863

Hastelton and Christler were today transferred to the sloop of war *San Jacinto*. Two marines from her are coming here in their places. She is going to sea soon. Went with them to help carry their baggage. Saw Darling and all the boys.

Sun Jun 21, 1863

General muster in the morning. Marines in full uniform. The longest day in the year, bean soup for dinner.

Mon Jun 22, 1863

On liberty. Fresh beef for dinner. After dinner went over to New York. Went to the Belmont and had dinner. Went to Baum's [Barnam's] Museum. Saw Gen'l Tom Thumb and wife. Commodore Nut and Minnie Warren. Got on board about seven PM.

Tue Jun 23, 1863

Weather warm. Guard inspected in the forenoon in full uniform. Cameron and Lane came on board from the barracks, have been transferred to us. Went on the *San Jacinto* in the morning. Saw Darling and all the boys. They expect to sail tomorrow.

Wed Jun 24, 1863

Rec'd a letter from Father. Wrote to Mary. The guard went over to the yard for drill at 9 o'clock AM. I did not have to go as I was on post at the time. Had nearly an hour extra on post however. The *San Jacinto* left in the morning. Father writes that he is going to build a plaster mill.

Thu Jun 25, 1863

Visiting day. Weather very warm. A draft of sailors went on board the *Governor Buckingham*. She is going after the privateers.

Sat Jun 27, 1863

Cleaned up our traps for tomorrow's inspection. In the afternoon about twenty of our guard with some marines from the

21. Commodore Nutt, Minnie Warren, Giant, Tom Thumb. Library of Congress

barracks went over to New York to conduct Admiral Foot's remains from the Astor House to the New Haven Steamboat.

Sun Jun 28, 1863
On liberty but not feeling well did not go out. Wrote to Father.

Mon Jun 29, 1863

Weather very warm. In the afternoon Serg't Alexander told me to get ready to go to New Haven to attend the funeral of Admiral Foote. Got ready accordingly. At half past nine with seventeen other privates and the band in charge of Serg't Alexander, we left the ship and marched to Fulton ferry, crossed over to New York and went on board the New Haven boat *Elm City*. Left the wharf at eleven o'clock. Turned in about midnight.

Tue Jun 30, 1863

Turned out about half past four in the morning and found we were alongside the dock at New Haven. We left the boat about six o'clock. Headed by the band we marched to the "Tremont House" where we had breakfast. Remained there until 10:00 AM when we marched to Admiral Foote's residence and conducted his remains to the City Hall where they were received by hundreds of people. At 3:00 PM we conducted them to the church where a funeral sermon was preached. After that the corpse was put into a hearse and a procession formed which marched through the principal streets and to the cemetery. Marines marching on each side of the hearse, at reverse arms, then marched back to the hotel where we had a tip-top supper. After supper Cameron and I took a walk about town. Saw Yale College. The buildings are of brick and look very old, but the grounds about them are very pleasant. We marched down to the boat about nine o'clock in the evening and I turned in immediately.

Wed July 1, 1863

Woke up about 5 o'clock and found we were alongside the New York dock. Got on board the ship about six o'clock. Captain Meade gave us twenty-four hours liberty. Rec'd a letter from Mary and answered it. Went over to New York in the afternoon and had supper at the Belmont. Got back to the ship about 7 o'clock.

Sat Jul 4, 1863
The most-quiet "Fourth" I ever spent. The North trimmed out with more than a hundred flags. A salute of twenty-one guns was fired from the coal dock battery at sunrise. At ten o'clock in the forenoon, all hands were mustered oft on the spar deck and Captain Meade read the Declaration of Independence.

[Richard W. Meade, III, was the son of Capt. Richard W. Meade, USN and proud descendant of Revolutionary War patriot and a nephew to General Geo. Gordon Meade. He retired after ranking to Rear Admiral. His brother, Robert Leamy Meade, USMC, later ranked to Brigadier General. (D. Sullivan, 2019)]

Sun Jul 5, 1863
Weather damp and rainy. Received a *Courier* from home. Wrote to Val.

Mon Jul 6, 1863
Rec'd a letter from Mary. Wrote to her and to Ed Church. On liberty. Went out for a short time in the afternoon, got back about 5 o'clock.

Tue Jul 7, 1863
Warm and pleasant. War news encouraging for our side. Lee knocked all to pieces by Gen. Meade.

[This was the uncle of Brother's Captain Meade. Victory in the Battle of Gettysburg.]

Wed Jul 8, 1863
Shot another dead man today. Twenty marines in full uniform left the ship at twelve o'clock. Went up the river in the Barge to the foot of 11th Street, New York. Marched to 2nd Ave. and up to the 17th Street. There we accompanied the mortal remains for somebody to a church for about half an hour, then brought out and buried in the church yard. We marines had the pleasure of smutting our muskets by firing over the grave. Then marched

22. Admiral Porter, USN, and General Meade. Library of Congress

back to the foot of 10th St, got aboard the Barge and started for the North. On the way a rain shower came up and were pretty thoroughly wet. Got on board about three o'clock.

["Shot a dead man" is slang for a gun salute at the funeral.]

Thu Jul 9, 1863
Visiting Day. Ship full of visitors as usual.

Sun Jul 12, 1863
On liberty. Went over to New York in the afternoon. Went to the Belmont and had something to eat, then went over to Brooklyn and took a car for Ft. Hamilton and look up Frank Smead.

Reached there about half past three o'clock, found him after some trouble. Mary Becker and an Aunt of hers a Mrs. Scott from Albany was with them, went by way of the South Ferry. Walked up to Vesey Street and got into an up town car. The Beckers now live in 46th St, and have a much nicer place than they had in 36th street. I had supper with them and stayed all night.

[Here is another clue about Mary Becker. She knows the Smead family. This is Benjamin Franklin Frank Smead.]

Mon Jul 13, 1863

Had breakfast in the morning with the Beckers, also another one at the Belmont when I got into town, got on board a few minutes past eight and in time for muster. A great riot in opposition to the draft broke out in New York during the day. About two o'clock PM twenty of us marines were ordered to fall in on starboard side of berth deck with our belts and muskets. Were each given thirty rounds of ball cartridges and marched over to New York. Halted at the guard house and stacked arms. In a short time we were joined by about fifty marines from the barracks, in command of Captain Greyson and Lieuts Mead and Stillman.

About three o'clock we marched to Fulton Ferry. Crossed over to New York. Marched up to Fulton St. to Broadway, up Broadway to Leonard St. a short distance and came to a halt. There Capt. Grayson received some orders from someone and we marched through Leonard Street to west Broadway where we stopped two upward bound street cars, drove the passengers out and taking possession started up town.

[John Contee Grayson, age forty-three, was commanding the Marine Guard. Born in Kentucky. He was often attached to barracks with long bouts of sick leave, perhaps the reason he did not advance his military career during the Civil War. (D. Sullivan, 2019)]

Got off the cars at 37th St. and proceeded to the Arsenal corner of 35th St. and 7th Ave. There we loaded our muskets and

23. Fort Hamilton. Library of Congress

accompanied by a company of Regulars with two small pieces of artillery, marched down Broadway and around through several streets to the 5th Avenue Hotel, and we were ordered to charge bayonets on them. We did so and cleared the park in a very short time.

After returning to the Arsenal we had some soft tack and raw beef to eat. About eleven o'clock in the evening we were roused out and marched down to the central police station in Mulberry St.

The rain poured down all the time so we have a very pleasant time of it. When we arrived there we were told to make ourselves as comfortable as possible for the night, so picking out a soft board in the floor I laid down in my wet clothes and was

24. Arsenal on 7th St. New York. Library of Congress

---

soon asleep. In our march from the Arsenal to the 5th hotel we passed some fine residences that had been set on fire by the mob and were still burning, though the firemen were then at work trying to put out the fire. In the night the dead body of a negro was brought to the police station. He had been hung to a lamp post and then set on fire.

[The African American children from an orphanage were at the 35th St. Police Station.]

Tue Jul 14, 1863
At about eight o'clock in the morning we were marched into the Bowery to an eating house where we had a good breakfast.

Then marched back to the police station. About ten o'clock we again fell in and marched through a great many streets in search of the rioters. Halted at the corner of Delaney [Delancey?] and some other St and waited for about an hour for them but saw nothing of them. The weather was very warm and we suffered a good deal from the heat. Some ladies in the neighborhood tore up some sheets and gave us each a piece of the muslin for a handkerchief, for which we were grateful.

We went back to the police station and after waiting there a while marched down Broadway to the St. Nicholas hotel. Halted in front of the hotel on the opposite side of the street and after staying there about an hour went back to the police station. There we had for dinner some raw ham, soft tack, butter, cheese, and coffee. Very good grub for marines. About 5 o'clock PM we again fell in and marched down Broadway to the City Hall where we took up our quarters in the "Governors Room." Slept all night very well on a velvet carpet.

[St. Nicholas Hotel was located at 507–527 Broadway]

[Navy Secretary Gideon Welles wrote on July 16, Thursday: "It is represented that the mob in New York is about subdued. Why it was permitted to continue so long and commit such excess has not been explained. Governor Seymour, whose partisans constituted the rioters, and whose partisanship encouraged them, has been in New York talking namby-pamby. This Forcible Feeble is himself chiefly responsible for the outrage." (Welles and Welles, 1911)]

Wed Jul 15, 1863
Went over to French's Hotel in the morning and had a good breakfast. Went there for dinner also. High living for marines. Beef steak, soft tack, pie and pudding. Pretty waiter girls. In the afternoon about 5 o'clock we marched up to North St. between Church Street and West Broadway. There we found about fifty sailors from the North Carolina who had three howitzers and were guarding some buildings filled with muskets, ammunition and c. We went into one of the buildings, stacked arms,

25. Gideon Welles, Navy Secretary. Library of Congress

stationed sentinels at the corners of the streets and then laid
down for a nights rest. Were roused up once in the night but it
was a false alarm.

Thu Jul 16, 1863
Nothing unusual occurred with us. Everything quiet in Worth
Street.

Fri Jul 17, 1863

Everything quiet during the day. In the morning Charley Mc-
Graney the drummer and McDonald the fifer came over from
barracks and we had retreat at Sun set and tattoo at nine o'clock
in regular garrison style. About half past eleven at night the
long roll was beat and of course all hands turned out and were
soon arrived and equipped. We formed in two companied
and marched up to Broadway, then down to the City Hall and
through the park. In front of the City Hall we halted an gave
three cheers, then marched around the block in which is *The
New York Times* office, then up Broadway to Leonard Street,
down Leonard to West Broadway, and then to our quarters in
Worth Street, where we turned in. What the fuss was about is
more than I can tell.

Sat Jul 18, 1863

About 5 o'clock in the afternoon we were ordered to get ready
to go home. We all obeyed with a will and gave three cheers at
the prospect of again sleeping with belts and clothes off. We
marched up to Broadway where we were met by the *North Carolina's* guard, fell out and went on board the ship, went out on the
Coal dock and discharged our muskets.

Sun Jul 19, 1863

General muster in the morning. Marines fell in on the spar deck
with side arms. I did not go up. Serg't Alexander wanted to
know the reason why, told him my belts were not clean enough.
Hadn't time to clean up since coming back.

Mon Jul 20, 1863

Inspection in the morning on the spar deck. My musket was
rusty so I of course got the usual compliment from the Sergeant. Wrote to Mother.

Wed Jul 22, 1863

Another inspection and drill on the coal dock. My musket still
not clean enough to suit the Sergeant. Wrote to Mary.

Thu Jul 23, 1863

No liberty list. All hands restricted to the ship. Don't know what's the matter.

Sat Jul 25, 1863

In the afternoon as I was out on the coal dock cleaning my belts word was passed for all marines to muster on the spar deck. We all fell in and the Sergeant read off the following names to get ready to leave the ship at 4 o'clock pm, bag and baggage. Davis, Fleming, McGee 1, Gleason, Carroll, Stein, Wilcox, Dolan, Malloy, Day, Mulchrone, Clark, Fletcher, Daly and Brother, fifteen of us in all, about five o'clock we went over to the Navy Yard and were paid off, then went back to the ship, put on our belts, took our muskets and marched over to the barracks. Were put in room No. 21. At roll call at tattoo found I was in Company A.

Sun Jul 26, 1863

Wrote a letter to Val. Rec'd a letter and *Courier* from Mary. It is reported we are going to Port Royal. That there is to be a battalion of marines sent there. Serg't Deemer says we are not for duty, and can get no liberty. Davis went over the fence last night, will probably never come back.

Mon Jul 27, 1863

Wrote to Mary. One hundred marines arrived from Washington, thirty from Philadelphia, and about forty from the Frigate *Sabine* Gleason and Daley deserted last night. Clark, Dolan, Stein, and Mulchrone are on the sick list, so the *North Carolina* guard is dwindled down somewhat.

Tue Jul 28, 1863

In the cook room all day, could get no liberty in the evening. Wrote to Mary. Extra sentries on to keep men from deserting.

Wed Jul 29, 1863
About forty men arrived from Boston and Portsmouth. I got out about eight o'clock PM. Went over to New York and stayed all night at the Belmont Hotel.

Thu Jul 30, 1863
Got up in the morning about eight o'clock. Walked about town until noon and took dinner at the Belmont, after dinner went up into the Bowery. Saw Serg't Wall. He said there were over a hundred absent at roll call last night. Went up to 46th Street to see Mary Becker. She was not home. Mrs. B. Said that she and a friend had gone to the Navy Yard to see me. She came home about seven o'clock with her friend Miss Marshall of Albany. Stayed there to supper, left there about ten o'clock. Went down town and crossed at the Fulton Ferry and got into a Flushing Avenue car. A Sergeant of police came up and asked me if I belonged to the Marine Corps, told him yes. Wanted to know when I left the barracks and I told him, asked if I was going back there and I told him I was. He said he had orders to arrest all marines who were out but as I was bound for the barracks he would let me go. When the car was opposite the guard house I got off and started for the gate. It was locked, and before the corporal could open it Serg't Richmond came up and walked in with me. Was put in cell with eleven others.

Fri Jul 31, 1863
We were marched out to breakfast in the morning. About sixty of us. After breakfast was put into another cell with eight others. Stayed there all day. The longest day I ever saw.

Sat Aug 1, 1863
Prisoners all released this morning. The Battalion left about noon. I did not have to go with them as the *North Carolina's* guard have been ordered back to the ship. I wanted to go with the battalion but Serg't Deemer said I would have to go on board the *North* again.

Sun Aug 2, 1863
On guard at Navy Yard. Post No. 1, 1st relief. Serg't Bhenson Officer of the day. Countersign "Active." The warmest day we have had. 105 in the shade at Navy Yard gate. Rec'd a letter from Val.

Mon Aug 3, 1863
Was sent back on board the North after being relieved off guard. The boys all seem glad to see me again.

Tue Aug 4, 1863
Fleming came back from the hospital in the afternoon.

Sun Aug 9, 1863
Very warm. Rec'd letters from Mother, Father, and Val. Wrote to Mother and Ed Church.

Mon Aug 10, 1863
Nineteen years old today. Serg't Alexander issued blouses to all who had none. We are to wear them instead of fatigue coat.

Tue Aug 11, 1863
Five men came from Barracks this morning to fill up our guard. We are still short six or seven men.

Fri Aug 14, 1863
In the morning seven of us in charge of Sergeant Alexander went on board of two steam tugs to take charge of some sailors who are going to New Orleans on the transport Continental. Left the North about nine o'clock and steamed down the river and up to Pier 43-North River where the Continental lay. We lay out in the stream until about two o'clock when she came out and the sailors were transferred to her. We then steamed up to the Fulton ferry landing, Brooklyn side when we went ashore and walked back to the North. Got there about three o'clock.

Sat Aug 15, 1863

The French flag was hoisted at our fore peak all day. At 8:00 AM, at noon, and at sunset a salute of twenty one guns was fired from the Coal dock battery. Could not find out what it was for. About five o'clock in the afternoon the French admiral steamed up the river in the steam yacht. Cleaned our accoutrements for Sunday's inspection.

Sun Aug 16, 1863

All hands in full uniform in the morning. About nine o'clock we fell in on the poop and all hands were mustered oft to hear something that the Captain had to say. Don't know what he said. After he had had his say he inspected us and we went below. After remaining on the gun deck about an hour we again went on the quarter deck to receive the admiral. We gave him a present as he came over the gangway with Commodore Radford.

Mon Aug 17, 1863

Attended the funeral of Commodore Morris today. Twenty of us in charge of Serg't Lola left the ship about nine o'clock in the morning. Went up the river in the Barge to the foot of 14th Street New York. Then marched to the commodore's residence in 17th St. Waiting there until eleven o'clock when the corpse was taken to a church. We waited outside about an hour when it was brought out and placed in a hearse, and forming a procession, marines taking the lead and band playing the dead march we started for Broadway. Went down Broadway to the South Ferry, where the corpse was taken on board the ferry boat, and we marched back to the Navy Yard by way of Fulton Ferry. Got on board the ship about three o'clock.

Tue Aug 18, 1863

Orderly Sergeant Lilly died this afternoon at three o'clock. Has been sick a long time. Hess was discharged today, his time being out, says he will join the volunteers.

26. Rear Admiral William Radford, USN, NHHC NH 47261

[Orderly Sergeant Eliakim Lilly died while attached to the USRS *North Carolina*. (D. Sullivan, 2019). Eliakim Lilly, age fifty-five, was born in Massachusetts. Some believe he invented the Lilly Handcuff or Lily Irons, used by escape artist Harry Houdini and by Marines holding Lincoln's co-conspirators after his assassination. In their research, they discovered Lilly died of "congestion of the brain" or meningitis. Lilly lived in the 5th Ward with a livery stable at the end of his block. Because there was on the next day a public health order for livery and tanneries in the ward to be removed, it is suggested that there was some connection. (See "Lilly Research" compiled by Ron Spitz, September 2017). Mr. Spitz was also investigating a myth about Lilly dying with the handcuffs on. Or, as his symptoms called for restraints, perhaps they used them on him. The term Lilly-Irons also refer to a type of whaling harpoon, but more can be found out about Lilly from Spitz's post.]

Fri Aug 21, 1863
Sergeant buried. In the morning about nine o'clock, twenty of us in charge of Serg't Alexander in full uniform, and the band, left the ship and marched to Serg't Lilly's residence No 23 Stanton Street Brooklyn. We stacked arms in the street and went into the house to view the remains. The Serg't was dressed in full uniform and appeared very natural. About ten o'clock the coffin was placed in the hearse and we started for Greenwood Cemetery. The band playing the dead march. Arrived there about twelve o'clock, fired three volleys over the grave, then took the cars for home. Got on board about three o'clock pretty well tired out with our long march. Rec'd a letter from Mary.

Sun Aug 23, 1863
Mustered on the berth deck in the morning with side arms. No full uniform. Wrote to Mary.

Mon Aug 24, 1863
Inspection on coal dock in the morning, we got through with it without much growling.

Tue Aug 25, 1863
Fell in on the coal dock in full uniform in the morning about 9 o'clock. The band also came in uniform. The band marched past us a few times, then we all took turns around the dock, and after humbugging about an hour we broke ranks and went on board again. The band was kept on board until late in the afternoon, playing all the time, as punishment for being late in the morning.

Wed Aug 26, 1863

Weather quite cool. Jumpers and white pants are put aside and fatigue coats and blue pants worn instead. The sloop of war *Brooklyn* 24 guns (?) arrived this morning. She fired a salute which was returned by the coal dock battery. She has on board the dead bodies of Commodore Rogers and another officer who were killed in the attack on Ft. Sumter.

Thu Aug 27, 1863

Serg't inspected our muskets at muster in the forenoon, growled as much as usual. Rec'd a letter from Ed Church.

Sat Aug 29, 1863

Rec'd a letter from Mary. Cleaned belts and c. for Sunday inspection. All hands in jumpers and white pants again. Weather warm.

Sun Aug 30, 1863

Very unwell in the morning and got excused from muster for the purpose of seeing the doctor. Saw him at nine o'clock but he would not put me on the sick list. I am not near enough dead. A fellow must be clear dead here before they will pay attention to him. The *New Burne* arrived this morning.

Mon Aug 31, 1863

The side wheel steamer *Ft. Jackson* left in the afternoon. At nine o'clock in the morning Serg't Alexander inspected the guard on the coal dock. Jumpers and white pants. I was on post, he passed the word for inspection in full uniform on Wednesday. Masters Mate Lane was sent on shore today. The band playing the rogue's march as he went over in the scow.

[A scow is an open, flat bottom utility boat.]

Tue Sep 1, 1863

Secretary Welles on board today. In the morning about nine
o'clock marines formed on the quarter deck, starboard side in
full uniform. The band was on the port side in uniform. About
eleven o'clock Sec'y Welles, with Admiral Paulding, Commodore Radfords and several other officers came on board. We
gave them a present as they came over the gangway. The band
struck up "Hail Columbia" and the coal dock battery fired a
salute. They all went into the cabin and then went below to
inspect the other decks. After they came on deck again the
drummer of the band played for them on his "German Piano."
One of the men with the Secretary gave the drummer a roll of
greenbacks. The Glee club then sang a few songs, after which
the whole party left the ship as they left the camel (?) in the
barge our crew maned the rigging and gave three cheers. Father
Gideon is large, with long, curly white hair, and heavy white
beard. He looked sleepy, looks very much like the pictures of
him in the comic newspapers.

Gideon Welles wrote on Aug 29, 1863:

*Have reluctantly come to the conclusion to visit the navy yards. It is a
matter of duty, and the physicians and friends insist it will be conducive
to health and strength. If I could go quietly it would give me pleasure, but
I have a positive dislike to notoriety and parade, —not because I dislike
well-earned applause, not because I do not need encouragement, but there
is so much insincerity in their showy and ostentatious parades, where the
heartless and artful are often most prominent.* (Welles and Welles, 1911)

Wed Sep 3, 1863

On liberty. Seven men and a Sergeant came on board from the
barracks for duty. Our guard is now nearly full again. Went
over to New York in the afternoon. Had dinner at the Belmont.
Went to Churchills in Chambers St. and saw Mr. Lipe, asked
him if Mr. Sutherland was in town but he did not know. Went

to Underhills in Duane Street and saw Mr. Wilcox. He said Mr. Sutherland was in the city. Thought he stopped in Hudson Street. Went back down town. After a while went to Hudson St. Walked up as far as Prince Street, then took a car and rode down town. Got into a 3rd Ave. car and rode up to 22nd St. Crossed over to Madison Ave., took a stage and rode down to Duane St. Went to see Mr. Wilcox again but he had seen nothing of Mr. Sutherland, since I was there. Went to the Belmont and had supper. Then started for a stroll up Broadway. Met Mr. Sutherland coming down, was very glad to see him and he seemed pleased to see me. Went with him to 118 Hudson St. where he is stopping. Stayed there a short time. Then he went to the City Hall park with me where we parted. I went to the Frankfort House, got a bed and turned in about eleven o'clock.

[Brother writes of James Sutherland, his old boss and tailor in Bath. Underhills was a clothing store.]

Fri Sep 4, 1863
Turned out about half past six in the morning. Went to the Belmont and had breakfast, then to the Claremont and had another one. Went to the United States Hotel and saw Mr. C. H. Barron of Bath. Had a short talk with him then started for home. Got on board about half past eight. A short drill on the coal deck at nine o'clock. The Union came in early this morning.

[Charles Haydon Barron opened his hardware store in 1857, when Brother was about twelve. Barron, who was a neighbor to another Brother family friend, George Knight, was active at the Freemason lodge with Val Brother. Barron was happy to see Brother. He hired him after the war. Reputable hotels published the names of their guests; newspapers show that C. H. Barron stayed often at this hotel. "The United States Hotel, opened in 1833 as Holt's Hotel, stood at Fulton and Water Streets, an area now part of the South Street Seaport Museum. The landmark, which had a steam-powered elevator for carrying luggage, was demolished in 1902. Several instantaneous stereoscopic negatives were made for it for E. Anthony in the early part of 1860, and from its

roof panoramic views were taken of the waterfront a few years later."
(Johnson and Lightfoot, 1880)]

Sat Sep 5, 1863
Received a letter from Mary. Expected Mr. Sutherland on board
but he did not come. Thomas, the old sailor who fell down the
ladder yesterday, was so badly injured that he died this morning. Was buried at the Hospital cemetery.

Sun Sep 6, 1863
Marines in full uniform at muster in the morning. Was on post
from 8:00 to 10:00 so got clear of it. Wrote to Mary.

Mon Sep 7, 1863
The guard ordered on the quarter deck in full uniform at 10:00
AM. Stayed there about half an hour and then went out to the
coal dock. The band accompanied us. The band marched past us
a few times after we formed in line. The Sergeant then inspected
our muskets and we went back on board again. On liberty in the
afternoon. Went over to New York and to the Belmont and had
Dinner. Then went to the Claremont and had another one. Went
to 118 Hudson Street to see Mr. Sutherland but he had gone
home on the five o'clock train. Strolled around New York a while
then went back to the ship, getting on board about 8 o'clock.

Tue Sep 8, 1863
Serg't Alexander drilled us in the morning on the coal dock for
about two hours and a half. Wish the coal dock would sink. It's
too handy.

Wed Sep 9, 1863
Sergeant Alexander, Corporal Brown and Privates Gilligan,
Weldon and Euchehart, went to Washington this morning with
a draft of sailors. We were mustered on the coal deck in the
morning by Serg't Lolla, who as usual made monkeys of us.

Thu Sep 10, 1863
Received letters from Mary and Ed Smead, a paper from Mother. Visiting day, ship crowded with visitors. The *Peterhoff* was brought from the Atlantic docks to the yard in the morning by the tug *Vanderbilt*. She will be converted into a gun boat.

[Edward Smead, age twenty-three, enlisted three times, starting with the 1st enlistment in Cowan's Battery E. NY Light Artillery. He was a Freemason and baker who relied on the Brother mill for flour. Smead's brothers were Frank, Florence, and James or "Jim."]

Fri Sep 11, 1863
Serg't Alexander came back last night but left again this morning with a draft of sailors from Baltimore. Corp'l Jensen and Private Nissen left with a draft for Philadelphia.

Sat Sep 12, 1863
Jensen and Nissen returned last evening. Cleaned up accoutrements from Sunday inspection. Captain Mead received news of his son Robert having been taken prisoner at Charleston.

Sun Sep 13, 1863
The guard mustered on the main deck in the morning in fatigue coats, white pants and side arms. Words passed for inspection on Monday morning in full uniform. Locke went on liberty and I went cook in his place. He did not go out until after dinner so I had nothing to do but get supper. Got through with it very well. Wrote to Mary and to Ed Smead. Services on the main deck. Starboard side.

Mon Sep 14, 1863
Got along with the breakfast very well with some assistance from Rowe. Locke came in a little after six bells, mustered out on the coal dock in the morning at nine o'clock with fatigues and muskets. Had a short drill, word was passed for dress parade Tuesday morning, provided the weather is clear. On the pass but did not go out. Cameron went out to Fort Hamilton

and came near being kept there by the officer of the day because he had no pass. Came on board mad as a hornet.

Tue Sep 15, 1863
The order was passed in the morning to muster out on the coal dock in clean fatigues at two bells, about ten minutes before that time we were ordered to get in full uniform immediately. We did so and were marched over into the yard to received General Dix. After marching about the yard for about fifteen minutes we came to a halt near the ordinance department. Admiral Paulding came along and we gave him a present, then stacked arms and after waiting nearly an hour were told that we could go on board again. Were ordered to put our muskets in the rack but remain in uniform. In about fifteen minutes were ordered up on the quarter deck, formed in line on the starboard side. Stayed there about half an hour. While we were there Gen'l Dix passed the ship in the Barge. Our Sailors manned the rigging and gave him three cheers. We were then allowed to go below and get out of uniform. Captain Mead is in Washington when he went to see about his son who was taken prisoner at Charleston. Lieut. Com'nder Mead has been ordered to one of the Atlantic Squadrons.

Wed Sep 16, 1863
Had a short drill on the coal deck in the morning. Asked Serg't Alexander if he could have me sent to sea. Says he will speak to the commanding officer about it. Hope I may be sent out on a good ship. Am tired of this old hulk.

Thu Sep 17, 1863
Visiting Day. A great many on board. Rec'd a letter from Mary.

Sat Sep 19, 1863
On the pass. Weather cold and rainy. Went out about 5 o'clock in the afternoon. Went over to Grand Street New York and had a tooth pulled. It was a very large one and came out very hard. The dentist had to pull three times on it. Went to see Locke in

27. General John A. Dix. Library of Congress

the evening but he was not at home. Got on board about eight
o'clock.

Sun Sep 20, 1863
Weather quite cool. Muster on the quarter deck in the morning
at nine o'clock. Word passed for inspection in full uniform on
Tuesday morning. Wrote a letter to Mary. In the afternoon two
sisters and a brother of young Brotherson came on board with
another young man. Asked me to show them around the ship.
Did so as well as I could.

Mon Sep 21, 1863
In the morning the Guard turned out in full uniform to receive
Admiral Farragut. Gave him a present as he came over the gang
way and he turned our salute very pleasantly. He appears much
younger than any admiral I have seen. Steps around as spry as
a boy.

Tue Sep 22, 1863
Dress parade on the coal deck in the morning, but as I was on
post I escaped it. Colors hoisted at nine o'clock AM. Tattoo at
8:00 PM. Rec'd a letter from Ed Smead.

Wed Sep 23, 1863
On the pass. In the morning drilled on the coal dock for about
an hour. Went out about half past twelve. Crossed over to
New York at Cath' St. Ferry. Went to Vandyke's and had an apple dumpling. Then went up to Grand street and had a tooth
pulled. Dentist broke it and did not get it all out. Took a car and
rode up to Harlem, then came to Peck Slip by steam boat. Got
back to the ship at eleven o'clock.

Thu Sep 24, 1863
Serg't Alexander, Corp'l Jensen and several privates went away
with a draft by Serg't Sullivan at nine o'clock. Visiting day. Ship
full of visitors.

Fri Sep 25, 1863
A short drill on the coal dock in the morning. Rec'd a letter
from Azel Gould. He is at Sweeny's Hotel and wants to see me
but I can't get ashore.

Sat Sep 26, 1863
Cleaned belts and c. on the orlop deck. In the afternoon about
twenty of us were take up to the Navy Yard gate to salute some
Russian officers. Gave them a present as they rode out in two
carriages.

28. Admiral Farragut, USN, NHHC NH 49516

Sun Sep 27, 1863
Muster in full uniform on the main deck in the morning. Word
passed for knapsacks on Monday morning. And full uniform
inspection on Tuesday morning. This ship is getting to be more
and more a place of torment. Services on the gun deck twice
today.

Mon Sep 28, 1863
Knapsack inspection and inspection of muskets on the coal
deck in the morning. About five hundred sailors left the ship
for the *Richmond*. *Grand Gulf* and *Sanoma*. The *Paul Jones* came

in again today. On the pass, did not go out. Cleaned musket, belts, and c.

Tue Sep 29, 1863

Drill for about an hour and a half on the coal dock in the morning. Word passed for full uniform inspection tomorrow morning.

Wed Sep 30, 1863

Uniform and dress parade on the coal dock in the morning. Rec'd a letter and paper from home. The English flag was hoisted at the fore and saluted in the afternoon. Guard ordered on deck to receive someone who did not come. The *Paul Jones* went out.

Thu Oct 1, 1863

Just a year ago today I left Bath. Visiting day, a great many visitors on board. Among them I saw Willard Knight and his sister. Weather very pleasant. The *Richmond* pulled out into the stream in the forenoon. The Guard paid off in the afternoon.

Sat Oct 3, 1863

On liberty. Sent a letter to Mary. Went over to New York about one o'clock. Got back on board about seven o'clock.

Sun Oct 4, 1863

Muster in full uniform on the spar deck in the morning. Service on the main deck in the afternoon. Rec'd a letter from Ed Church.

Mon Oct 5, 1863

Guard in uniform at 9 o'clock. Went up to the Navy Yard gate to receive the French admiral. He came in a carriage about half past eleven. We stayed there until he left at about one o'clock. Then went back to the ship. The *Sonora* went out in the afternoon.

Tue Oct 6, 1863

A short drill on the coal dock in the morning. The gun-boat *Nyack* was launched in the afternoon. The Russian flag was at our fore and a salute fired from the coal dock battery.

Fri Oct 9, 1863

The guard in full uniform on the quarter deck in the forenoon to receive Admiral Farragut. He came about half past ten o'clock. On liberty list, went over to the Navy Yard in the afternoon with Cameron. Went all over the yard and on board for a transport. Got back to the ship about half past three. After supper went over to New York. Went to the Belmont and had supper. Walked up Broadway as far as Niblo's and back. Had another supper at the Belmont, then back to the ship getting on board just after gun fire.

Sun Oct 11, 1863

The guard in uniform at muster on the poop in the morning. Wrote to Mary, Ed Church, and Ed Smead. The *Grand Gulf* went out in the morning.

Mon Oct 12, 1863

A French frigate came to the yard this morning. She is a very fine looking ship. Is going into the dry dock. Drill on coal deck in the morning.

Wed Oct 14, 1863

The guard in full uniform on the quarter deck in the morning to receive Admiral Paulding. He came on board about half past eleven o'clock accompanied by General Haggerty and several other gentlemen. After they came on board marines and the band were sent out on the coal dock. The howitzers were maned and the three companies of sailors with muskets were drilled and altogether we made quite a show. The admiral came out and received us. We were then sent on board and Captain Mead's "Performing Negroes" went out and went through with their usual evolutions. The admiral seemed very much pleased with them.

[Major Peter Haggerty was attached to General Butler.]

Thu Oct 15, 1863

Visiting day. The ship as usual crowded with visitors. Word was passed early in the morning for the marines to be on the quarter deck in full uniform at half past ten AM. About half past nine, before half of us were ready we were ordered to go on the quarter deck as soon as possible. We went up, stacked arms and waited until dinner time but no one came, we went below and had dinner and went on deck again, waited there until half past three and were ordered to go below and get out of uniform. Went below and had supper. Just after supper we were ordered on deck again in a great hurry, part of us were in uniform, part in fatigues and some with blouses, but up we went just as we were and the long expected French admiral came on board. We gave him a present and were then allowed to go below once more. Being on the pass I went on shore as soon as possible. Went over to New York and had supper at the Belmont. Then to the Claremont and had another supper. Walked up Broadway as far as Canal Street and back. Then over to Brooklyn and up Fulton St. as far as Hooley's and back to the ferry. Took a car for the Navy Yard. Got on board a little before gun fire (8 o'clock). After I left the ship the guard had to fall in again.

Fri Oct 16, 1863

Weather rainy and very unpleasant. The marines ordered the deck at half past nine to receive the Russian admiral, waited on deck about half an hour but he did not come. Then we were marched up to the Navy Yard gate, waited there about half an hour in the rain and then were mercifully allowed to go into the guard room out of the wet, were in there about forty-five seconds when we were ordered to fall out and fall in and were marched on board the ship on the quarter deck. In about fifteen minutes the Russian admiral came over the side accompanied by about forty Russian officers, most of them quite young, probably cadets. They stayed on board about three quarters of an hour. Meantime we had gone below to get our dinner. Just as we had about one potato comfortably settled we were ordered on deck to give them a salute as they left the ship, as soon as they were all over the side we were sent over to the Navy Yard gate again. Waited under the arcade about half an hour but as no one came, went inside the guard house and stayed until about three o'clock, then went back on board the ship and were permitted to take off our wet uniforms and get something to eat. Such days as this tend to make a fellow sick of life on the *North Carolina*.

Sat Oct 17, 1863
No admirals to bother us today. Cleaned belts and c. on the coal dock in the forenoon. Rec'd a letter from Vep Darling.

Sun Oct 18, 1863
Muster on the quarter deck in the morning. Wrote to Darling. He is now on the steamer *Ft. Henry* at Key West.

Tue Oct 20, 1863
Full uniform and drill on the coal dock in the forenoon. On the pass. Went on shore after supper and got back about eight o'clock.

Wed Oct 21, 1863
Rec'd a letter from Mother containing some medicine for my tooth ache. A short drill on the coal dock in the morning. Cameron went on board the *Union* and says that little Bob Brotherson fell under a car and had one of his feet badly mashed.

Thu Oct 22, 1863
Inspection of hammocks in the morning. Visiting day. Was very much surprised in the afternoon by receiving a visit from Mr. Young and Mr. Clark. They stayed a short time. Invited me to call and see them.

[His brother-in-law was James Young, who married his sister Ellen on November 1, 1860. Mr. Young hired a substitute to avoid war service.]

Fri Oct 23, 1863
Muster on the coal dock in the morning by Serg't Sullivan. Serg't Alexander gone to Cairo.

Sun Oct 25, 1863
Muster on the main deck in the morning. Were inspected by acting Master Coffin. Wrote to Mother.

Mon Oct 26, 1863
US Steamer *New Berne* came in the morning. On the pass, went on shore after supper but the Serg't at the Navy Yard gate would not let me go out as he could not find the pass. Came back on board and got another pass and went out.

Thu Oct 29, 1863
Sergeant Alexander came back yesterday, visiting day, ship full of visitors. The gun boat *Peoria* was launched at half past ten AM. She is a side wheel double-ender.

Fri Oct 30, 1863
Guard drilled about an hour on the coal dock in the morning. Received a letter from Mary telling of the death of Joel—

[Text erased. This should be a note about the death of Joel Pratt, the stepson of his sister Cornelia and a cousin who lived in Prattsburgh. The boy was thirteen years old.]

Sat Oct 31, 1863
The guard paid off in the afternoon. Traded liberties with Godfrey. He is on the day in my place. Sergeant Alexander tells me that I will be sent to sea on the *Hartford* when she goes into commission. Very welcome news for me as she is said to be a fine ship, and I am sick of this one.

Sun Nov 1, 1863

Inspection on the quarter deck in the morning, as my belts were not white enough my bayonet scabbard black enough, nor my coat brushed clean enough to suit the Sergeant I received a lecture. On liberty, went out about half past two. Went to Rice's at the ferry and had some roast veal and bread pudding. Then went over to New York to the Claremont Hotel where I got some more roast veal and break pudding. Walked up Broadway. While passing the St. Nicholas Hotel saw Ed Cook of Bath on the steps. Got back to the ship just after gun-fire. The *New Berne* left in the forenoon for the South Atlantic squadron.

[Edwin C. Cook, age twenty-five, was later a vestryman for St. Thomas Church. His father, Judge Constant Cook, provided leadership and funding, including acreage, for a new church. Judge Cook was a pioneer of prominence and fortune, involved with railroad development early. Edwin later went to work with the First National Bank of Bath and served in many public roles for the village, including president and the agricultural society. He was attached to the Bath Fire Department in his organization of the Edwin Cook Hose Company, which drilled other fire houses, including the one Brother joined after the war.]

Mon Nov 2, 1863

Parade on the coal cock in the morning in full uniform. Wrote to Mary. Gilligan, Fray and Hayes were put in the brig in the evening for selling whiskey to sailors. Colonel Harris was on board in the afternoon.

Tue Nov 3, 1863

About thirty landsmen left the ship today for the Marine barracks. Are going to enlist as marines. More are to go tomorrow.

Wed Nov 4, 1863

One year ago today the *Vanderbilt* went into commission. Wish I was on her now. A draft of 250 sailors left today for *Philadelphia* in charge of Serg't Alexander. A corporal and eleven privates. The *Emma* sailed this PM.

Fri Nov 6, 1863
Guard in full uniform at half past eleven. Paraded on the coal dock with the band for about a half an hour. Then went on the quarter deck, but a storm of wind and rain coming up we were allowed to go below and get out of uniform, and so we were all very glad of the storm.

Sat Nov 7, 1863
Another draft of sailors was going to Philadelphia today, but when they were all ready it was postponed until Monday. On the pass, went out about 3 o'clock. Bought some sand paper and emery paper and rotten stone in Brooklyn. Then went to Rice's and had a good meal. Went over to the New York Post Office. Then to the Claremont Hotel and had another good meal. Walked up Broadway and back, then went over to Brooklyn. Walked up Fulton Street as far as the City Hall and back to the ferry. Got back on board about 7 o'clock.

Sun Nov 8, 1863
Full uniform on the poop deck in the morning. A Russian gunboat is at the buoy, came up last night.

Mon Nov 9, 1863
No drill today. At noon a draft of about three hundred sailors left for Philadelphia in charge of Serg't Alexander and twelve privates. Hayes, Fay, Gilligan is cleared from the charge of selling Whisky, but the other ship is ready to go to sea, then they will be sent away on her. Perhaps I will be sent on the same ship.

Tue Nov 10, 1863
One year ago today I left New York harbor on the *Vanderbilt* for my first voyage. No drill today. The marines who went with the draft came home this morning.

Wed Nov 11, 1863
A short drill in the coal dock in the morning. Rec'd a letter and paper from Mary.

29. Col. John Harris, USMC, NHHC NH 100174

Thu Nov 12, 1863

Visiting day, wrote to Mary. On the liberty list but did not go out. Sold my liberty to Diegan for 4/-. Cameron was relieved off the cabin door in the evening. He had some trouble with the first Luff. Will probably be back soon.

Fri Nov 13, 1863

A draft of sailors left today for the gun boat *Gov Buckingham*. The gun boat *Flag* arrived in the afternoon from Charleston. Cleaned uniform hat and epaulettes.

Sat Nov 14, 1863
Weather damp and foggy. Cameron was put on the duty on the gangway this morning.

Sun Nov 15, 1863
Weather damp and rainy. Inspection on the berth deck in the morning in clean fatigues.

Mon Nov 16, 1863
Full uniform on the coal dock in the morning. On the pass. Went out about half past four. Went to see Locke. Stayed about an hour. Saw his wife and baby. The baby is two weeks old. Then went over to New York. Went to the Belmont Hotel and had supper. Went to the Claremont and had another one. Went back to Brooklyn. Took a Navy Yard car. Got there just five minutes after gun fire so could not go down. Waiting about half an hour when Corporal Ryan came in and as he had the countersign I went down with him, got on board about nine o'clock.

Tue Nov 17, 1863
Weather damp and rainy. No drill. Wilcox came down from the Hospital yesterday. Carroll was caught carrying out three Navy Blankets, and was put in the brig, others were found in his trunk. This old soldiering is getting played out on this ship. Heard today that Captain Heywood is going as marine officer on the *Hartford.* Hope it is true. The men who have been with him say he is a good man. An alarm of fire was given in the Yard in the evening, a false alarm.

[Rufus E. Wilcox (1842–1909) from Danbury, CT]

Wed Nov 18, 1863
Rainy weather. Rec'd an *Advocate* from home. A schooner mounting seven guns arrived today.

Thu Nov 19, 1863
Visiting day. A great many on board. Main deck crowded. The Russian gunboat left the buoy in the forenoon. Weather pleasant.

Fri Nov 20, 1863
On the pass but did not go out. Gave my musket a good cleaning. The steamer *Fort Jackson* arrived in the morning and went under the shears.

Sat Nov 21, 1863
Rec'd a letter from Mary. We had a fire on the orlop deck for the first time this season. Damp and rainy weather.

Sun Nov 22, 1863
Marines in full uniform on the poop in the morning.

Mon Nov 23, 1863
Drilled about an hour on the coal dock in the morning. Word passed for full uniform parade tomorrow morning. Foley was put in the brig this morning for being slightly intoxicated. Wrote to Mary.

Tue Nov 24, 1863
On the pass but did not go out. Saw a notice in today's paper that the *Peterhoff*'s cargo sold for $300,000. Rainy Weather. No inspection.

Wed Nov 25, 1863
The guard ordered in uniform at nine o'clock. Mustered on the berth deck. As soon as roll was called Sergeant Alexander went over to the barracks and we got out of uniform. Nobody knows what it was all about. Carroll received a worthless discharge today.

Thu Nov 26, 1863

Thanksgiving day. All work in the Yard suspended. Captain Mead released twenty three prisoners from the brig. News this morning of a great victory at Chattanooga by General Grant. He is a fighter and will stand a good chance for the White House if he keeps on. Had beef soup and boiled beef for Thanksgiving dinner.

Fri Nov 27, 1863

Muster on the coal dock in the morning.

Sat Nov 28, 1863

On the pass but did not go ashore. The *New Berne* came in early in the morning.

Sun Nov 29, 1863

Muster on the berth deck in the morning in clean fatigues. The steamer *Grand Gulf* came in.

Mon Dec 7, 1863

On liberty. Went to Griffin Bros dentists in Fulton St. Brooklyn and had two teeth filled. Went over to New York and after eating two or three suppers went back to the ship.

Mon Dec 14, 1863

Rainy weather. No parade or inspection. The steamer *Union* came in towards evening. In the afternoon all hands were mustered out on the coal dock and then mustered on board again. The police were looking for a criminal, but I believe did not find him.

Tue Dec 15, 1863

Went on post as the brig at eight o'clock. Was relieved about nine and ordered to get in uniform and get any luggage ready to go to the barracks. Wilcox, Hayes, and Fay were ordered to do the same. About half past ten we went to barracks in charge of Sergeant Sullivan. Stayed there until about two o'clock when

30. USS *Hartford*. Library of Congress

with about forty other marines were marched down to the Navy Yard on board the sloop if war *Hartford*. She went into commission shortly after we came back on board. Captain Haywood and Lieut. Commander Kimberly execution officer. The *Hartford* is to be Admiral Farragut's flag ship. I have been appointed one of the orderlies to the admiral and commodore. There are four of us. Rece'd a letter from Darling. Wrote to father in the evening.

[Rules and regulations stated: "Orderlies will invariably be dressed and conduct themselves with becoming propriety, will receive all communications appertaining to their post, and deliver the same promptly. They are not allowed to sit down on post or amuse themselves by reading of any kind. The orderly on the admiral's door will report the time each half hour to the orderly on the Captain's door and by him reported to the officer of the deck." (D. Sullivan, 2019).]

CHAPTER 6

USS *Hartford*

Wed Dec 16, 1863

We were divided into messes and numbered off today. My mess is No. 4. We are still alongside the Navy Yard dock. Hayes left sometime in the afternoon. We will probably never see him again. Fay is complaining and will probably be sent to the Hospital. Cameron came on board in the afternoon and brought

31. USS *Hartford*, view of the main deck looking aft from the forecastle, 1864, NHHC NH 53680

32. Rear Admiral James S. Palmer, USN, NHHC NH 47589

me a paper from home. Admiral Farragut and Commodore Palmer were on board a short time today. Pork and bean soup for dinner.

Thu Dec 17, 1863
Rain and hail all day. Wilcox and I selected what we needed out of Hayes's outfit and left the rest. Roast beef for dinner.

Sat Dec 19, 1863
Cameron came on board bringing me another paper from home, and my wash clothes. Cleaned belts and brasses. Pork and beans for dinner.

Sun Dec 20, 1863
Weather very cold. Wrote to Mother. Bullion beef for dinner.

Mon Dec 21, 1863
Rec'd a letter from Mary and one from Father. We pulled out into the stream in the afternoon and anchored just ahead of the North Carolina. Pork and beans for dinner.

Tue Dec 22, 1863
Wrote to Mary. General stores were served out in the PM. I drew a bar of soap, scrub brush and box of blacking. Duff for dinner.

Fri Dec 25, 1863
Ship surrounded with ice, wrote to father. Rec'd letter from Mary. Fresh grub for dinner.

Tue Jan 5, 1864
The admiral and commodore and fleet Captain Drayton came on board about half past ten AM. We got up anchor and under way about noon. Steamed down the bay and out to sea. Weather quite rough the first part of the night. Duff for dinner. Wrote a letter to Father to send on shore by the pilot but did not send it.

33. Capt. Percival Drayton, USN, NHHC NH 88386

[Percival Drayton was appointed midshipman at the age of fifteen in 1827 and sent to sea. Very "physically fit, patient, loyal, and ever willing to learn and serve." Farragut stated that he was "An energetic fellow, full of zeal." He had more than the required skill of handling ships, Drayton was keen on discipline of gunnery for accuracy. . . Being "of a most healthy and hardy constitution: his tall, sinewy frame. . .gave him uncommon capacity to resist fatigue. . .I do not know whether or not he was a religious man, but a purer man I never knew." (Barratt, 2018)]

Wed Jan 6, 1864
Weather a little warmer. We are steering south west. Had the afternoon watch. Pork and beans for dinner. Passed a schooner bound north in the afternoon.

Thu Jan 7, 1864
Had the first dog and mid watches. Sea quite rough. Ship rolling heavily. Mr. Jones officer of the deck had a fire while on watch. Passed a brig bound North in the afternoon. She showed English colors. Bullion beef for dinner.

Sun Jan 10, 1864
Weather very pleasant. General quarters for inspection at half past two AM. Marines under arms in clean fatigues. The commodore looked at us pretty sharp. After retreat all hands were mustered on the quarter deck and Mr. Mason the commodore's clerk read some passages from the Prayer Book. All the sailors were then mustered around the captain. Passed Abaco in the PM. Bullion for dinner.

Mon Jan 11, 1864
Weather very pleasant. We sent up the main royal yard in the morning, sent it down again in the afternoon. Could see the island of Cuba from the poop in the evening. Pork and beans for dinner.

Tue Jan 12, 1864
A Key West pilot came on board about six o'clock. Came to anchor off the town about 8:00 AM. Admiral Bailey with his flag captain and lieut. came on board about nine o'clock. He has to hoist a red flag now as one admiral is his senior. All hands commenced coaling ship about noon. Saw a marine on the dock belonging to the steamer *Ft. Henry.* Said he knew Vep Darling and would tell him to come and see me. Wrote to Father. Duff for dinner.

Wed Jan 13, 1864

Hammocks piped up and 4 o'clock AM. Commenced coaling ship at seven o'clock. Admiral came on board in the morning. Also his flag Captain and the Colonel commanding the fort here with his staff. A sailor died in the sick bay last night, was buried on shore this morning. In the afternoon a marine from the *Ft. Henry* came on board and told me that Darling could not get off. He stayed a short time and then left saying he would try and get Darling off. In about half an hour he came on board again and Darling with him. Of course was very glad to see Darling and had a long talk with him. At about four o'clock PM we pulled out from the dock, got up anchor and steamed out to sea. We are probably going to Mobile. Fresh grub for dinner.

Thu Jan 14, 1864

Steaming NNW weather very pleasant. Marines had a short drill on deck in the morning. Also another at night. Had the afternoon watch. Bullion beef for dinner.

Fri Jan 15, 1864

One month since we went into commission. A rain squall in the afternoon. Had the mid and 1st dog watches. Duff for dinner.

[Watches were stood from midnight to 4:00 a.m. (the mid watch); 4:00 to 8:00 (morning watch); 8:00 to 12:00 noon (forenoon watch); 12:00 to 4:00 p.m. (afternoon watch); 4:00 to 6:00 (first dog watch); 6:00 to 8:00 p.m. (second dog watch); and 8:00 to 12:00 midnight (night watch). The bell was rung to mark the passage of each half hour of the watch: one bell was rung a half-hour after the watch commenced, two bells after an hour, and so on, until eight bells marked the end of the watch. (U.S. Navy, 1971)]

Sat Jan 16, 1864

Had the morning and 2nd dog watches, weather cool. Still steering North by west. Pork and Beans.

Sun Jan 17, 1864
Had the forenoon and 1st night watches. Came to anchor for a pilot about one o'clock this morning. I sleep under the compressor and had to turn out and lay my hammock on deck. Weighed anchor about six and anchored off Pensacola Navy Yard at half past seven. We were visited during the day by a great many officers from the vessels laying here. We are anchored in full view of Santa Rosa Island, Ft. Pickens and the Navy Yard. Most of the buildings in the yard were burned by the rebels and nothing but bare walls are standing. Williams and Thackery and some sailors were sent on shore to the hospital. Some marines from the Frigate *Potomac* came on board in the afternoon. Had services on the quarter deck in the morning. The guard in full uniform. Bullion for dinner.

Mon Jan 18, 1864
Weighed anchor about nine o'clock. As we were leaving the harbor Ft. Pickens and Ft. Barrancus fired a salute. Were in sight of land all day. Had the afternoon watch. General quarters in the afternoon. Sailors were given their small arms. cutlasses and muskets, pikes, revolvers, and c. Marines received 40 rounds of ball cartridges and 50 caps each. My station at quarters is at the cabin door. Some of the guard are stationed in the tops, took down the railings around the cabin and ward room hatches. It looks as if we expected to see some hot work soon. The guns loaded with solid shot. Came in sight of the blockading fleet off Mobile Bay about 4'oclock. Came to anchor about half past seven. Pork and beans for dinner.

[Arriving off Mobile Bay, Admiral Farragut was laser focused to inspect his ships, know his enemy's position, and test his men and hardware. He was glad to return to his command of the West Gulf Blockading Squadron and his base at New Orleans." (U.S. Navy, 1971).]

Tue Jan 19, 1864
Had the mid and 1st dog watches. Weighed anchor about 9 o'clock AM. Are off Mobile Bay. Can just see land above the

horizon. The sloop of war *Richmond* and several smaller vessels are in sight. Can see the smoke from the Rebel ram inside the bay. Dropped anchor about half past ten. Remained at anchor all day. The gunboat *Oneida* came in and anchored just off our starboard quarter at night. At night fall several of the gun boats got under way and moved in toward land. Duff for dinner.

Wed Jan 20, 1864
Weather very pleasant. Had the morning and 2nd dog watches. The *Jasmine* a dispatch boat arrived from New Orleans this morning. Bought a pilot for us. General quarters in the morning at 3 bells. The admiral, Cap't Drayton, Lieut. Watson and the pilot who came from New Orleans went on board the gun boat *Octorara* and steamed up the Rebel forts. They returned about noon. In the afternoon two targets were set adrift and all our guns had a shot at them. Some close shots were made but neither of the targets were struck. We weighed anchor and got under way about seven o'clock in the evening. Port and beans for dinner.

[Lieut. John Crittenden Watson was two years older than Brother. Born in Kentucky, at fifteen he was appointed acting midshipman with the US Naval Academy. Farragut wrote to his son Loyall, "I am almost as fond of Watson as of yourself." Likewise, Watson was quite attached to Farragut. When Watson showed up for duty, Farragut, in the company of other officers, "took me a little aside and told me, in the kindest possible way, that he was sorry to have to tell me I was not to remain on the *Hartford*, but was to be relieved by another master (a grandson of Mr. Crittenden). His kind sympathy touched me, and I smilingly told him I was that fortunate Master who would stay aboard his flagship and hoped and trusted that with the discharge of my duties I would win his confidence." (Watson, 1916)]

Thu Jan 21, 1864
Had the forenoon and first watches. We were boarded by a Mississippi South-West Pass pilot about nine o'clock, came to anchor just outside the bar about eleven o'clock. Got up anchor

34. Lieut. Com. John C. Watson, USN, with Adm. Farragut, 1866, NHHC NH 53391

and crossed the bar at two PM and started up the Mississippi River. Past Forts Jackson and St. Philip at half past seven in the evening. Ft Jackson brought us to the first firing a blank cartridge and then sending a shot across our bows. We were boarded by an officer from the fort. About eight o'clock the fog became very heavy so that neither shore could be seen from the deck except when we were very close in. The pilot was stationed at the fore top mast head. About half past eleven we were forced to drop anchor as the pilot could not see his way any longer. Came to anchor at Lawrence's upper plantation forty miles below New Orleans. Bullion for dinner.

Fri Jan 22, 1864

Had the afternoon watch. Duff for dinner. Got up anchor and got under way at ten o'clock. Arrived at New Orleans and anchored at 4:00 PM. The *Pensacola* and several gun boats are here. Commodore Bell with his fleet captain came on board immediately. Just before we came to anchor the *Pensacola* fired a salute of thirteen guns and we returned a salute of eleven guns. Had to wear full uniform at the cabin door in the afternoon. I wore my fatigue cap and Commodore Palmer ordered me to wear the uniform hat. He must want us to put on all the style possible.

Sat Jan 23, 1864

Weather warm and pleasant. Scrubbed hammocks at 4 o'clock AM. Water very cold but it seems nice to have all the fresh water we want to scrub and wash with. In the afternoon cleaned belts brasses and c. for tomorrow's inspection. An English Captain commanding the British gun boat here came on board. Pork and beans for dinner. The admiral had a reception on shore in the evening at the residence of General Banks.

Sun Jan 24, 1864

Had the morning and 2nd dog watches. Marines at muster in the morning in full uniform. Several of the boys got extra duty because their epaulettes were not clean. My musket not very clean but it passed. Services on the quarter deck in the forenoon. The captain's clerk read the Episcopal morning service and a minister from shore made a short address. Wrote to Mother and sent a paper to Val. Bullion and coffee for dinner.

Mon Jan 25, 1864

Had the morning and first watches. Was kept very busy in the morning. A great many people on board to see the admiral. Pork and beans for dinner. The steam transport *Arkansas* arrived from Pensacola in the evening.

Captain Drayton's letter to his friend Hamilton for January 26, 1864

I am going through the old story of the Ordinance. So busy from morning to night as to have no enjoyment in life, and I shall really not be sorry for a little outside work, merely to give me a continuance of the rest I had a taste of coming-down. There are in the Squadron more than sixty vessels, and the reports applications, regulations etc. constantly pouring in from them, are without end, to say nothing of the personal applications for everything under the sun from morning to night. Wyckham Hoffman is here, on Franklin's staff, looking very well, and pleased with his duty and full of zeal. I don't know why it is that most of the army officers seem to rather improve under their hardships, while the Navy ones break down and look care worn and haggered without exception, and although little known North from unimportance of the persons, I have been surprised to learn how many of the Masters and Ensigns have died during the last summer from Yellow fever, particularly in the small vessels.

[Drayton wrote about General William B. Franklin (1928–1903) and former attorney and diplomat, Wickham Hoffman (1823–1900). (Drayton, 1906).]

Tue Jan 26, 1864

Had the afternoon watch. Very busy but not so much so as yesterday. Boatswain's mates Graham and Wiley were put in the brig for being drunk and disorderly. A fireman got drunk and struck the Corporal and Sergeant of the guard and the Chief Engineer. He was put in double irons. Will probably be court-martialed. Fresh grub for dinner.

Wed Jan 27, 1864

Had the mid and 1st dog watches. There is a report that Commodore Palmer is to leave the ship. Am afraid it is too good to be true. Pork and beans for dinner.

Thu Jan 28, 1864

Should have had the morning and 2nd dog watch. General quarters in the morning at half past nine. Drilled a short time with muskets. Bullion and coffee for dinner. The fireman who struck the Chief Engineer has been taken on board the sloop of war *Portsmouth* for a court-martial.

Fri Jan 29, 1864

The Commodore is packing up all his things and I think he is going to leave sure. Had a forenoon and first watches. Fresh grub for dinner.

Sat Jan 30, 1864

Marines in uniform all day. General Banks was expected on board but he did not come. Thompson, McSweeney, and Mundell were transferred from orderly put to day and Pagnello, Bowling, and Langdon, put in their places. I am left as orderly and hope I may remain so, for I like the duty much better than "Sentry go." Had the afternoon watch. Pork and beans for dinner.

Sun Jan 31, 1864

Weather warm and pleasant. Marines in uniform at muster in the morning. Services on the quarter deck at 10:00 AM. A gentleman from shore officiating. Had the forenoon and first watches. Bullion beef for dinner. Wrote to Mary.

Mon Feb 1, 1864

Had the afternoon watch. The pilot who brought us up the river came on board in the morning so I think we will leave before many days. General Banks on board. Pork and beans for dinner.

Wed Feb 3, 1864

Weather cool. Wrote to Cameron. Small stores served out in the afternoon. I drew a clothes brush, bar of soap, bottle of pepper, and six skeins black sewing silk. All hands aired bedding and word was passed to scrub hammocks tomorrow morning. Had the morning and 2nd dog watches. Lawrence 2nd received a letter from Brooklyn which said that the *Vanderbilt* had arrived there and the guard was expected at the barracks. Sorry I could not have stayed on her. Pork and beans for dinner.

Thu Feb 4, 1864

All hands scrubbed hammocks in the morning. A cold job. Water cold as ice. Had the forenoon and 1st watches. Commodore Palmer was on board in the afternoon as stiff as ever. Bullion beef for dinner. Word was passed at quarters to get tie-ties ready for the new hammocks.

Fri Feb 5, 1864

Weather warm and pleasant. Some ladies and gentlemen from the city came on board in the afternoon to see the admiral. Heard him say that we are to leave here tomorrow. Had the afternoon watch. Fresh grub for dinner. The *Lackawana* went out.

Sat Feb 6, 1864

Wrote to Val. We got up anchor about half past five PM, and steamed down the river. Had the mid and 1st dog watches. Pork and beans for dinner. Weather pleasant.

Sun Feb 7, 1864

Was roused out of my billet at one o'clock AM by the men heaving back the starboard compressor. We came to anchor about half past one. At day light I found that we were just about the forts Guard in full uniform at quarters. No inspection. Most of our officers have gone to visit the forts. Got up anchor about twelve o'clock, and started down the river again. Crossed the bar about three o'clock in the afternoon. General muster in the afternoon and the first Luff read the proceedings of some general court martial. Had the morning and 2nd dog watches. Bullion beef for dinner.

Mon Feb 8, 1864

Came in sight of the blockading fleet off Mobile Bay about day light. Came to anchor near the *Richmond*, about half past eight.

Cap't Strong of the *Monongahela*, Captain Le Roy of the *Oneida* and Captain Jenkins of the *Richmond* soon came on board. The *Lackawanna* arrived at eleven o'clock. Captain Marchand came on board and brought quite a large mail for the vessel here but none for us. Had the morning and first watches. Pork and beans for dinner.

Tue Feb 9, 1864

Weather pleasant. Got under way about half past twelve last night. Arrived at Pensacola and anchored about half past ten AM. Had the afternoon watch. Duff for dinner. We bent the new sails and bent our old ones. In the afternoon sent down top gallant masts and riggings. The ship as usual boarded by many officers wanting to see the admiral. He and Captain Drayton went on shore about half past three. Had to wear uniform at the cabin door. Suppose we are stripping ship for the coming attack at Mobile. Hope we may have good luck there. Had to sleep on deck again last night because my hammock was in the way of the capstan bars.

Wed Feb 10, 1864

Had the mid and 1st dog watches. The *Oneida* came in the AM. Our men at work making splinter nettings. Sent all our spare spars on shore. Quarter gunners painting our guns black. Pork and beans for dinner.

Thu Feb 11, 1864

Hoisted out all the boom boats in the morning. A mortar schooner got foul of our jile boom in the afternoon. We got clear of her by paying out more chain. After we were clear, manned capstan bars and took up slack chain. Am feeling very unwell, shall see the Doctor tomorrow if I am not better. Some Brigadier General was on board and took dinner with the admiral. Captain Drayton is in command of this ship now. He told Bolling during the 1st dog watch that we orderlies should not take our caps off. We like him much better than we did Commodore Palmer. Had the morning and 2nd dog watches. Bullion beef for dinner.

Fri Feb 12, 1864

Went to see the doctor this morning and he put me on the sick list and gave me a pill. Capt Haywood called me to the quarter deck just after quarters and asked me if I knew an Acting Master Howell. Said that he saw on shore yesterday and he inquired after me. Six of our guard, Sullivan 2, O'Sullivan, Penterry, Parker, Logen and Calahan were sent on shore to the barracks yesterday, and six from the barracks came on board in their places. We expected two more in the place of Williams and Thackery but did not get them. The new men are better looking than those who went on shore and seem to be better men. Sullivan was back a short time today. Says he likes the barracks very well. Duff for dinner. The steamer *Tennessee* came in the afternoon. She towed the admiral's steam barge the *Loyal* from New Orleans. She also brought our mail. I received a letter which was written in January '63 when I was on the *Vanderbilt* at Hampton Roads. Someone has forwarded it but I don't know who. Probably one of the *Vanderbilt*'s boys.

[Master Howell was John A. Howell, the nephew of Ed Howell, the man who discouraged Charley Brother from joining the Marines.]

Sat Feb 13, 1864

On the sick list, took two doses of quinine, 10 grain each. Went into St. Thomas one year ago today. Pork and beans for dinner.

Sun Feb 14, 1864

Still on the sick list. Marines in full uniform at muster. No services on board. Wrote to Father. Word passed for Marines to pack knapsacks for inspection tomorrow. The *Tennessee* left today. Weather warm and pleasant. Bullion beef for dinner.

Mon Feb 15, 1864

Two months today since we went into commission. Got our boats in about half past seven in the morning. Shipped Capstan bars, hoisted up smoke stack and started fires about nine o'clock. It is reported that we are going to New Orleans again.

Still on the sick list. Marines fell in on the quarter deck in the morning with packed knapsacks. Capstan bars were unshipped after dinner so we will probably not leave today. Pork and beans for dinner.

Tue Feb 16, 1864
Still on the sick list. The *Richmond* came in from the blockading fleet in the morning. Two Rebel soldiers, deserters from Mobile were on board all day. Duff for dinner. Wrote to Darling.

Wed Feb 17, 1864
Still on the binnacle list, but returned to duty at the cabin door. Had the afternoon watch. Got up anchor about nine o'clock and left Pensacola. In the afternoon sighted a steamer. Came up with and hailed her. She proved to be the *De Sota*. Her Captain came on board of us and stayed a short time. Came to anchor with the blockading fleet off Mobile Bay at half past 4 o'clock PM. When I turned out this morning found one of my shoes in a spit box. Couldn't find the other one at all. Got the Sergeant to break out a new pair for me. Pork and beans for dinner.

Thu Feb 18, 1864
Weather very cold. Got up anchor at six o'clock in the morning, arrived at Ship Island and anchored at half past twelve. The sloop of war *Vincennes* and several transports are here. Had the mid and 1st dog watches. Bullion beef and coffee for dinner. Came off the sick list. The Doctor says I had better come in and take my medicine for a few days longer. Ship Island at this end appears to be perfectly barren and is covered with white sand. There is a light house here and several other buildings probably used for the troops and prisoners. They're building a good sized brick fort here.

Fri Feb 19, 1864
Very cold this morning. Thermometer down to 28. Wind went down in the forenoon and the afternoon was somewhat warmer. All hands aired bedding, had the morning and 2nd dog watches.

Duff for dinner. At quarters in the forenoon the 30 pound rifle on the forecastle was discharged. Carried about a mile and a quarter. The army transport *Clyde* left for New Orleans.

Sun Feb 21, 1864

The ships letters were distributed this morning by the Master of Arms and I got two more. Marines at quarters in full uniform. We got some beef and vegetables from the supply steamer and had fresh grub for dinner. Had the afternoon watch. The steamer *Admiral* left for the New Orleans about 2:00 PM. The steamer *Queen* arrived in the morning and left for the north in the PM. Some sailors and marines from the *Vincennes* came on board in the afternoon. The Marines seem to have very good times on the *Vincennes*, do not have to drill nor wear white belts. They want to change with some of us, think it would be nice to be on the flag ship. Word passed for knapsack inspection tomorrow.

Mon Feb 22, 1864

Washington's and Father's birthday. Flags hoisted at our fore and main. The admiral, Captain Drayton, Lieut. Watson and Mr. Davis went on an expedition up the sound this morning. Will probably be gone two or three days. General quarters at three bells. Marines in the tops and I at the cabin door. Knapsack inspection after retreat. Inspected muskets, boxes and c. Sherman ordered us to stack arms before we had fixed bayonets, then tried to lay the blame on us. Had the mid and 1st dog watches, fresh grub for dinner. New hammocks were served out in the forenoon. At noon a national salute was fired by us and the *Vincennes*.

Tue Feb 23, 1864

Turned out at 2:00 AM and scrubbed my hammock on the forecastle. We had a long drill on the quarter deck after quarters. Had the morning and 2nd dog watches. Fresh grub for dinner. Our mess got a barrel of spuds yesterday and we had potato scouse for breakfast. The steamer *Tennessee* arrived about four o'clock from off the Mobile blockade. Turned in scrubbed hammocks at night. Mine fortunately was clean enough to pass.

Wed Feb 24, 1864

The gunboat *Jackson* came in the morning. Came alongside of us and took off our 30 Pd's rifle gun and a lot of ammunition. We can distinctly hear firing up the sound, where the admiral is bombarding some Rebel batteries. Had the forenoon and 1st night watches. Fresh grub for dinner and potato scouse for breakfast. In the afternoon a guns crew of marines exercised at one of the broadside guns. They did first rate and can beat any gun crew on the ship. Wrote to Ed Smead, cleaned belts and accoutrements. Came across an *Albany Journal* at the Cabin door the only one I have seen since leaving home. It was like meeting an old acquaintance.

Thu Feb 25, 1864

One year since I left the *Vanderbilt*. Weather warm and pleasant. A long drill on the quarter deck in the morning. Can hear the bombarding again today. Had the afternoon watch. Coffee and hard tack for dinner. The colonel commanding on the island came on board with a major in the afternoon. General quarters at 5:00 PM. Word passed for washing clothes tomorrow morning. Got up clothes lines. Steamer *Jackson* went up the sound in PM. The *Tennessee* left and took our mail. She is going to New Orleans. Steamer *Arkansas* arrived in evening from New Orleans.

Fri Feb 26, 1864

Scrubbed and washed clothes in the morning. Steamer *Arkansas* came alongside of us in the forenoon and we took a Sawyer gun off of her and quantity of ammunition. There were some ladies on the steamer and Captain Haywood and some of the other officers went on board as soon as she came alongside. Had the mid and 1st dog watches. The tug boat *Glascow* arrived at 5 o'clock and immediately left for Grant's Pass. About seven o'clock the admiral and staff returned on board. Came down on the *Calhoun*. Duff for dinner.

[Another typed version reads: "About seven o'clock and immediately left for Grant's pass."]

Sat Feb 27, 1864

The steamer *Jackson* came in about seven o'clock and came alongside of us. The *Jasmine* came in about the same time. We put our Sawyer gun on board the *Jackson* and took our 30 pd'r rifle out of her. Also a Sawyer gun that had burst. After she hauled off the *Arkansas* came alongside and we put the busted [bursted] Sawer on board her. Had the morning and 2nd dog watches. Pork and beans day. The admiral has another secretary named McKinley. Mr. Adams went to New Orleans in the afternoon, also the pilot Freeman. Cleaned belts and c. for tomorrow's inspection. Wrote to Mary.

Sun Feb 28, 1864

Warm and pleasant. Had the morning and 1st night watches. Pork and beans for dinner. Wrote to Mother. In the evening the supply steamer *Admiral* arrived from New York via Key West, thirteen days on the way. Her captain and paymaster came on board and brought a large mail for us and other vessels of the squadron. While Mr. Davis and Mr. Heingenbothom were distributing the mail I got two myself. One from Mary written Jan 2nd and one from Ed Church written April '63 and directed to the *Vanderbilt*. An army transport came in about ten o'clock.

Sun Feb 28, 1864

Warm and pleasant. Marines in full uniform at quarters. Had the forenoon and 1st watches. Bullion beef and coffee for dinner. The admiral and staff left about four o'clock for Grant's pass on the gun boat *Calhoun*. A guns crew from this ship goes with them. The *Tennessee* arrived about 5:00 PM from New Orleans. Bought a small mail but nothing for me. Word passed for knapsack inspection tomorrow morning.

35. Pilot Martin Freeman, USN, NHHC NH 49432

Mon Feb 29, 1864

A target was set adrift about a mile off and all the starboard guns had two shots each at it. Jimmie Smith's gun and one of the rifles made the two best shots. After quarters we had knapsack inspection, then a short drill. In the afternoon the different divisions practiced with small arms at a target. Had the afternoon watch. Pork and beans day.

Tue Mar 1, 1864

Had the mid and 1st dog watches. At two o'clock in the morning Bickford [George W. Bickford] was brought to the mast for refusing to go on post. Officer of the deck (Mr. Jones) ordered him put in the brig. Am afraid it will be a court martial for him. Steamer *Gertrude* came in about three bells in the morning watch. Steamer Jackson came in about the same time. She has burst the other Sawyer gun that we put on her. About seven o'clock called all hands up anchor. Got up the starboard anchor and let go the port anchor. Steamer *Glascow* came in at twelve last night. Went away immediately. About two o'clock wind began to blow very hard, let go the other anchor. The admiral came on board about three PM. We started fires and got up steam immediately. It is reported about the ship that two rams have come out from Mobile. Duff for dinner.

Wed Mar 2, 1864

Weather cold all night. Mercury down to 36. Had the morning and 2nd dog watches. The *Gertrude* went out about half past five. After quarters we had quite a long drill by Lieut. Sherman. Boatswain called all hands up anchor and he dismissed us, got up anchor. The Army transport Clyde arrived in the afternoon from New Orleans. She said that the *Metacomet* had left New Orleans with the mail three hours before she did. Pork and beans for dinner. Capstan bars were shipped so when hammocks were piped down I could not swing in my billet. At eight o'clock I spread my bed down by the orderly mess table. Was roused up at ten o'clock by the gong beating to general quarters. We do not have to lash (?) up for quarters at night. Got dressed and on deck as soon as possible, relieved Langdon at the cabin door. Drew drilled a short time at the port battery. Retreat at 10:40.

Thu Mar 3, 1864
Had the forenoon and 1st night watches. Bullion beef and coffee for dinner. The last of our potatoes for breakfast. Got up anchor at nine o'clock and sailed from Ship Island. Closely followed by the *Tennessee*. About half past ten a steamer was discovered on the starboard quarter. Came up with us at 12:30. The *Tennessee* passed us about half past five. We arrived off Mobile bay and anchored at seven o'clock. I stowed my hammock in the port netting near the gang way this morning. Couldn't get it at night when hammocks were piped down so had to spread my watch coat on deck and sleep that way. Lights were seen in the night apparently on shore making signals.

Fri Mar 4, 1864
Turned out at six o'clock none the worse for having slept on deck all night. Weighed anchor at half past eight, anchored again at nine. A mail received on board in the morning. I received a letter from Mary and one from Val. Fire quarters at three bells. After retreat marines drilled about three quarters of an hour. Our pilot Freeman came on board again this morning. Had the afternoon watch. Duff for dinner. We have not seen anything of the ram yet. The admiral visited one of the gunboats this afternoon. Wrote to Mary.

Sat Mar 5, 1864
Got up anchor at half past eight AM. Think we are going to Pensacola. All hands aired bedding at 10:30. Had the mid and 1st dog watches. Pork and beans day. Cleaned belts, brasses and muskets. Came to anchor off Pensacola Navy Yard at 3:30 PM. Commodore Smith soon came alongside in the *Loyal*. The steamer *Admiral* came in about five o'clock.

Sun Mar 6, 1864

Had the morning and 2nd dog watches. The tug *Glasgow* came in about seven o'clock. Brought a small mail also two rebel deserters and a rifle cannon shell weighing about 80 pounds which was fired into one of the "bumers"(?) at Grant's Pass but did not explode. It is of English make. The deserters say that the gun that fired it has since burst. Rec'd a *Courier* from Mary. Marines at full uniform at muster. Inspected first by Captain Drayton and then by the admiral. Bickford was brought by the *Admiral*. Boling stood my watch from 6:00 to 8:00. The *Admiral* sailed for the North taking our mail. Word passed for knapsack inspection tomorrow.

Mon Mar 7, 1864

Breakfast at six o'clock. The Launch and 1st and 2nd cutters were hoisted out. A coal bark came alongside at 7:30 and shortly after all hands commenced coaling ship. Had the forenoon and 1st night watches. Steamer *Kennebec*, *Mettamora*, and *Genesee* came in in the forenoon. The *Glascow* left for New Orleans at noon taking our mail. Pork and beans for dinner but no hard tack, we have a plenty of everything except bread. Stewed dried apples for supper. I ate so many I nearly made myself sick. The two deserters from the rebel army left us today. I think they went on the *Glascow*. No knapsack inspection this morning. No general quarters. In the evening a gentleman lately from Mobile came on board and had a long talk with the admiral. It is reported about the ship that the Rebels are going to attack the Navy Yard tonight.

Tue Mar 8, 1864

Weather warm and pleasant. Had the afternoon watch. Rebels didn't attack the Yard last night. The boat *Bermuda* came in at 8:00 o'clock AM. We got a lot of beef, ice, and potatoes from her. Our mess got two barrels of spuds. More potato scouse in prospect. All hands on called this morning at 5:00 o'clock. Breakfast piped as soon as hammocks were stowed. All hands coaling ship. Got done at 3:00 PM. All hands scrub and wash clothes. I was on post but Lawrence relieved me. No supper until two bells. Heard we are to sail early tomorrow morning. Soft tack for supper. Struck a howitzer and some ammunition into the launch to be used in case the Rebels attack the yard. Bickford tried by court martial.

Wed Mar 9, 1864
All hands called at five o'clock. Breakfast as soon as hammocks were stowed. The *Loyal* was kept maned and ready all night. The Rebels didn't come. Weather cold and stormy, rained nearly all day. Paymaster served out the green backs. I got five dollars, the first money I have had in some time. Had the mid and 1st dog watches. Fresh grub for dinner. Washed clothes piped down before they were dry for fear of their being blown away. At 5 o'clock, PM ship began to drift towards shore. Had to let go the starboard anchor.

Thu Mar 10, 1864
Weather clear and pleasant. Had the morning and 2nd dog watches. The *Mettacomet* went out about 8 o'clock PM. Wash clothes triced up again in the morning. A line was got up on the starboard side for wet watch coats and pea jackets. Fresh grub for dinner.

Fri Mar 11, 1864
Had the forenoon and 1st night watches. Duff for dinner. Cleaned belts in the afternoon. About three o'clock marines ordered on the quarter deck with cross belts and muskets. Commodore Smith of the Navy Yard soon came alongside and we gave him a present as he came over the side. Shortly after Brigadier General Asboth and another officer came on board. The gen'l wore a yellow blanket and the other officer a blue one. We gave them a present as they came over the side. They took dinner with the admiral and Captain Drayton. Gen'l quarters in the forenoon at three bells. Lieut. Sherman drilled the guard sometime after retreat. As I was on post I got rid of it. The sailors are scraping the gun carriages, are going to polish them.

Marines on the quarter deck again to salute the general as he left the ship. In the evening saw Bickford's sentence on the log slate. He is to have solitary confinement in double irons on bread and water with loss of pay for thirty days and afterward to have three months extra police duties. Rather a hard sentence. I hear that he is to be sent on shore here.

Sun Mar 12, 1864
Weather pleasant. In the morning about half past eight all hands aired bedding. The steamer *Cowslip* came in about one o'clock. Steamer *Glascow* arrived shortly after. She brought a mail but only one or two letters for this ship. Had the afternoon watch. Pork and beans for dinner. Serg't Marks and Corp'l Eagan had a quarrel in the afternoon. Eagan slapped Marks and Marks stabbed him three times with his sword. The wounds are not deep and not much harm done. Both have been placed under arrest.

Sun Mar 13, 1864
One of the warmest days we have had yet. Marines in full uniform at quarters in the forenoon. Ship's company with white cap covers. A chaplain came on board from the frigate *Potomac* and after quarters we had services. Captain Gibson of the *Potomac* the captain of the *Genesee*, the chaplain and another officer a Lieut. Commander took dinner with the Admiral and Captain Drayton. Had the mid and 1st dog watches. Bullion and coffee for dinner. Wrote to Val. Sent to publishers for 1st ten *New York Ledgers* for the year 1864.

[Brother began a new diary on March 14, 1864. (U.S. Navy, 1971)]

Mon Mar 14, 1864
Had the morning and 2nd dog watches. Pork and beans for dinner. General quarters in the forenoon at three bells. Took my station at the cabin door as usual. Retreat at half past ten. Knapsack inspection on the berth deck after quarters, were inspected by Lieut. Sherman. Captain Haywood is sick. Bickford was sent

on shore in charge of Sergeant Caversish (?) is to remain there until his punishment is over. At six bells all hands triced up the propeller. They are going to put a knife in it but for what purpose I don't know. The supply steamer *Union* arrived about one o'clock. Brought a mail, received a letter and paper from Mary.

Tue Mar 15, 1864
Got up washed clothes in the morning. Bolling washed for me while I stood post duty for him. The *Union* went out about seven o'clock. Had the forenoon and 1st night watches. Wash clothes piped down at four bells in the afternoon. We were cheated out of our duff and given bullion beef for dinner instead.

[The second draft of the IU Lilly Library transcription has more for this entry. The next sentence reads, "Piped down, washed clothes at four bells in the afternoon, found several dead inhabitants on my shirt. Cheated us out of our duff and gave us bullion beef for dinner." The same version also says this entry is on a Tuesday, not a Thursday. With the second draft, there is no word "instead."]

Wed Mar 16, 1864
Marks and Eagan were tried by Summary Court Martial. Quarters and drill in the afternoon at three bells. Had the afternoon watch. Pork and beans for dinner.

Thu Mar 17, 1864
St. Patrick's Day. Weather cool. Came near freezing in the mid watch. Duff for dinner. The steamers *Oneida* and *Tennessee* came in today. A Sergeant Smith belonging to the barracks was buried and our drummer and fifer were sent on shore to attend his funeral. They came on board just after sun set pretty full. The cooper and armorer in the same condition.

Fri Mar 18, 1864
Had the morning and 2nd dog watches. Duff for dinner again. The gunboat *Ossipee* came in about six bells in the morning. John Howell is her executive officer. Word passed that a mail

would leave the ship at two PM. Wrote a letter to Father and took it off at half past one but the mail had gone. The *Ossipee* left about half past two. Fire quarters at 6:00 PM.

[Someone erased this sentence from the original diary: "John Howell is her executive officer." John Howell, from Bath, NY, later invented the Howell Torpedo.]

Sat Mar 19, 1864
Had the afternoon and 1st night watches. Pork and beans for dinner. Marks and Eagan have received their sentence and are on duty again. Marks is to lose one month's pay and receive three months extra duty. Eagan forfeits two-months' pay and gets three months extra duty. I wonder what the extra duty will be. The *Glascow* came in about two o'clock. The *Pembina* at noon. Cleaned belts and c. in the afternoon. Wrote to Father.

Sun Mar 20, 1864
Marines in full uniform at quarters. Ships company in clean blue and white cap covers. Serg't Behrensen gave orders to clean and mark our uniform hats and turn them in to him as they are to be done away with for the present. Had the afternoon watch. Bullion and coffee for dinner. The *Bermuda* came in at 3:00 PM.

Mon Mar 21, 1864
Cold and rainy all day. Had the mid and 1st dog watches. Pork and beans for dinner. All hands scrub and wash clothes. Williams came back from the Hospital this afternoon. Colors hoisted at 8:00 AM. The *Jasmine* came in about 5:00 PM. Brought no mail. Several gun boats arrived during the day. Weather reported very rough outside.

Tue Mar 22, 1864
Had the morning and 2nd dog watches. Duff for dinner. Ship *Courier* went out in the morning. Gunboat *Sebago* arrived in the afternoon. General quarters at 5:30 PM. This morning found

36. Lieut. John A. Howell, USN, was about twenty-four years old in 1864, and later ranked Commodore, NHHC NH 48913

that my belts were black. Several other belts were in the same fix though not as bad as mine. They say it is caused by the bilge water in the hold. The paint work about the hat lockers is also blackened. Weather cold.

Wed Mar 23, 1864

Had the forenoon and 1st night watches. Pork and beans for dinner. Bought a bucket from the bum-boat for 60 cents. Loosened sail in the forenoon. At three bells cleaned belts.

Thu Mar 24, 1864

Had the afternoon watch. Bullion and coffee for dinner. The last of our spuds for breakfast. Rain and wind in afternoon.

Fri Mar 25, 1864

Had the mid and 1st dog watches. Duff for dinner. General quarters in the forenoon at four bells. All the port guns fired at a target five times. Some splendid shots were made. Distance eleven hundred yards. The *Glascow* arrived in the evening brought a mail from New Orleans. Rec'd a letter from Mary dated March 6th.

Sat Mar 26, 1864

Warm and pleasant. Last night Bolling was taken sick while on watch at the cabin door and was relieved by Lawrence 2nd. While I was out on my hammock a short time last night someone stole my blanket. This makes three I have lost in the service besides the comforter sent me from home. Fire quarters in the forenoon at 4 bells. Gen'l quarters at 6 bells and target practice. Each of the starboard guns had two shots at the target. The shooting was good but not as good as yesterday. Cleaned belts and epaulets in the afternoon. Had the morning and 2nd dog watches. Pork and beans day. Wrote to Mary.

[Brother's note about his blanket being stolen and his complaint about similar incidents before are erased from the original diary but appear in a typed transcript at the Lilly Library, Indiana University]

Sun Mar 27, 1864

Weather warm and pleasant. Marines at muster in full uniform with fatigue caps and white cap covers. Ships company in clean blue and white covers. The chaplain from the *Potomac* came on board and held services after quarters. Had the forenoon and first night watches. Bullion beef and coffee for dinner. Several motor schooners arrived during the day. Rec'd a paper from Mary. The New York papers say that Farragut is to be relieved from here to take command of the South Atlantic squadron. Hope it is not so, or if it is that he may take us with him. In the morning a ship was seen outside sending up rockets. She afterwards went farther out and anchored.

Mon Mar 28, 1864
One year ago today we arrived at New York on board the *Peterhoff*. Heard yesterday that she had been sunk off Galveston. Rain all day. Had the afternoon watch. Pork and beans for dinner. Gun boat *Itasca* arrived in the afternoon.

Tue Mar 29, 1864
Had the mid and 1st dog watches. Duff for dinner. At 11:15 am the starboard anchor was let go because the wind was blowing strong from the northwest. At 6:30 got up starboard anchor. General quarters at three bells and a long drill for us after retreat. Wind blowing hard all day. No boats ashore except the *Loyal*. An army transport arrived in the afternoon.

Wed Mar 30, 1864
All hands called at three bells. Breakfast at six o'clock. Had the morning and 2nd dog watches. Pork and beans for dinner. The sloop of war *Richmond* arrived in the afternoon. She has encountered a heavy storm and lost two of her boats. Captain Jenkins came on board as soon as she had anchored. We orderlys now have charge to the keys of the magazine.

Thu Mar 31, 1864
All hands called at three bells. Breakfast at four bells. Had the afternoon and first night watches. Bullion and coffee for dinner. The *Jesmine* came in about eleven o'clock in the evening. Marines fired at target in the afternoon. I fired five times and hit it the last time. Weather pleasant.

37. Farragut's dinghy Loyal, NHHC NH 53391

Fri Apr 1, 1864
All hands called at three bells. Breakfast at four bells. Scrubbed and washed clothes. The mail came on board from the *Jesmine*. Rec'd a letter from Mary and one from Ellen W. Had the afternoon watch. Duff for dinner. I ate my own duff and Wilcox's too. Corporal Eagan sent on shore to barracks and a private sent on board from there in his place.

Sat Apr 2, 1864
All hands called at the three bells. Breakfast at four. Mason was made acting corporal today to take Eagan's place. Cleaned belts in the afternoon. Had the mid and 1st dog watches. Pork and beans for dinner. The admiral, Cap't Drayton, Lieut. Watson, Mr. McKinley, Mr. Davis, Mr. Brownwell and, Willis, Wilson, and Brooks went on board the steamer *Tennessee* and left for New Orleans. We now fly a long pennant at the main instead of a blue one at the mizzen. Mr. Kimberly is now in command of the ship. It is said the admiral will be gone a month or more. We now strike a bell after the *Richmond*. Wrote to Mother.

Sun Apr 3, 1864

Weather warm and pleasant. Quarters at 4 bells in the forenoon. Marines in full uniform and white cap covers. Ships company in clean blue with white cap covers. General muster after quarters. First Luff read articles of war. Ships company mustered around the capstan. Had the morning and 2nd dog watches. Bullion and coffee for dinner. In the afternoon some of the marines and sailors went on board the *Richmond*. Some of the *Richmond*'s men came on board of us. Her marines have 10 and 12 hours off, have no drill, never wear full uniform and wear no belts but waist belt when on post. So it seems that Lieut. Powell is a pretty good officer.

Mon Apr 4, 1864

Had the forenoon and 1st night watches. Pork and beans for dinner. General quarters at three bells. Retreat at four. Marines ordered to wear no box belts on post in future. Signed account for $37.01.

Tue Apr 5, 1864

All hands called at two bells. Breakfast at three bells. All hands scrub and wash clothes. Ship *New England* went out in forenoon quarters at 3 Bells. A long drill after retreat. Had the afternoon watch. Duff for dinner.

Wed Apr 6, 1864

Warm and pleasant. All hands called at two bells. Scrubbed hammocks after breakfast. Had the mid and 1st dog watches. Pork and beans for dinner. General quarters in the forenoon and 3 bells. A short drill afterwards. Double quick to the tune of "Pop goes the weasel." Scrubbed hammocks piped down at one o'clock.

Thu Apr 7, 1864

Had the morning and 2nd dog watches. Bullion, coffee, and soft tack for dinner. The supply steamer *Admiral* arrived at 7:00 AM. Mail came on board in forenoon. Rec'd a letter and several

New York Heralds from Cameron. Commenced raining at about 7:00 AM. Rained all day. No gen'l quarters. We got a lot of fresh beef and vegetables from the *Admiral*. Our mess got two barrels of spuds.

Fri Apr 8, 1864
Rainy and stormy all day. Fresh grub for dinner and potato scouse for breakfast. Had the forenoon and 1st night watches. Dispatch boat *Glascow* arrived in the PM from New Orleans. Brought us a small mail but none for me. A ship said to be the *Pensacola* has anchored outside with her Jack up for a pilot.

Sat Apr 9, 1864
The *Pensacola* came in this morning. She is homeward bound. Has been out here about two years. It is reported she has three hundred sick men on board and two hundred whose times are out. Wrote to Val.

Sun Apr 10, 1864
Marines at quarters in full uniform with fatigue caps with white covers. Ships company in clean blue and white cap covers. Had the mid and 1st dog watches. Fresh grub for dinner. A number of our men went on board the *Richmond* in the afternoon.

Mon Apr 11, 1864
Warm and pleasant. Marines had quite a long drill after quarters. Then knapsack inspection on the berth deck. Had the morning and 2nd dog watches. The *Pensacola* went out in the PM. The *Jesmine* arrived. Bought us a small mail, none for me. An attack upon the Navy Yard being anticipated we were ordered to have our belts and muskets in readiness to go on shore at a moment's notice. An evening quarters the guns were loaded with 10 second shell. When hammocks were piped down word was passed for the men to stand by for a call to general quarters during the night. Pork and beans for dinner. Bickford came on board.

Tue Apr 12, 1864

All hands scrub and wash clothes. The rebels didn't disturb us last night. Quarters in the forenoon at three bells. Marines drilled after quarters. Wash clothes piped down in the afternoon at seven bells. In the morning we were ordered to put away our fatigue coats and put on jumpers. Weather quite warm. The warmest day we have had yet. Had the forenoon and 1st dog watches. Duff for dinner.

Wed Apr 13, 1864

Had the afternoon watch. Pork and beans for dinner. Drill on the quarter deck in the morning. An attack is expected on the Navy Yard tonight. The ship *Sportsman* and a bark have moved out of the way.

Thu Apr 14, 1864

Had the mid and 1st dog watches. Firing was heard on shore in the direction of Fort Barrancus between and three o'clock AM. The *Potomac* and *Richmond* beat to quarters and then we did. The guns were cast loose, and the boats sent on the shore with the Marines. Some of the sick and myself were left on board. I being on watch at the cabin door. The men stayed at the guns until about 5 o'clock when they were piped down. Soon after the boats returned with the marines. Breakfast at half past six. Quarters at two bells. No drill. It is reported that we are going on shore tonight with knapsacks. Rain began to fall about noon. At about 5:30 PM marines fell in with cross belts, muskets and watch coats, and went on shore in the first cutter. We marched up to Barracks and stacked arms, broke ranks and all went to the canteen which was opened for us. A marine who I used to know in Brooklyn loaned me a mattress and watch coat, and spreading them on the floor I turned in about eight o'clock. Turned out at nine to answer roll call. Turned in again but could not get to sleep for some reason on account of the fleas. Pork and beans for dinner.

Fri Apr 15, 1864

Turned out at Reveille. Faley was locked up during the night for being drunk and disorderly. In the morning took a walk around the yard with Knox. We fell in about 6:30 and marched down to the basin where the first cutter was waiting for us. Sullivan and McCristle could not be found so we went off without them. Got on board about seven o'clock, and after a little delay got breakfast. No coffee. The *Glascow* arrived last evening. Brought us a mail which was distributed this morning. Received a letter from Mary dated March 29th. Hunt is cook in place of Sullivan. In the forenoon cleaned belts brasses and c. Had the 2nd dog watch. Duff for dinner.

Sat Apr 16, 1864

Had the forenoon and 1st watches. Sullivan and McCristle were brought on board in the afternoon. Both were put on double duty immediately. Pork and beans for dinner. Hunt makes a good cook. Hope he will stay there.

Sun Apr 17, 1864

Had the afternoon watch. Quarters at four bells. Marines in full uniform, fatigue caps and white cap covers. Ships company in clean blue and white cap covers. The secretary of the Commodore belonging to the yard came on board with his wife, a very pretty woman. Wrote to Mary. In the afternoon some of the marines and sailors went on board of us. The *Arkansas* arrives in the evening. Had bullion beef and boiled spuds for supper. Sullivan is off double duty and is cook again.

Mon Apr 18, 1864

Weather pleasant. No knapsack inspection. General quarters in the forenoon at two bells. Relieved Bolling and took station at the cabin door. Retreat in about fifteen minutes. I went below and did not fall in for drill. The rest of the guard drilled about an hour. Had the mid and 1st dog watches. Pork and beans for dinner. The *Seminole* came in about six PM. She is from off Galveston. Word passed to wear white pants next Sunday.

Tue Apr 19, 1864

Had the morning and 2nd dog watches. Duff for dinner. In the morning about seven bells the schooner *Kittatinny* and bark *Anderson* at the bayou (?) fired several times toward shore. Don't know what it was about.

[Smith's transcription of the diary says: "I don't know what the firing was for." Smith's transcription of the diary says: "Rice and Beans for dinner."]

Wed Apr 20, 1864

Had the forenoon and 1st watches. Pork and beans for dinner. The supply steamer *Admiral* arrived in the forenoon from New Orleans. Brought a mail. Rec'd a letter from Mary and a number of *New York Ledgers* from publishers. Kelly and Williams went on board the *Admiral* are going North by orders of the doctor. Williams with a blind eye and Kelly with varicose veins in his legs and feet.

[Smith's 1964 transcription of the diary says, "Duff for dinner."]

Thu Apr 21, 1864

Warm and pleasant. Had the afternoon watch. Bullion beef and coffee for dinner. Drill on the quarter deck in the forenoon. Those of the guard who need them drew white pants and jumpers. Langdon came off the sick list.

Fri Apr 22, 1864

Wash morning. Had the mid and 1st dog watches. Duff for dinner. Fire quarters at two bells in the forenoon. A short drill for marines afterwards. Captain Haywood taught us how to stack arms without bayonets. Wrote to Mary.

Sat Apr 23, 1864

Cleaned belts and c. in the afternoon. Had the morning and 2nd dog watches. Pork and beans for dinner.

Sun Apr 24, 1864

Had the forenoon and 1st watches. Marines at muster in full uniform and white cap covers. Ships company in clean blue and white cap covers. An army transport loaded with soldiers arrived in the morning. Rec'd a paper from Mary. Boiled rice for dinner.

Mon Apr 25, 1864

Warm and pleasant. General quarters at two bells in the forenoon. Drill after quarters. Had the afternoon watch. Pork and beans for dinner. Deveaux [Devoe] came on board from the hospital.

Tue Apr 26, 1864

Scrub and wash clothes. The *Tennessee* came in and anchored at six PM. Suppose the admiral will be back on board of us tomorrow. Received a *New York Times* from Mary. Had the mid and 1st dog watches. Pork and beans day.

Wed Apr 27, 1864

The admiral, Captain Drayton and all of the staff came on board this morning and once more we fly the blue pennant from our mizzen mast. General quarters at two bells in the forenoon and drill after. The awning post were put up and the awning bend on. It is new and very nice. The *Seliago* came in. Had the morning and 2nd dog watches. Pork and beans for dinner.

Thu Apr 28, 1864

Had the forenoon watch. Bullion and coffee for dinner. The schooner *Rachel Seaman* came in about one bell in the 1st watch. It is said she has a lot of spuds on board. The *Tennessee* went out at 4:00 PM.

Fri Apr 29, 1864

General quarters at two bells in the forenoon. After retreat all hands aired bedding. Wash morning. Had the afternoon watch. Wrote to mother. Duff day.

Sat Apr 30, 1864
Weather pleasant. Cleaned belts and c. for Sunday inspection. We got up anchor at 10 o'clock AM and steamed out to sea. Arrived off Mobile Bay and anchored with the blockading fleet about seven o'clock. The Captain of the *Ossippee* came on board immediately. Had the mid and 1st dog watches. Pork and beans for dinner.

Sun May 1, 1864
Got up anchor and got under way this morning at 12:30. A Pensacola pilot boarded us about seven o'clock AM. Said that the steamer *Union* had gone into Pensacola about an hour before. We anchored off Pensacola Navy Yard about eight o'clock. Got some fresh beef, vegetables and ice from the *Union*. She left in the evening for New Orleans. Quarters for inspection at six bells in the forenoon. Marines in full uniform and white cap covers. Ships company in clean blue and white cap covers. Had the morning and 2nd dog watches. Bullion beef and rice for dinner. Clean hammocks served out at evening quarters and word passed to scrub in the morning.

Mon May 2, 1864
Scrubbed hammocks in the morning. Had the forenoon and 1st watches. Fresh grub for dinner. Scrubbed hammocks piped down at seven bells in the afternoon. Small stores served out. Drew a bar of soap, cake of beeswax, and bottle of pepper. Clean hammocks turned in at evening quarters. The *Glasgow* went out.

Tue May 3, 1864
Had the afternoon watch. Duff for dinner. Quarters at the usual hour. About a dozen sailors whose times are out were sent here from the Schooner to take their place. Wrote to Mary. The *Ossipee* came in.

Wed May 4, 1864
Weather pleasant. Langdon on the sick list. Thompson takes his place. The anchor chains were got and cleaned to day and sent below again. The boom boats were got out. Think we will lay here for some months. Had the mid and 1st dog watches. The *Mettacomet* came in about 6:00 PM.

Thu May 5, 1864
Had the morning and 2nd dog watches. Pork and beans for dinner. Quarters at the usual hours but no drill. Drew a pair of shoes.

Fri May 6, 1864
Warm and pleasant. The *Union* came in about 5:30 AM. Brought us a mail from New Orleans. Rec'd a letter from Mary and one from Vep Darling. Cleaned belts in the afternoon. Had the forenoon and 1st watches. Duff for dinner. The *Richmond* went out about eight o'clock in the morning. She is bound for the blockading fleet. The *Glascock* came in about 5:00 PM. Brought us a mail. Rec'd a letter from Mary written about a month before the one I got this morning.

Sat May 7, 1864
Had the afternoon watch. Pork and beans for dinner. Loosed sails in the morning. Paymaster served out money. I drew five dollars. Warm and pleasant.

Sun May 8, 1864
Marines at muster in full uniform with white cap covers. Ships company in clean blue and white cap covers. Ships company in clean blue and white covers. Were inspected by Captain Drayton and then by the Admiral. Weather very pleasant. In the afternoon about twenty men and boys went on shore on liberty until sunset, came off in the sun down boat nearly all slightly intoxicated. We are all to have liberty here, a few every day. Had the mid and 1st dog watches. Bullion and rice for dinner. Wrote to Mary.

Mon May 9, 1864

General quarters and fire quarters in the morning. Some more of the ships company went on shore in the afternoon. Had the morning and 2nd dog watches. Pork and beans day.

Tue May 10, 1864

Gun boat *Penguin* came in the morning. Scrub and wash clothes. In the forenoon the bark *Henry Booth* of New York came along-side loaded with coal and all hands commenced coaling ship. There is a report that Gen'l Grant has gained a great victory in Virginia. Had the forenoon and 1st watches. Sea pie for dinner. About thirty more men ashore on liberty. The *Seminole* came in.

Wed May 11, 1864

Still coaling ship. Knocked off about half past twelve. Lieut. Howell [John A. Howell] was on board this morning. I saw him on the quarter deck but not to speak to him. Had the afternoon watch. Pork and beans for dinner. More men ashore on liberty. Langdon came off the sick list.

Thu May 12, 1864

Had the mid and 1st dog watches, more men ashore on liberty. The coal bark hauled away from us this morning. John Howell came on board while we were at quarters. After we dismissed he sent for me, went on the quarter deck and had a short talk with him. He looks well in uniform. He said his ship is to sail soon or he would ask me to come see him. The *Albatros* came in. Bullion beef for dinner.

Fri May 13, 1864

Had the morning watch. Sea pie for dinner. On liberty, went ashore in the 2nd cutter about one o'clock with Corporal O'Conner [O'Connor], Knox, and Taylor. We first took a bath on the beach at the Navy Yard. Went up to Ft. Barrancus. The woods are full of black and white soldiers and refugees. The soil is sandy and loose which makes walking hard work. The town at the yard doesn't amount to much. Only a few small buildings and shantys in it. Got back there about half past five. Bought some ink, paper, envelopes, thread, needles, and sewing silk. Went on board the *Bermuda* to see Corporal McCandles but he had gone on shore. Got back on board about seven o'clock. The *Bermuda* came in in the morning. We got some fresh beef, ice, and vegetables from her. The *Buckthorn* arrived in the PM. Brought mail for the squadron, none for me.

Sat May **14, 1864**
More men ashore on liberty, general quarters in the morning and target practice. One shot hit the target. Had the forenoon and 1st watches. Pork and beans for dinner. Cleaned belts and c.

Sun May **15, 1864**
Marines at muster in full uniform and white cap covers. Ships company in white shirts, white cap covers and blue pants. After quarters all hands mustered oft to listen to some remarks from the Chaplain of the *Potomac*. More men ashore on liberty. Had the afternoon watch, fresh grub for dinner. Dandy funk for supper.

Mon May **16, 1864**
General quarters in the morning at two bells. Had the mid and 1st dog watches, fresh grub for dinner, wrote to Val. Bolling went on shore to barracks, and a man there came on board in his place. Marines drilled about an hour in the afternoon. The *Tennessee* came in.

[Smith diary transcription states first line of entry is this: "Weather pleasant."]

Tue May **17, 1864**
Wash morning. Quarters at the usual hour. Had the morning and 2nd dog watches. Fresh grub for dinner. Wrote to Ellie, Cameron, and Darling. Sergeant Mackie of the *Seminole* on board in the afternoon. The *Port Royal* came in in the forenoon.

Wed May 18, 1864

The *Itasca* and another double ender arrived from Mobile in the forenoon. The *Itasca* was disabled and was towed in by the other boat. The *Glasgow* went out in the evening. Pork and beans day. Had the forenoon and 1st watches.

Tue May 19, 1864

The *Galena* came in in the afternoon. Had the afternoon watch. Bullion and coffee for dinner. Clean hammocks served out at evening quarters with orders to scrub dirty ones in the morning.

[The Smith transcription has the start of the entry for May 19th: "Weather pleasant. The *Galena* came in in the afternoon.]

Fri May 20, 1864

All hands scrubbed hammocks and washed clothes. Duff for dinner. Had the mid and 1st dog watches. General quarters last night and eleven o'clock. I did not hear the alarm and did not wake up. After all the rest were on deck the Orderly Serg't came down and waked me. While at quarters the tug boat *Narcissus* came in. Her captain came on board and reported that the ram were out at Mobile, which caused considerable excitement on board of us. Retreat beat about half past eleven. Lawrence on the sick list. Taylor goes on the cabin door in his place.

Sat May 21, 1864

Had the morning and 2nd dog watches. Steam was up when I went on watch. We got underway and left Pensacola about half past six AM. About ten o'clock we met the *Glasgow*. She brought a mail. Rec'd a letter and a *New York Times* from Mary. Cleaned belts in forenoon. Arrived off Mobile Bay and anchored with the fleet in the afternoon. Weather very warm. Pork and beans for dinner.

Sun May 22, 1864

Had the forenoon and 1st watches. Wrote to Mary, muster in the morning at 10 o'clock. Marines in uniform coats, white pants and cap covers. Ships company in blue pants, white frocks and cap covers. In the afternoon our two one hundred pound rifles guns were put up on the forecastle and the 30 pounder put on the poop. It is reported that we are going in to feel the forts. Bullion and dandy funk for dinner.

Mon May 23, 1864
Weather very warm. Marines in jumpers and white pants. All hand aired bedding in the morning. Splinter netting put up. That looks as if we might expect some hot work soon. The *Glasgow* came alongside in the morning. Came from Pensacola. Brought a small mail, none for me. In the afternoon about six o'clock we with nearly all the other vessels of the blockading fleet, got under way and stood away in a Southerly direction, and then back again to nearly the same place we started from. Had the afternoon watch. Pork and beans day.

Tue May 24, 1864
The steamer *Admiral* arrived last night. We got some ice, fresh beef and vegetables from her. Duff for dinner. Had the mid and 1st dog watches. The *Ossipee* and several other ships practiced firing at a target. From what I heard the admiral say I think we are going to run past the forts soon.

[Smith transcription states, "Weather very warm. Washed a shirt, pair of socks and pr. of white pants. The admiral came in last night. Got some ice, fresh beef, and some vegetables from her. Had the third and first dog watches. Duff for dinner. The *Ossippee* and several other ships fired at target. . ."]

Wed May 25, 1864
The *Bermuda* arrived last night. She brought us a mail. Rec'd letters from Father and Mary. There is a report that Grant has taken Richmond. Fresh grub for dinner. Had the morning and 2nd dog watches. Wrote to Father.

[The Smith transcription has a different sentence: "Recd a letter from Father & Mary containing sad news about Henry, also rec'd a *NY Times* for April 16th." When Henry ("H.H.") returned from Australia in 1865, he was in very poor condition. According to oral history via Marjorie (nee Brother) Peterson, family members were shocked by his appearance; his hair was white and he refused to talk about what happened there except that he developed a profound respect for English government. His time in Australia met with "varying fortunes" and he returned "with shattered health at last that when he was carried on ship-board for his return passage he had slight expectation of serving any other purpose in this world than that of deep sea surroundings. Crossing the Southern Ocean direct to Liverpool via Cape Horn, he was impressed with the vastness of the watery waste from six long weeks without a single glimpse of 'terra firma.'" (*Prattsburgh News*, Jun 24, 1884)]

Tue May 26, 1864
Marines in clean blue clothes. Had the forenoon and 1st watches. Fresh grub for dinner. Sullivan has sore finger and Smith is cook in his place.

Fri May 27, 1864
Had the afternoon watch. Cleaned musket and bayonet in the forenoon. Marines in clean blue and white cap covers. In the evening about half past five the fleet got under way and drilled and maneuvered about two hours. Came to anchor a little closer in. Fire quarters in forenoon. Loosened sail in evening.

Sat May 28, 1864
Had the mid and 1st dog watches. About one bell in the mid watch a light was seen bearing W.S.W. Cap't Drayton and the admiral came on deck. It blazed up once very bright and disappeared shortly afterwards. The *Seminole* went to quarters about two bells, gave no signal. Cleaned belts brasses and c. in the forenoon. About three bells in the 1st dog watch the fleet got under way. Drilled a short time, anchored again at the old place. Pork and beans dry.

[The Smith transcription shows the name of the ship is erased; the Lilly transcript has it typed.]

Sun May 29, 1864
General quarters at four bells. Marines in uniform, white pants and cap covers. Ships company all white. Wrote to Mother. Had the morning and 2nd dog watches. Bullion and dandy funk for dinner.

Mon May 30, 1864
Had the forenoon and 1st watches. Pork and beans for dinner. Some rebel prisoners were brought down from up the sound by the tug Narcissus in the afternoon. As evening quarters the guns were cast loose and the men ordered to stand by their guns during their watch on deck. About one bell in the first watch a bright light was seen in the vicinity of Fort Gaines. About an hour after, two green lights were seen near Fort Morgan. They disappeared about four bells. A picket boat went out about one bell, in charge of Lieut. Munday and Masters Mate Childs. Gen'r quarters in the forenoon.

Tue May 31, 1864
All the watch scrub and wash clothes. Turned out to wash clothes at four o'clock. Marines in white pants and cap covers. Ships company in white frocks and cap covers. The Glasgow arrived in the morning from Pensacola. Brought Deneaux and Perry the quartermaster. Pentony's sentence is three years penitentiary at hard labor. The Brooklyn came in about four o'clock PM and anchored near us. She fired a salute of sixteen guns. Wrote a note to Dora Harris and sent by the cockswain of the Brooklyn's gig.

Wed June 1, 1864
The fleet got under way in the forenoon and drilled about three hours. Received a note from Josiah Gregg in the afternoon. He and Harris and Bandfield, Angus, Smith, and Oviatt are on

38. Capt. Drayton and Adm. Farragut. Library of Congress

board the *Brooklyn*. Oviatt is a corporal. The *Port Royal* came in in the afternoon. Had the mid and 1st dog watches. Pork and beans for dinner. All the captains of the fleet were on board in the afternoon.

Thu Jun 2, 1864

Sent a note to Gregg on the *Brooklyn*. Had the morning and 2nd dog watches. Bullion and coffee for dinner. The *Kanawha* arrived and brought a large mail for the fleet.

Fri Jun 3, 1864

Had the forenoon and 1st watches. Duff for dinner. The admiral and Captain Drayton went on board the *Brooklyn* in the afternoon. Sergeant Canendish was transferred to the *Ossipee* yesterday. He is to be her Orderly Sergeant. The sergeant from the *Ossipee* comes to us. His name is Beard [Robert G. Baird].

Sat Jun 4, 1864

Had the afternoon watch. Cleaned belts and c. in the forenoon. The steamer *Admiral* arrived in the morning from New Orleans. Brought some mail, none for me. While on her way from Galviston to New Orleans she captured a prize. Was taking her up to New Orleans when she sank in the river. It is thought that her captain scuttled her to prevent her captors getting anything for her. Pork and beans day.

Sun Jun 5, 1864

Had the mid and 1st dog watches. Fresh grub for dinner. At quarters marines in full uniform, white pants and cap covers. Ships company all in white. Rec'd a letter from Gregg. Wrote to Mary.

Mon Jun 6, 1864

This morning during the mid watch a great commotion was seen among the vessels in shore. Lights were shone and rockets fired, in the morning the *Mettacomet* and one or two other vessels were not to be seen. About half past eight the *Metacomet* came up with a good sized side wheel tried to run in last night but was turned back by our gunboats and the *Metacomet* chased her and captured her after a run of five hours. She is said to be from Havana and a valuable prize. The supply steamer *Circasian* arrived in the forenoon. Brought us a small mail. Rec'd a *New York Times*. Pork and beans day.

Tue Jun 7, 1864
The *Glasgow* arrived from New Orleans in the afternoon. The *Mettacomet*'s prize left for Philadelphia. Duff and fresh grub for dinner. Had the forenoon 1st watch.

Wed Jun 8, 1864
Captains Alden, Jenkins, and March and LeRoy came on board and dined with the admiral and Captain Drayton. Rec'd a letter from Mary. Had the afternoon watch. Fresh grub for dinner. All hands aired bedding in the forenoon. Piped down in the afternoon at two bells.

Thu Jun 9, 1864
Had the mid and 1st dog watches. Fresh grub for dinner. The *Circassian* arrived in the morning.

Fri Jun 10, 1864
Had the morning and 2nd dog watches. Salt horse for dinner but no duff.

Sat Jun 11, 1864
The *Glasgow* arrived in the forenoon. Brought some mail. Rec'd a *Steuben Courier* from Mary, wrote her a letter. Cleaned belts, brasses, muskets and c. in the afternoon. Cleaned hammocks served out at evening quarters. Had the afternoon and 1st watches. Pork and beans.

Sun Jun 12, 1864
Had the afternoon watch. About two o'clock some of the *Brooklyn*'s men came on board. Harris and Gregg among them. Was of course very glad to see them and we had a good visit. Bullion and dandy funk for dinner. Marines at muster in full uniform, white pants and cap covers. Ships company in all white.

Mon Jun 13, 1864

Scrubbed hammocks in the morning. General quarters in forenoon. Have the mid and 1st dog watches. Pork and beans.

Tue Jun 14, 1864

Port watch scrubbed hammocks. Duff for dinner. Had the morning and 2nd dog watches.

Wed Jun 15, 1864

The *Glasgow* arrived from Pensacola and left in the afternoon for New Orleans. Marines had drill in the afternoon. Wash morning. Pork and beans for dinner. Had the forenoon and 1st watches.

Thu Jun 16, 1864

Saw Lieut. John Howell on board in the forenoon. The *Genesee* arrived and left again. Bullion and coffee for dinner. Had the afternoon watch.

Fri Jun 17, 1864

The *Glasgow* arrived in the afternoon. Brought a mail. Rec'd a letter from Val with some postage stamps I sent for some time ago. General Canby came on board and took a dinner with the admiral. Left at four o'clock. Marines at present arms as he went over to the side. He is bound for Pensacola. Had the mid and 1st dog watches. Sea pie for dinner, aired bedding. Lieut. Sherman transferred to the *Richmond*.

[Edward Richard Sprigg Canby, age forty-seven, was born in Boone County, Kentucky, on the Ohio River. Canby went to West Point. "Canby was heading back to Lake Pontchartrain. As the General crossed the deck, Capt. Heywood's 44 Marine guards gave him a snappy salute." Farragut wasn't aware that Canby was coming on this day. They met in Farragut's "spacious cabin" that was located under the poop deck. Farragut was animated to be making progress with the plan, knowing that the Army and Navy were together outlining the attack now from land and sea. (Friend, 2001)]

39. Gen. Edward R. S. Canby. Library of Congress

■ *The Boys of Bath*

Sat Jun 18, 1864
Had the morning and 2nd dog watches. Pork and beans for dinner, fire quarters in the forenoon. Cleaned belts and c.

Sun Jun 19, 1864
Rained in the morning. Quarters for inspection at the usual hour. Ships company in blue pants, white frocks and cap covers. Marines in clean blue. Had the forenoon and 1st watches. Bullion and coffee for dinner. Wrote to Val.

Mon Jun 20, 1864
Had the afternoon watch. Pork and beans for dinner. Wrote to Ed Church and Ed May. The *Glasgow* arrived in the forenoon and left for New Orleans. Drill in the PM by Capt. Haywood.

[According to the 1860 Census, Edward S. May was the son of S.S. May, a master carpenter. The May family lived up the street from the Hess family and the Brother family.]

Tue Jun 21, 1864
Had the mid and 1st dog watches. Sea pie for dinner. Drill in the PM by Cap't Haywood. Wrote to Will Hess.

Wed Jun 22, 1864
Drill in the afternoon by the orderly Sergeant. Sent for some New York Ledgers. The *Lackawanna* came in from Pensacola. Pork and beans for dinner. Had the morning and 2nd dog watches.

Thu Jun 23, 1864
The *Circassian* came in the morning. Mr. Davis left us. Had the forenoon and 1st watches. Bullion for dinner. *Circassian* left in the afternoon.

Fri Jun 24, 1864

Had the afternoon watch. Duff for dinner. The *Glascow* and *Genesee* arrived and both left for Pensacola in the afternoon. Brought us some mail. Rec'd a letter from Mary and one from Tom Seymour. Cavenaugh came on board in the afternoon from Pensacola, aired bedding. Cleaned muskets in forenoon.

Sat Jun 25, 1864

Cleaned belts and c. for Sunday's inspection. Pork and beans day. Had the mid and 1st dog watches.

Sun Jun 26, 1864

Very warm. Bullion and boiled rice for dinner. Had the morning and 2nd dog watches. Marines at muster in uniform and white pants. Ships company in white. Wrote to Mary and Tom Seymour. The *Richmond* and *Mettacomett* came in from Pensacola in the morning.

Mon Jun 27, 1864

The *Glasgow* and *Phillippi* came in the forenoon. *Glasgow* left for Ship Island and the *Phillippi* for New Orleans. Had the forenoon and 1st watches. Pork and beans for dinner. General quarters in the evening.

Tue Jun 28, 1864

Had the afternoon watch. Duff for dinner. Drill in the afternoon by the Orderly Sergeant. The *Glasgow* and *Cowslip* arrived. The *Clyde* left for Pensacola.

Wed Jun 29, 1864

Had the mid and 1st dog watches. Pork and beans for dinner. Steamer *Clyde* passed us this morning on her way to New Orleans. Drill in the afternoon by Captain Haywood.

Thu Jun 30, 1864
Drill in the afternoon by Captain Haywood. Had the morning and 2nd dog watches. Bullion and coffee for dinner.

Fri Jul 1, 1864
Had the forenoon and 1st watches. Last night a steamer tried to run in but was run ashore by the *Glasgow*. She can be seen plainly about a mile from Fort Morgan. Several of the gun boats are firing at her and at a four gun battery on the beach, but they do not seem to hit her. The fort has fired at the gun boats several times but done no damage. In the afternoon the admiral and Captain Drayton went on board the *Glasgow* and went in to where the gun boats were firing. In the evening an armed boats crew left the ship in charge of Lieut. Adams and Ensign Dana. I suppose they are going to try and board the steamer or destroy her. The supply steamer *Bermuda* arrived.

Sat Jul 2, 1864
Lieut. Adam's boat returned this morning. They went so near the blockade runner that they could hear the men talking who were at work unloading her. They did not try to board her. Some of our guns boats fired at the steamer at intervals all day but we could not see that they did any damage. This evening another boat left us in charge of Lieut. Munday. I believe they will board the steamer tonight sure. Had the afternoon watch. Fresh grub for dinner. The *Philippi* arrived last night from New Orleans. Cleaned muskets, belts, and c. The *Ossipee* arrived from Pensacola in the afternoon.

[Farragut was by now getting news that Grant had ordered Canby to send troops to Fort Morgan, Virginia. A disappointed Farragut transferred his frustration to "the destruction of the stranded blockage runner." (Friend, 2001)]

Sun Jul 3, 1864
The blockade runner is there yet. During the mid watch shots were fired from our gun boats in shore and from Ft. Morgan,

but the steamer does not appear to be damaged any. Mr. Munday's boat apparently did no more than Mr. Adam's did. Marines at quarters in full uniform, white pants and cap covers and packed knapsacks. Ships company in all white clothes. Wrote to mother in the afternoon. Had the mid and 1st dog watches. Fresh grub for dinner.

Mon Jul 4, 1864

All ships of the fleet display at national flag at each masthead. All fired a salute at noon. In the afternoon the admiral went on board the *Cowslip* and went in quite near the blockade runner. The *Galena, Monongahela, Seminole* and several other gunboats were there firing at the batteries on shore which returned their fire. Ft. Morgan fired occasionally. The *Monongahela* sent some shells into the fort. Had the morning and 1st dog watches. Fresh grub for dinner.

Tue Jul 5, 1864

The *Glascow* arrived in the afternoon. Brought some mail. Rec'd a letter from Mary and one from Mrs. Metcalf. This is Admiral Farragut's birthday. He is sixty three years old. He had all the ships officers in the cabin drinking his health. Had the forenoon and 2nd dog watches. Duff day.

[Mrs. Metcalf's family ran the first tavern in Bath, NY, and was a welcome beacon for the early, weary travelers through town. She was like a grandmother to Charley. The letter was a touchstone of home.]

Wed Jul 6, 1864

Had the afternoon watch. Pork and beans for dinner. Two boats went from this ship last night in charge of Lieut. Watson and Ensigns Whiting and Dana. They boarded the blockage runner and set her on fire. She burned in two hours, but we can still see her so it looks as if she did not burn much. The *Glasgow* arrived in Pensacola, the *Tennessee* left for there. It is reported that two monitors are expected down here soon.

40. Maj. Gen. Gordon Granger. Library of Congress

Thu Jul 7, 1864
Had the morning and 1st dog watches. Bullion and coffee for dinner. Wrote to May and Gregg. An expedition is going in tonight to blow up the steamer {Ivanhoe}. Marines drilled at quarters.

[Farragut found it difficult to ask Watson to go in again to blow up the Ivanhoe. (Friend, 2001)]

Fri Jul 8, 1864
The boats that went in last night to blow up the steamer were fired upon by some men on board of her. One of our men, Haw-

kins of the main top, was dangerously wounded. None of the others were hurt. Had the forenoon and 1st dog watches. Duff for dinner. In the forenoon at nine o'clock the *Jasmine* arrived from Pensacola. Brought news of the arrival of the *Bienville* and the monitor *Manhattan*. The admiral is in high glee about it. The *Glasgow* left for New Orleans with our mail. About half past two PM the sailor Hawkins died in the sick bay. He was unconscious from the time he was hit. Rec'd a letter from Gregg with his photograph for me to forward to Mary, a good likeness. In the afternoon about five o'clock a steamer arrived from New Orleans bringing Major Generals Canby and Granger and several other officers. They came on board of us. They left about seven o'clock.

[From Gregg's diary, we know this is William Hawkins. Canby's party (Maj. Gen Gordon Granger, Commo. James S. Palmer) "arrived at Farragut's ship. Canby said that despite the transfer of troops to Virginia, causing the delay of the attack, he had found other troops to invest with the attack on the forts." (Friend, 2001).]

Sat Jul 9, 1864
Had the afternoon watch. Rained in the forenoon. Cleaned belts, muskets and c. after supper. The *Philippi* left for Pensacola in the morning taking the corpse of Hawkins for burial. Mr. Herrick and four sailors went with it. Pork and beans for dinner.

Sun Jul 10, 1864
Had the morning and 1st dog watches. Have been on duty irregularly of late because Langdon having a black eye did not want to do any duty in day time. Today he takes his regular turn again. Bullion and coffee for dinner. Marines at inspection in uniform and white pants. Ships company all white. Just after day light in the morning a blockage runner was discovered on shore about a quarter of a mile from Ft. Morgan. The *Galena*, *Monongahela* and *Genesee* were ordered in to shell her. They made some splendid shots and hit her several times though they had to fire at long range. Men could be seen busily unloading her. In the afternoon at steamer came out from behind the fort and

went alongside the blockage runner apparently to pull her off or tow her in. The *Mettacomet* and *Seminole* were sent in to shell her. They soon drove the gun boat inside. Wrote to Father, Mrs. Metcalf and Gregg. The *Glasgow* arrived from New Orleans bringing a mail. Rec'd a *New York Times*. In the evening a picket boat was sent in charge of Mr. Herrick. Bickford and Wilcox were blacklisted for not having clean muskets at inspections.

[The blockade runner was a paddle wheeler run aground, but the enemy was able to save her. (Friend, 2001)]

Mon Jul 11, 1864
Had the morning and 2nd dog watches. The *Glasgow* left for New Orleans. A steamer came out from behind the fort and towed the blockade runner in. The Admiral Lieut. Watson and the steward, cook and waiters went on board the *Tennessee* in the afternoon. It is said we will leave for Pensacola tonight. Pork and beans for dinner.

Tue Jul 12, 1864
Got up anchor and got under way in the morning about three o'clock. Had the forenoon and 1st watches. A Pensacola pilot came on board about eight o'clock. We came to anchor in the bay off the Navy Yard at 11 o'clock. The monitor *Manhattan* is here and several of our gun boats. We are not allowed to have any communication with those on shore. Bolling and Leodan came alongside at noon but were not allowed on board. About half past two PM a coal bark came alongside and the port watch commenced coaling ship. Lawrence 2nd was sent on shore to the hospital. About seven o'clock in the evening an officer came on board from the *Manhattan* and said that she was on fire below and they could not get at the fire to put it out, we could see her men all crowded on her deck and smoke coming out of her smoke stack. Captain Drayton went off to her in the 3rd cutter. Came back about half past ten. Said that the fire was out and that nothing was injured. That only some oil and waste had burned.

U.S. Flagship *Hartford*,
Off Mobile Bay, July 12, 1864
General Orders, No. 10

Strip your vessels and prepare for conflict. Send down all your superfluous spars and rigging. Trice up or remove the whiskers. Put up the splinter nets on the starboard side, and barricade the wheel and steamer with sails and hammocks. Lay chains or sand bags on the deck over the machinery, to resist a plunging fire. Hang the sheet chains over the side, or make any other arrangement for security that your ingenuity may suggest. Land your starboard boats or lower and tow them on the port side, and lower the port boats down to the water's edge. Place a landsman and the pilot in the port quarter boat, or the one most convenient to the commander.

The vessels will run past the forts in couples, lashed side by side, as hereinafter designated. The flagship will lead and steer from Sand Island, N. by E. by compass, until abreast of Fort Morgan; then N. W. half N. until past the Middle Ground; then N. by W., and the others, as designated in the drawing, will follow in due order until ordered to anchor; but the bow and quarter line must be preserved to give the chase guns a fair range, and each vessel must be kept astern of the broadside of the next ahead; each vessel will keep a very little on the starboard quarter of the next ahead, to enable the stern guns to fire clear of the next vessel astern.

It will be the object of the admiral to get as close to the fort as possible before opening fire. The ships, however, will open fire the moment the enemy opens upon us, with their chase and other guns, as fast as they can be brought to bear. Use short fuzes (sic) for the shell and shrapnel, and as soon as within 300 or 400 yards give them grape. It is understood that heretofore we have fired too high, but with grapeshot it is necessary to elevate a little above the object, as grape will dribble from the muzzle of the gun.

If one or more of the vessels be disabled, their partners must carry them through, if possible; but if they cannot then the next astern must the required assistance; but as the admiral contemplates moving with the flood tide, it will only require sufficient power to keep the crippled vessels in the channel.

Vessels that can must place guns upon the poop and topgallant forecastle and in the tops on the starboard side. Should the enemy fire grape, *they will remove the men from the topgallant forecastle and poop to the guns below until out of grape range.*

The howitzers must keep up a constant fire from the time they can reach with shrapnel until out of its range. (ORN, Series 1 #21)

Wed Jul 13, 1864
Twenty months since I enlisted. All hands called and hammocks piped up at four o'clock in the morning coaling ship. Breakfast at seven. Had the afternoon watch. Pork and beans for dinner. Hoisted up propeller in the forenoon. Wrote to Val.

[Val was Charley's brother, seventeen years his senior and running the family mill.]

Thu Jul 14, 1864
Still coaling ship, watch and watch. Had the mid and 1st dog watches. Bullion for dinner. In the mid watch about one bell a rocket was sent up by a vessel outside. Proved to be the supply steamer *Admiral*. She came in after daylight, brought news of the distribution of the privateer 290 by the USS *Kearsarge*. The *Estelle* arrived in the PM.

Fri Jul 15, 1864
Had the morning and 2nd dog watches. Fresh grub for dinner, got a barrel of spuds from the steamer *Admiral*. Finished coaling ship about two PM. Got through coaling ship about two o'clock in the Afternoon, washed down decks. Seven months to day since we went into commission.

Sat Jul 16, 1864
Had the forenoon and first watches. Fresh grub for dinner. Potato sauce for breakfast. Loosed sail at eight AM. The *Narcissus* came in during the afternoon, got in a lot of provisions & stores, a quantity of Marine clothing also came on board. The *Bermuda* came in in the afternoon.

Sun Jul 17, 1864

Had the forenoon watch. Ten of our sailors and one fireman went on board the *Bermuda*. They are going North. Quarters in the forenoon at ten o'clock. Marines in jumpers, blue pants and white caps. Sixteen sailors came on board from the Potomac." Dandy-funk for dinner.

Letter from Capt. Drayton to Rear-Admiral Farragut

US Flagship *Hartford*
Off Pensacola, July 17, 1864

My DEAR ADMIRAL: As you said you wanted pilots, I have picked up one highly recommended by Freeman as knowing every foot of Mobile Bay, and who besides is a pretty good bar pilot. He would, perhaps, do for the Manhattan or Brooklyn. He was in General Asboth's employ, who was very loath to part with him. He is entirely without clothes and you will be obliged to order some given him. Yours, very respectfully, P. Drayton.
(Department of the Navy 1894–1922)

Mon Jul 18, 1864

Had the mid and 1st dog watches. Pork and beans for dinner. Got in a lot of provisions. Ammunition and c. Doctor Gibson is detached from this ship. I hear he goes aboard the *Seminole*. Another doctor comes here in his place.

Tue Jul 19, 1864

The wash woman was alongside yesterday with the wash clothes. I was asleep and did not know she was here so she took my clothes ashore again. Had the morning and 2nd dog watches.

Wed Jul 20, 1864

The *Bienville* and *Manhattan* left about seven AM. We left Pensacola about nine AM. About half past ten we met the *Brooklyn* bound for Pensacola. Passed the *Manhattan* in tow of the *Bienville* at noon. The *Manhattan's* deck was under water. Arrived off Mobile Bay and anchored at about the same place about four PM. Had the forenoon and 1st watches. Pork and beans for dinner. The *Bienville* and *Manhattan* arrived about an hour after us. The admiral and staff came on board before dark. Several army officers were on board in the evening.

Thu Jul 21, 1864

Had the afternoon watch. Bullion and coffee for dinner. Wilcox and McCrisle were let out of the brig. The *Manhattan* went in near sand island and anchored. Wrote to Mary.

Fri Jul 22, 1864

The *Glasgow* left for New Orleans, weather very warm. Had the mid and 1st dog watches. Sea pie for dinner.

Sat Jul 23, 1864

The *Phillippi* arrived from Pensacola. A severe rain squall came up about seven PM. The admiral was out in it and got wet through. Had the morning and 2nd dog watches. Pork and beans for dinner.

[Brother managed his correspondences like a clerk. A letter from Ed Church has notes to himself: "received July 20, 1864" and "answered July 24, 1864."]

Sun Jul 24, 1864

Wind blowing hard all last night and today. Weather cooler. Ship rolls heavily. Had the forenoon and 1st watches. Bullion and coffee for dinner. Wrote to Ed Church. Marines at inspection in uniform, blue pants and white caps. Ships company in clean blue. The *Glasgow* arrived from New Orleans in afternoon. No mail for us. Clean hammocks served out at evening quarters.

[Brother's letter to Ed Church was in response to the following, held in the family archives. Parts were cut out with scissors.]

Charles Brother Esq.
New Orleans or Elsewhere.

Dear Sir - Enclosed please find amt of interest due you from Miss Jennie Barnes which please acknowledge by receipt of same and oblige. Yours resfly, E. L. Church Collector & Atty at Law, West side of Liberty St., Bath, NY

[Some text cut out with scissors]

But she said the within would be enough for you to keep to remember her by. Don't you think I would make a good pettiforger from the style of the above. I ask a thoughs and pardons for my negligence in writing you but it has been impossible for me to do so, not because I was to busy, but I was indisposed I suppose. I know of nothing else but however I will try to do better in the future. I cannot give you a detailed account of matters and things since I last wrote you but will commence later. I suppose you have heard of Judge Barnes death. Jennie was home to his funeral and stayed about one week. Then was the time I did my dinning for you. Lid Rumsey, Lizzie Ogden and Sarah McCay are all home from the City at present. Rob Campbell and Will Dutcher are having some great times about Lizzie Odgen. Lizzie's and Rob's mother's would rather Rob would be her "gallant." She likes Will the best and so they have it. That is the only excitement of the kind that is going on now days. I suppose... [text cut out]
. . .Glee Club but I will suppose you have not and tell you a little about it. Will Dutcher, Carter Robie and myself are the soprano singers. Louis Boardsman – Tenor – Will Howell – Bass – from the Club we have been singing about two months. We (the Club) are going to give a picnic on the Fourth if the weather admits. We expect to have one good time. I have wished you were here hundreds of times so as to go in with us. Charlie I cannot write all I would like to in one letter (for I am writing in business hours) and I cannot think of all I would like to say but will try to write more in my next answer to you. Don't you wait 6 months to answer this

because I did for I will try answer promptly after this. With many wishes for you good luck I remain as ever.

Your friend, E. L. Church, Bath, NY

PS. I shall not read this over and correct it for it would tempt me not to send it. It looks so bad I written in such a hurry. Yours truly, E.L.C.

Mon Jul 25, 1864
Had the afternoon watch. Pork and beans for dinner. The *Glasgow* left in forenoon for New Orleans. General quarters in the morning.

Tue Jul 26, 1864
The *Ossipee* left at 2:30AM for Pensacola. Port watch scrubbed hammocks and I scrubbed mine. The steamer *Admiral* arrived from New Orleans about 6:00 AM. Brought mail. Rec'd a paper from Mary. Had the mid and 1st dog watches. Duff for dinner. The steamer *Admiral* left for the North at noon. Serg't Behrensen went home on her. He has been sick for some weeks. Wrote to Father. Baird is now orderly Serg't, McSweeney is acting corporal. The *Octorara* arrived in the afternoon and left in a short time.

Wed Jul 27, 1864
The *Oneida* came in from Pensacola. The *Glasgow* arrived in the afternoon from New Orleans. Had the morning and 2nd dog watches. Pork and beans for dinner. Aired bedding in PM.

Thu Jul 28, 1864
Had the forenoon and 1st dog watches. Bullion and coffee for dinner. Guard at quarters and eight o'clock relief in fatigue coats. The captain wanted to see who had them and who had not. The *Glasgow* left for New Orleans about eleven AM. About 10:00 AM a tug boat arrived with dispatches for the admiral. The *Brooklyn* about four PM. The *Buckthorn* arrived in the evening.

Fri Jul 29, 1864

Marines in white pants. Had the afternoon watch. Duff for dinner. Got sheet anchor chain up and commenced hanging it on, the starboard side for protection of the boilers when we go into action. Shifted Nos 1 and 2 port broadside guns over to the star board side.

GENERAL ORDERS, No. 11.
FLAGSHIP *HARTFORD*
Mobile Bay, July 29, 1864

Should any vessel be disabled to such a degree that her consort is unable to keep her in her station, she will drop out of line to the westward and not embarrass the vessels next astern by attempting to regain her station. Should she repair damages, so as to be able to reenter the line of battle, she will take her station in the rear as close to the last vessel as possible.

So soon as the vessels have passed the fort and kept away N.W., they can cast off the gunboats at the discretion of the senior officer of the two vessels, and allow them to proceed up the bay to cut off the enemy's gunboats that may be attempting to escape up to Mobile. There are certain black buoys placed by the enemy from the pules on the west side of the channel across it toward Fort Morgan. It being understood that there are torpedoes and other obstructions between the buoys, the vessels will take care to pass to the eastward of the easternmost buoy, which is clear of all obstructions.

So soon as the vessels arrive opposite the end of the pules, it will be best to stop the propellar of the ship and let her drift the distance past by her headway and the tide, and those having side-wheel gunboats will continue on by the aid of their paddle wheels, which are not likely to foul with the enemy's drag ropes. D.G. Farragut, Rear-Admiral. (ONR Series 1 #21)

Sat Jul 30, 1864

Had the mid and 1st dog watches. Pork and beans for dinner. The *Glasgow* arrived from New Orleans in the afternoon. Cleaned musket in forenoon. Belts and c. in afternoon. Marines stationed at the two after broadside guns. The *Manhattan* (monitor) taken around to the other side of sand island in the forenoon. Another monitor for the *Tecumseh* is at Pensacola. Came down in tow of the *Eutaw*.

Sun Jul 31, 1864

Weather warm. Uniform and white cap covers for marines at quarters. Ships company in clean blue and white cap covers. The *Mettacomet* arrived about 9:30 AM. In the afternoon an iron clad from New Orleans a two turreted (?) monitor arrived and went around inside of sand island. The *Tennessee* arrived in the PM from New Orleans with some mail. Rec'd a bundle of *New York Ledgers* that I sent for some time ago. Had the morning and 2nd dog watches. Bullion and coffee for dinner.

[Smith diary states only *Ledgers* and not *New York Ledgers*. Smith diary has more to this line, "which I sent for some time ago but no letters. I guess the people at home have forgotten me altogether." The Lilly version does not have this last sentence.]

Mon Aug 1, 1864

Had the forenoon and 1st watches. Pork and beans for dinner. Another two tenited (?) iron clad arrived from New Orleans and went around inside sand island. In the afternoon about three bells we were all hustled into uniform coats, blue pants, fatigue caps, waist belts and muskets and hurried up on deck to receive General Granger. He came after we had been up about half an hour and we gave him a present as he came over the side. A Colonel and Captain were with him. We were then allowed to break ranks but must stay on the quarter deck until he left. He went over the side about half past five. We then got out of the uniform and had our supper.

[Smith diary states, "The other monitor from New Orleans arrived to-day and went around inside Sand Island."]

Tue Aug 2, 1864

Had the afternoon watch. Duff for dinner. The *Glasgow* arrived from New Orleans about two o'clock. Brought us some mail. Rec'd a letter and paper from Mary. Letter from Tom Seymour and Ed May. Mary writes that Mother's health is improving which is indeed good news. Think we are going to fight soon. Everything is being got ready for fighting and a few days more will probably tell whether we are to take Mobile or not. Transports loaded with troops are at Ship Island. Wrote to Mary. Small stores served out. I drew a scrubbing brush, bar of soap and four pocket handkerchiefs.

Colby M. Chester's Comments on Watson

On the Sunday night preceding the battle, Lieutenant Watson took charge of a large cutter, armed and equipped for action, and, with muffled oars, entered the Bay, in spite of the strong picket guard maintained by the Confederates to prevent such incursions. He tackled the long line of torpedoes strung across the channel, which were held in place and at a distance of about 10 feet below the surface of the water by a number of buoys placed at intervals in prolongation of the line, and sunk one or more of them. This daring exploit was repeated by Watson on Monday night and again on Wednesday night. . .

On this last, or Wednesday, night that it was possible to act before the fight, Watson's boat crew worked so long and assiduously to drill a hole in one of the most important iron buoys he had to deal with in order to sink it, in spite of the danger of drawing the attention of the enemy to his work by the sound of "his big bass drum," that daylight caught him in the act, and he was forced to make a precipitous retreat to regain his ship and take part in the Battle of Mobile Bay. How far he entered the Bay on these several occasions in the darkness of the night I doubt if the admiral knew himself; but as Tuesday morning he brought back with him "five deserters from Fort Gaines," he evidently was in close touch with the enemy."

Wed Aug 3, 1864

Had the mid and 1st dog watches. Pork and beans for dinner. In the morning some officers and men belonging to the army signal corps came on board. They are to be distributed among the ships in the fleet. Lieut. Watson was out on picket last night returned this morning with four deserters from Ft. Gaines. They are stout healthy looking men. In the afternoon the admiral and Captain Drayton sent their valuables on board the *Tennessee*. It begins to look as if we are to get some hard knocks pretty soon. Towards evening one of the New Orleans iron clads came out quite near us and went back again.

[Drayton was the administrator of the West Blockade Squadron and its sixty-eight vessels. The paperwork with plans on the USS *Hartford* was a huge concern. With his exercise, his mind may have also been on carefully storing the records as well, although they probably remained on the flagship. (Friend, 2001)]

Drayton wrote to his friend Hamilton on August 3, 1864

. . .The faults of the war are owing to the character of our people, too much comfort and consequent effeminacy. The southern people are just in that condition which is best for fighting, plenty of food and little pelf. How, if you are in favor of an energetic prosecution of the war, you are in favor of putting in that party which to a certain extent is opposed to it, is beyond my comprehension. However every man can only act according to his convictions and you are as much interested in the country and its integrity as I am perhaps more. However all the captains are on board to arrange for going into Mobile which we will do tomorrow if we can get the Tecumseh from Pensacola. Should all turn out right I will write you again, if not why no matter, and you will bid Mrs. Hamilton and everyone good bye for me. (Drayton, 1906)

Thu Aug 4, 1864

Had the morning and 2nd dog watches. Bullion and coffee for dinner. Our boats were got out in the afternoon. It is reported about the ship that we are going to fight tomorrow morning, and I think we are. I gave Father's address to Pegnola and Wilcox to be used in case I am hurt. They gave me the address of their parents. The monitor *Tecumseh* arrived about sunset from Pensacola. Capt. Craven, her commander came on board of us.

[According to pension records, Noel Pagnello enrolled on October 19, 1863, with the USRS *North Carolina* and was discharged at Portsmouth, New Hampshire, on November 6, 1867. A Catholic with three sisters who became nuns, Pagnello (possibly spelled Pagnuelo?) later moved to San Francisco and became totally deaf in the right ear due to a pistol shot round. Wilcox was never the same after the Battle of Mobile Bay. According to his pension records, he suffered from mental derangement and developed chronic dementia. According to the December 3, 1871, pension record notation, "His head was so affected by excitement of the engagement that he has since become insane and is now an inmate of St. Elizabeth Hosp. near Washington, DC." Farragut was frustrated with the delays of the *Tecumseh's* arrival. He was angry and embarrassed to report to the Army that the Navy could not deliver the *Tecumseh* on time. In order to meet the deadline, crews from the *Richmond* and the *Bienville* were sent to help coal her at Pensacola. (Friend, 2001)]

Letter from Admiral Farragut to his wife:

My Dearest Wife: -
I write and leave this letter for you. I am going into Mobile Bay in the morning, if God is my leader, as I hope He is and in Him I place my trust. If He thinks it is the proper place for me to die, I am ready to submit to His will, in that as all other things. My great mortification is, that my vessels, the ironclads, were not ready to have gone in yesterday. The army landed last night, and are in full view of us this morning, and the Tecumseh has not yet arrived from Pensacola.

God bless and preserve you, my darling, and my dear boy, if anything should happen to me, and may His blessing also rest upon your dear
mother, and all your sisters and their children.

Your devoted and affectionate husband, who never for one moment
forgot his love, duty or fidelity to you, his devoted and best of wives.
(Spears, 1905)

[Brother began a new diary on August 5, 1864. His pocket diary after the
Battle of Mobile Bay contains several blank pages right after the battle.]

Fri Aug 5, 1864 "Battle of Mobile Bay"
All hands called at 3 o'clock in the morning. At 5:30 the Mettacomet came alongside and made fast to us on our port side.
The other vessels of the fleet that went in paired off in the same
way, lashed together by two. We got under way about 6:30 and
steamed in toward Ft. Morgan. The Brooklyn and Octorara taking
the lead. The Hartford and Mettacomet next and the Richmond and
Port Royal next after us. The fort opened fire on us at about ten
minutes past seven, just after we commenced firing one of the
monitors, the Tecumseh sunk. It is supposed that she ran on a
torpedo and she went down like a shot.

We passed the Brooklyn and so had the honor of being the
first ship in. As soon as we passed the forts the rebel gun boats
pitched into us and the Mettacomet cast off from us and went
after one of them. About twenty minutes past eight we had
passed out of range of the gun boats and batteries and ceased
firing and anchored about 8:35. The rest of the fleet soon came
up with us. In a little while we discovered that the rebel ram
Tennessee was coming up after us. We signaled for the monitors
to go after her and got up anchor.

The admiral gave us orders to run the ram and run her
down if we could. We made for her but could not strike her
fairly. She swung around against us and fired a shell into us
which killed and wounded eight men on the berth desk. Her

other guns did not go off or she might have swept our berth deck clean. As she passed us we gave her our port broadside but I could not tell whether it damaged her any or not. Some of the other ships then engaged her and her smoke stack was shot away. She seemed to be disabled otherwise and to be making way towards the fort. We loaded our starboard guns with solid shot and got under way to go after her again, when the *Lackawanna* ran into us.

She struck us just abaft the main rigging, crushing in our bull works, dismounting two guns and causing great confusion on board of us. I thought sure she would sink us but she did us no damage below the water line. As soon as we got clear or her, disabled as we were we started for the ram again, but before we could get to her she hoisted the white flag. I was very glad to see it for I did not like the idea of another broad-side from her.

At this time the *Ossipee* was nearly on to her and one of the monitors close at hand. We then came to anchor about five miles above Ft. Morgan. Captain Johnson the commanding officer of the ram came on board with captain of the *Ossippee* and gave his sword to the admiral. He reported that Admiral Buchanan was on the ram and had lost a leg during the action. His sword was brought on board by one of the *Ossippee's* officers.

Our ship presented a fearful sight after the action. A shell burst in the steerage tearing everything to pieces. The powder division suffered more than any other. A great many shots came in on the berth deck. The shell from the ram *Tennessee* burst as it came through, killing the doctor's steward instantly, wounding the captain's clerk—Mr. Heiginbotham—and killing and wounding several others. Ensign Adams, Mr. Dickson the Boatswain and Masters Mate Herrick were slightly wounded. Not one of the marines were hurt. Boy Clark had both arms and both legs taken off but lived a short time. Seaman Alexander lost both arms and both legs and died shortly after, very few were slightly wounded. Our cockpit looked like a slaughterhouse.

(*opposite*) 41. Battle of Mobile Bay Chart. Library of Congress

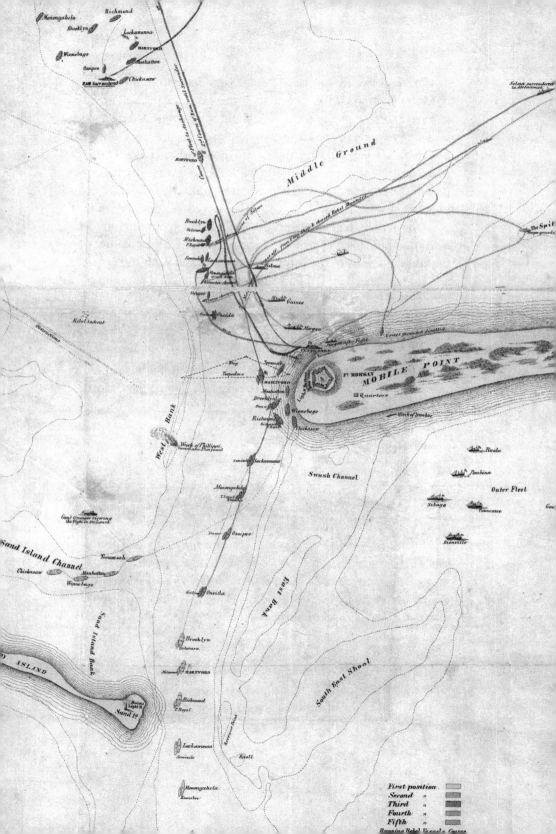

Monongahela
Richmond
Brooklyn
Lackawanna
Winnebago
HARTFORD
Ossipee
Manhattan
RAM Surrendered
Chickasaw

Selma surrendered
to Metacomet

Middle Ground

HARTFORD

The Spit

Brooklyn
Richmond
F. Royal
Seminole
Lackawanna

Selma

Monongahela
Kennebec

Ossipee

Gaines

Drake
Oneida

Ft. Morgan

Rebel Lookout

Observations

TENNESSEE
Surrender after Fight
Gaines grounded & demolished

Fort Morgan
MOBILE POINT

Wing
Tecumseh
Torpedoes
HARTFORD
Manhattan
Brooklyn
Ossippee
Richmond
Kennebec
Winnebago
Chickasaw

Quarters

Ditch of Ironsides

West Bank

Wreck of Philippi
burned after Fleet passed

Seminole
Lackawanna

Rinola

Pembina

Swash Channel

Monongahela
Tecumseh

Gen'l Granger viewing
the Fight in Steamboat

Outer Fleet
Sebago
Tennessee

Sand Island Channel

Tecumseh

Ossipee

Bienville

Chickasaw
Manhattan
Winnebago

Gati
Oneida

East Bank

SAND ISLAND

Sand Island Bank

Brooklyn
Petrara

Metacomet
HARTFORD

South East Shoal

Sand Island

Sand Is.

Richmond
F. Royal

Kennebec Shoal

Lackawanna
Seminole

Knoll

Monongahela
Kennebec

At night twenty-one dead bodies were sewed up in hammocks, sent on board the *Selma*, the prize captured by the *Mettacomet*, and taken away for burial, about thirty wounded were sent to Pensacola on the *Mettacommet*. At night the Rebels abandoned Ft. Powell, burning and destroying all they could. The monitor *Tecumseh* was blown up by a torpedo during the first part of the engagement and immediately sunk. Only about ten of her crew were saved.

One of our small gun boats the *Phillippi* which was left outside attempted to run past Fort Morgan after we had got in, but finding the fire from the fort too hot she turned back and got aground on a bar. Her Captain and crew took to their boats and abandoned her, leaving their signal books and everything else to fall into the hands of the rebels. The rebels boarded her and after taking what they wanted set her on fire.

[Farragut's original plan had him leading the column, but his captains expressed concern that the *Admiral* was too exposed here. (Friend, 2001)]

Drayton wrote to his friend Hamilton on August 5, 1864

We are inside of Mobile Bay after a pretty sharp scrimmage, in which you will see from the papers that a good deal of injury was done to us and one monitor blown up by a torpedoe. We understand that the bay was strewn with them, but the only one which fairly exploded was the cause of this frightful accident to the Tecumseh. You may suppose I am busy and since three this morning I cannot say that I have been unoccupied for more than a quarter of an hour, and now that it is dark snatch a few moments to write you a few lines for yourself and the family, generally. . . Long live the Republic and down with traitors. (Drayton, 1906)

[The following account of the battle, written by Charles Brother many years later, was not found in the original pocket diary in Mobile, Alabama, at the University of South Alabama. It was included in the typed transcript held by the Lilly Library at Indiana University.]

Battle of Mobile Bay

The above account of the occurrences of August 5, 1864, which included the battle of Mobile Bay, was written probably the day after. I have been sorry that I did not write a more minute description of the events of that day, at that time or soon after, but I did not then realize the importance of those events and times.

The following account of the battle is written many years after from memory, but I think is correct as far as it goes. I of course have forgotten much, and so cannot give a complete account, but I have not stated as fact anything except as I actually remember it.

On the *Hartford*, we had been preparing for the fight all summer, and particularly during the days immediately preceding August 5th. We had taken down all our sails, our top-gallant masts and all our yards, and all rigging and ropes and blocks belonging to the yards and sails, in fact everything of that kind that could be dispensed with, sent away some of our boats, took down all railings around hatches, all ladders except those actually needed, everything movable put away and out of the way. We had hung anchor chains on our starboard side to protect our boilers and machinery. Splinter nettings were put along inside our bulwarks, all the extra port holes on the starboard side, supplied with guns from our port battery, so that we could fight more than half of our guns, while we of the rank and file were not officially notified that we were going into the bay the next morning, we seemed to feel, by the preparations made on the 4th that that was the programme.

Many of our men gave addresses of their parents or near relatives to some of their chums, so that if they were killed the survivors would know who to inform.

On the morning of the 5th all hands were called at three o'clock. We had an early breakfast of coffee and hard tack. At 5:30 the *Mettacomet* came alongside and made fast to us on our port side. The other wooden ships that were going in paired off in the same manner as follows. The *Brooklyn* and *Octorara–Rich-*

mond and Port Royal–Lackawanna and Seminole–Monogahela and Kennebec–Ossipee and Itasca–Oneida and Galena. The following ironclads were inside sand island. The Tecumseh and Manhattan, both single turreted monitors with 15-inch guns, and the Chicasaw and Winnebago, two turreted monitors with smaller guns.

Some of the marines dressed for the fight in clean underclothes and their best fatigue uniforms, saying that if they were to be killed they wanted to die with their best clothes on.

We got under way about 6:30 and steamed in towards the entrance to the bay. The Brooklyn leading, we next and the Richmond next after us. The other ships following. Our drums to quarters with the long roll and we realized that the fight was coming. The Marines maned the two aftermast broadside guns.

I took my station at the cabin door relieving the orderly on watch. Captain Drayton, Executive Officer Kimberly, Lieut. Watson and several other officers were on the poop. Captain Drayton fought the ship, Kimberly giving the orders to the men, the first one being "Man the starboard battery."

Admiral Farragut was the last officer to appear on deck. He wore a fatigue sack coat and little navy cap. He did not wear a sword, but brought up a small straight sword which he laid on the skylight over the captain's cabin.

Just about this time Captain Jouette (?) of the Mettacomet called out to Captain Drayton and said that he had some hand grenades, and suggesting that some of them be sent to the men in our tops from them to use in case we came into close quarters with the rebel ram or gunboats. Captain Drayton assented and ordered a quarter gunner who was in the after division, and me, to go on board the Mettacomet after them. We climbed over on to her and the grenades were given to us in two ships buckets. As we started back someone on the Mettacomet demanded the return of their buckets, so other buckets were brought to us from the Hartford and we put the hand grenades into them. I remember that at this time the admiral was on the port hammock nettings between the main and mizzen shrouds, (?) for

42. Adm. Farragut, USN. Library of Congress

as I was changing the grenades into our own buckets I nearly dropped one, and thought that it was fortunate I did not drop it as it might have exploded and hurt the admiral.

About the time we went over to the *Mettacomet* the shot and shell from Ft. Morgan and the batteries began to reach us, and when we got back to the *Hartford* they were hitting us occasionally, and when one would come in on our spar deck our men at the guns would cheer as if they enjoyed it. At the cheering Kimberly smiled grimly and sung out, "Oh, you'll get enough of that before long."

About this time the admiral having made his way along the hammocks nettings to the main shrouds, began to ascend the main rigging and took a position in the rigging near the futtock shrouds. Captain Drayton or some other officer on the poop sung out to the admiral saying that he ought to be tied there to prevent falling, and signal Quartermaster Knowles was sent aloft with a small rope which I thought was a hammock lashing, and making it fast to the shrouds on one side of the admiral, passed it around his body and fastened it to the shrouds on the other side. The admiral remained there until we had passed the fast[fort] and gun boats.

Soon it was reported that the monitor *Tecumseh* had gone down. That she had probably struck a torpedo. Then the *Brooklyn* and her consort ahead of us stopped, and we passed them. The admiral or Captain Drayton ordered Captain Jouett to send one of the Mettacomet's boats and pick up if possible any survivors from the *Tecumseh* and a boat was sent immediately which picked up ten or twelve men. All that were saved of the *Tecumseh's* crew.

Farragut Reported

As I had an elevated position in the main rigging near the top, I was able to overlook, not only the deck of the Hartford. But the other vessels of the fleet. I witnessed the terrible effects of the enemy's shot, and the good conduct of the men at their guns; and although, no doubt, their hearts sickened, as mind did, when their shipmates were struck down beside them, yet there was not a moment's hesitation to lay their comrades aside, and spring again to their deadly work. (Porter, 1886)

Alexander McKinley, Admiral Farragut's secretary reported:

The admiral immediately gave the word to go ahead with the Hartford and pass the Brooklyn. We sheered to port, passing the Brooklyn on our starboard side and, as we cleared her bows, fired shell and shrapnel into the water battery like hail. We passed directly over the line of torpedoes planted by the enemy, and we could hear the snapping of the submerged devilish contrivances as our hull drove through the water—but it was neck or nothing and that risk must be taken. (McKinley, 1864)

After passed the Brooklyn and neared the fort and batteries, they had a better range of us and struck after us and with deadly effect. And now the battle was on in earnest. We returned their fire as rapidly as possible, our men working and fighting as if they had no fear and cheering whenever our shots seemed to strike with effect, and sometimes when we were struck.

And now they began to fall. Killed and wounded in every form.

I ran about with messages from Captain Drayton to the officers of divisions and between the captain and admiral.

Ensign Glidden stood in the main rigging about midway between the admiral and the deck and messaged for and from the admiral and the pilot were repeated by him.

The pilot, Martin Freemen, was in the main top, in both our fore and main tops were a howitzer and crew, when not busy otherwise I helped the powder boy (Pagnallo) at the after gun. The big shells were too heavy for him.

[Martin Freeman was a medal of honor for his bravery.]

Captain Heywood took the Lanyard (?) and fought one of the marine guns all through the action. As soon as we could bring our guns to bear fairly upon the fort and batteries we kept up such a heavy fire that their men were driven from their guns and could not then damage us much, but soon the rebel ram and gunboats had range of us and improved their opportunity.

Captain Jouett implored the admiral to let him cut loose from us and go after the gun boats, but he would not give his consent until we were out of range of the forts, then he told Jouett to go ahead and with axes the ropes were cut that bound us together and away went the *Mettacomet*. The rebel boat *Selma* started up the bay. The *Mettacomet* took after her and soon captured her bringing her back a prize.

We had now passed the forts and gunboats and came to anchor up the bay about 8:35. The rest of the fleet soon came up.

Boatson to signal to our ship to ram the ram, but they did not respond to suit him and he ordered Captain Drayton to ram her. She seemed to be making for us and we soon met. We tried to ram her but could not strike her fairly for she swung around as if to avoid us and we gave her only a glancing blow. As we passed we were close together and we gave her a broadside of solid shot from our port battery of eight or nine guns, but it did not appear to affect her any. She discharged only one of her four starboard guns, and that sent a shell in on our berth deck which killed and wounded eight men.

Ensign Heiginbotham, Captain Drayton's clerk, was struck by a piece of the shot. It shattered one of his legs at the knee so badly that it had to be amputated. He died before evening, the only officer killed on the *Hartford* in this engagement.

About this time the admiral seemed to be considerably excited. Apparently our ships were not attacking the ram to his
satisfaction, and as he ordered Captain Drayton to again go after her he said, "D—n it, if I want anything done I have to do it
myself." Captain Drayton said to him, "Aren't you afraid he will
lead us onto torpedoes," to which the admiral replied, "I don't
care a d—n for torpedoes. I can go wherever he can."

So we started again after the ram, but just then the *Lackawanna*, also after her, ran into us, she struck us on our starboard
side just abaft the main rigging, knocked over two of our guns
and crushed in our bulwarks nearly to the water. She immediately backed off and as soon as we could get clear of her we
started again after the ram, but before we could get very near
her she showed a white flag.

She had been disabled by a fifteen inch solid shot from the
Manhattan that pierced her side, disabling her steering gear,
and wounding her Admiral–Buchanan. Her smoke stack had
been shot away and she was damaged in other ways.

Our men cheered as her white flag appeared. She was
boarded by an officer from one of our ships that was near her–I
think the *Ossippee*–and her captain was brought aboard the
Hartford by Captain LeRoy. He had passed the fort and batteries,
captured the ram and gunboat *Selma*, struck the *Gaines* so hard
that she had been run towards shore and sunk in shoal water.
The *Morgan* ran back under the guns of the fort and at night ran
past our ships and escaped up the bay.

43. Richard D. Dumphy, coal heaver. Library of Congress

Our ship was struck often and our crew suffered terribly. Nearly as many men were killed on the *Hartford* as on all the other ships in the fleet except the *Tecumseh*, which took down more than a hundred men. Our heavy loss was owing no doubt to the fact that we were the first ship to pass the forts and so the first to receive the fire from them and the ram and gunboats. Twenty five of our men were killed, and about thirty more wounded.

The dead were sewed up in hammocks and taken away for burial that night on the captured steamer *Selma*. The wounded were sent to Pensacola on the *Mettacomet*. Some of our men were blown to pieces by the exploding shells.

A sailor–William Andrews—always wore a long sandy goatee, and only by that could his remains be identified.

[William E. Andrews, captain afterguard (D. Sullivan, 2019)]

A sailor–Alexander–had both legs and both arms shot off. [James Alexander, landsmen]

A coal heaver–Dumphy–had both hands shot off. He recovered and I saw him afterwards in New York.

The quarter gunner who went with me on board the *Mettacomet* after the hand grenades, was killed by a shot that cut him nearly in two at the waist.

A boy–Clark–lost both legs and died.

Of those who lost arms and legs, few survived. One of our assistant engineers lost an arm. Our wounded were taken below as soon as possible, but the dead were simply pulled out of the way and left until the fight was over. Our decks above and below were covered with blood, which by night gave out such a sickening smell that I slept on the spar deck to avoid it as much as possible. None of the Marines were hurt.

Langdon was knocked overboard by the shock when the *Lackawanna* struck us, but he caught a ropes end that hung over our port quarter and was pulled on board.

The time that I have given I noted by a clock that laid during the fight on the skylight over the admiral's cabin. Why our gunboat the *Phillippi* attempted to run in after us I never heard.

Dr. William Commons Recalled

. . . *Assistant Surgeon Wright was struck. A shell struck him "under one arm and plowing through his body, came out under the other arm. . .*

"As he sank to the deck. . . I looked at Daniel Example, expecting to see him dive into the hold again and stay there, but. . . he came bravely forward. With men falling all about us either killed or horribly mutilated, Daniel Example stayed with me to the end of the engagement and rendered great assistance in caring for the many victims of the slaughter. He was only a negro slave, who probably never had been freed, it might be said, he was without a country, and yet he was the brave as the bravest. . .

"Example helped when a man was decapitated by a passing shell. . . yet neither the head nor body was very much lacerated, the kind-hearted surgeon placed the head with the body so that they may be buried together. Another man's bones were stripped bare of flesh by a passing shell exposing his heart with was still beating. Dr. Commons says they ascribed this phenomenon to what they called windage, as the shell in either case did not come in actual contact with the body, but caused havoc by air pressure alone. . . . After the explosion of the last two shells thrown on the Hartford, not a man was left on his feet but himself and Daniel Example, the rest being hurried to the deck by the concussion."

Dr. Commons explained the African American's strange name. *"He did not even have a proper name. . . It was another officer who, when the black man said his last name was 'nothing,' an officer noted, 'Now that is a fair example of the southern negro . . . and he was called Daniel Example."*

—*Star Press*, Nov 19, 1911

Sat Aug 6, 1864
Captain Haywood with ten of our guard, ten from the *Richmond* and five from the *Brooklyn* were sent to Fort Powell to take possession. The *Mettacomet* left for Pensacola at day light this morning with the wounded of the fleet. The *Stockdale* arrived from New Orleans. Wrote a letter to father last night. In the af-

ternoon one of our iron clads went up to Fort Gaines and fired a few shots at her, then drew off. Cleaned belts and c. for tomorrow's inspection.

Sun Aug 7, 1864

Only three orderlys now because so many men are away at Ft. Powell and on the ram. Had the forenoon and 2nd dog watches. Bullion and coffee for dinner. Marines at inspection in full uniform, white pants and cap covers. Ships company in white. General muster after quarters. Paymaster read a psalm and prayer. Mr. Kimberly read a letter from the admiral thanking the men for their good conduct during the fight of Friday. Then read the articles of war. All hands mustered around the captain. Wrote to Mother. The *Mettacomet* arrived from *Pensaola*. General Granger and staff came on board. In the evening Captain Drayton and an army Colonel went over to Fort Gaines with a flag of truce.

Mon Aug 8, 1864

Had the morning and 1st dog watches. Pork and beans for dinner. In the morning about seven o'clock Captain Drayton, Lieut. Watson, Lieut. Tyson, Mr. Whiting, Mr. McKinney, Mr. Brownell, and Mr. Williamson and two army officers went over to Fort Gaines with a flag of truce. About ten o'clock the rebel flag was hauled down and the stars and stripes hoisted in its place. All of our ships in the bay, maned their rigging and gave three cheers. The boat returned about noon bringing the rebel officer's swords and a lot of other things including the rebel flag. With Ft. Gaines we get 850 prisoners. The fort mounts 28 guns. In the afternoon General Granger came on board. The *Buckthorn* came in a Pellican pass.

Tue Aug 9, 1864

Had the afternoon and 1st night watches. Duff for dinner. General Granger is landing troops in the rear of Ft. Morgan. In the afternoon the iron clads and several of the wooden vessels went in near Ft. Morgan and fired a few shots into her. She fired only a few shots into her. She fired only a few in return. The *Port*

Royal took the ram *Tennessee* in town and went near the fort, and anchored. About five o'clock we got under way and steamed up nearer the fort and anchored.

Wed Aug 10, 1864
My birthday, twenty years old, out of my teens. Had the forenoon and 2nd dog watches. Pork and beans for dinner. General Granger came on board in the evening. He says that deserters are already coming in to him from Ft. Morgan. A severe rain storm, nearly all day.

Thu Aug 11, 1864
A new smoke stack was rigged on the ram today. Had the morning and 1st dog watches. General Canby, General Arnold, and Commodore Palmer came on board in the afternoon. Wrote a letter for McCristle to his mother. Bullion and coffee for dinner. Slap jacks for supper.

Fri Aug 12, 1864
Commodore Palmer and the two generals stayed on board of us last night. They left this morning. An officer with a flag of truce came down from Mobile in the forenoon. Had the afternoon and 1st night watches. Salt horse and coffee for dinner, no duff, used all our flour making slap jacks last night.

Sat Aug 13, 1864
Cleaned belts and c. in the afternoon. Wrote to Tom Seymour. In the afternoon the *Tennessee* went in towards the fort and fired a few rounds into it. The fort returned the fire striking the *Tennessee* ten times but doing no damage except putting one shot through her smoke stack. One of the monitors shelled the fort all the afternoon. Had the forenoon and 2nd dog watches. Pork and beans day.

Sun Aug 14, 1864
Inspection in forenoon at four bells. Marines in jumpers and waist belts. Ships company in clean blue. Wrote to Mary. Rec'd

44. Capt. Drayton and Adm. Farragut on USS *Hartford* in Mobile Bay, Alabama, 1864, NHHC NH 49501

---

a letter from her, a paper from Mother and one from Mrs. Metcalf. Had the morning and 1st dog watches, coffee and dandy funk for dinner. One of the monitors shelling the fort at intervals. The marines who have been on the ram *Tennessee* came back in the afternoon. We now have four orderlies once more. In the afternoon Captain Haywood came alongside in a boat rowed by Finnisy, Simons, and a marine from the *Richmond* guard. They went back in the evening.

Mon Aug 15, 1864
It is reported about the ship that we are going North before long. In the forenoon the admiral and staff went on an expedition up the river on the *Mettacomet*. *Chickasaw, Winnebago, Port Royal* and one or two other gun boats. Had the morning and 2nd dog watches. Pork and beans for dinner. The *Manhattan* shelling the fort at intervals during the day. Two or (of) our nine inch guns sent on shore. They are going to erect a battery on shore for shelling the fort. The admiral and staff returned about nine o'clock PM. They went to within about four miles of the city. Found the channel destructed by a vessel filled with

bricks and sunk. The rebels have one or two gunboats up there inside Dog river bar.

Tue Aug 16, 1864
Wash morning. Had the forenoon and 1st night watches. Duff for dinner. Wrote to Mrs. Metcalf.

Wed Aug 17, 1864
Had the afternoon watch. Pork and beans for dinner. Wrote to Mary.

[Word on the boys of Bath reached home: "Josiah Gregg, 'Dora' Harris, and Charley Brother, three of our Bath Boys, were active participants in the great battle at Mobile. We are glad to learn that all escaped safely and hope they may ever be equally fortunate." *Steuben Courier*, Aug 17, 1864]

Thu Aug 18, 1864
The *Tritonia* arrived from New Orleans. Rec'd a letter from Mary written on the 2nd. Had the mid and 1st dog watches. Bullion and coffee for dinner.

Fri Aug 19, 1864
Had the morning and 2nd dog watches. Duff for dinner. The *Tritonia* left in the fore noon for New Orleans, took our mail. Our drummers time out today. He has been six years in the service. The Admiral is sick, has a boil that is in the way when he wants to sick down. A severe squall in the evening. Hammocks piped down about 10:00 PM.

Drayton wrote to his friend Hamilton on August 19, 1864:

. . .had the Tecumseh floated a little longer we should have had no after fight with the enemy's iron clad. How it is that all the other' vessels escaped from torpedoes is a mystery, for we see by the books captured at Fort James, that about ninety were planted on the 3rd and 4th alone. I suspect that their harmlessness consists in the great difficulty of keeping the pow-

der dry. At any rate it is a horrid kind of warfare, not worse than mines perhaps, although more efficacious. We are still beseiging Morgan, which will stand out longer than the army people imagine. They blow tremendously and seem to calculate all the time on what they call demoralization. . . I have never been so worked in my life. Why fighting is mere child's play compared to the preparations required for it, and the keeping ones forces supplied with food coal ammunition etc particularly when as in the present case the main avenue of communication is blocked up. I received a letter from Hoyt with one from you yesterday. He seems to despair of the Republic, we who are not within reach of politics view things in a better light. The admiral has not been well for a few days past suffering a good deal from your old enemy boils, and in the midst of it and of our incessant work we have had fixed on us one or two loafing curiosity hunters, one a son of V-, totally uninteresting, but who on the strength of a letter from Banks (all politeness of course, no friendship) quietly came on board with their baggage, and I understand from Palmer that it requires all his tact to save us from others. . . . (Drayton, 1906)

Sat Aug 20, 1864

The *Circassian* arrived outside yesterday. Had the forenoon and 1st watches. Fresh grub for dinner. Cleaned musket and c. in the afternoon. We drifted about half a mile last night during the squall. Made a duff bag for the mess.

Sun Aug 21, 1864

Had the afternoon watch. Fresh grub for dinner, inspection in the morning. Marines in uniform and white caps, ships company in white frocks and caps and blue pants. General Asboth with part of his staff arrived in the afternoon. Wrote to Mary and Ed May. The *Bermuda* arrived outside.

Mon Aug 22, 1864

Early in the morning three ironclads with seven or eight of the wooden vessels and our land batteries opened upon Fort Morgan and shelled it all the forenoon. The ironclads going close in the other vessels laying off at long range. In the afternoon only the iron clads and the ram *Tennessee* and the shore batteries fired. They gave the fort a terrible shelling and the fort did not return the fire. Towards night there seemed to be something on fire in the fort that made a very black smoke. Has the mid and 1st dog watches. Fresh grub for dinner.

Tue Aug 23, 1864

Had the morning and 2nd dog watches. Fresh grub for dinner. Early in the morning as the iron clads were shelling Fort Morgan there were two or three heavy explosions inside the fort, followed by a very heavy smoke. There seemed to be a fire moving along the whole length of the fort. Meantime the iron clads kept up their fire and about seven o'clock a white flag was hoisted upon the walls of the fort. All firing ceased, at once and Captain Drayton and Lieut. Watson went on board the *Cowslip* and went to the fort. At 2:30 pm the fort surrendered. The rebel flag was hauled down and the stars and stripes run up. We then fired a salute as did all the rest of the fleet. The crews then manned the rigging and gave three cheers. In the afternoon all the vessels came in that had been stationed outside, and the bay was once more open. We get over four hundred prisoners with the fort. They had spiked their guns before they surrendered, which it is said is contrary to the usages of war.

Wed Aug 24, 1864

Had the forenoon and 1st watches. Fresh grub for dinner. The admiral was taken quite sick in the forenoon. Had a fainting fit.

Thu Aug 25, 1864

Had the 2nd dog watch. My face badly swollen so Taylor stood the afternoon watch for me. In the forenoon two sisters and a niece of the Admiral came on board. They are from Pensacola, Florida. The Pilot Freeman with several boats was engaged all day taking up torpedoes. In the afternoon they took one up on the beach near Ft. Morgan and while they were examining it exploded, killing several men and wounding about fifteen others.

Freeman was badly burned about the face. The army transport *McClellan* left for the North in the afternoon. Sent a letter to Father by her. The *Tritonia* arrived from New Orleans but brought her no mail.

[Freeman reported to the pension office he was still blind for four months after explosion.]

Fri Aug 26, 1864
Had the mid and 2nd dog watches. Duff for dinner. Pilot Freeman sent to Pensacola hospital.

Sat Aug 27, 1864
The *Tritonia* left for New Orleans. Cleaned belts epaulets and c. Had the morning and 2nd dog watches. Pork and beans for dinner. In the afternoon a steamer arrived from the North. Said to belong to the Sanitary commission. Looks very much like the steamer *Admiral*, all hands aired bedding. The *Bienville* arrived from Pensacola.

Sun Aug 28, 1864
Had the forenoon and 1st dog watches. Bullion and coffee for dinner. In the afternoon Taylor–McKinney–Royal–Corporal–O'Conner and I went on shore. Some sailors, mostly petty officers went also. We of course visited Fort Morgan. Could not get inside at first so we went around the outside. After a while we got a pass and went inside. Nearly all the guns are dismounted, the carriages have been knocked to pieces by our shot and shell. Pieces of our shell were laying all around, and some that had exploded. A fire still burned inside where the stores had been kept. In many places the brick walls had been pierced through and through. The fort is in fact pretty well used up, and a good deal of time and labor will be needed to set it right again. The water battery seems to be uninjured. It mounts four ten inch guns, one eight inch, and two thirty two pound rifles. Shot and shell in abundance are laying near the guns which shows that they had plenty of ammunition. After we had finished looking

at the fort, Taylor, Royal, and I went down to the beach and had a swim. The water was very warm and nice. The atmosphere seemed much warmer on shore than on board ship. Came off to the ship about half past four. Priest the quarter gunner was in our boat and drunk. He fell overboard and lost his trousers and had to come on board ship without them. It is said that whiskey was sold on board an army transport steamer at the wharf. McKinney also partly full. Taylor and I didn't need any. At the fort we saw two of the guns that threw those heavy ribbed shell like the one that came in through our steerage. One of these guns had a trunion knocked off.

Mon Aug 29, 1864
Had the afternoon watch. Pork and beans for dinner. About twenty five men whose times are out went on board the steamer *Bermuda* for passage North. Royal our Drummer among them. The *Tritonia* due but did not arrive.

Tue Aug 30, 1864
Wrote to Mary. The *Tritonia* not in yet. Had the mid and 2nd dog watches. Fresh grub for dinner.

Wed Aug 31, 1864
The *Tritonia* arrived in the afternoon. Brought us quite a large mail. Rec'd a letter from Father, and Mary, and Will Ingersoll and Ed Church. Ed sent me twenty-five postage stamps that I had sent for. They all write that Jim Gould was killed in battle before Atlanta on the 20th day of July. Had the morning and 2nd dog watches. Fresh grub for dinner. Weather very warm. Thermometer at 90. Marines returned from Ft. Powell.

[Corporal Jim Gould was the brother of A.R. Gould, Jr. Jim was with the 78th NY Regiment before joining the 102, Co. F. and 21 years old when he was killed in action during the Battle of Peach Tree Creek, Georgia on July 20, 1864. He was buried five miles north of Atlanta. The *Steuben Courier* stated on August 10, 1864 that he was "a kind, generous boy, a favorite with the family, and his death will be mourned by a wide circle of friends." Survivors include his parents, a brother, and four sisters, and members of St. Thomas Episcopal Church. (Johnston, 1900).]

Thu Sep 1, 1864
Had the forenoon and 1st night watches. Fresh grub for dinner. Small stores served out. I drew a bar of soap, scrubbing brush, box of shoe blacking, bottle of pepper. The *Kennebec* arrived in the evening from Pensacola. It is reported that two more of our men have died there from wounds received in the fight, and that Admiral Buchanan's leg will not be taken off.

Fri Sep 2, 1864
The *Tritonia* left for New Orleans. The *Mettacomet* arrived from Pensacola. Had the afternoon watch. Duff for dinner. Freeman the pilot came on the *Mettacomet*. He is not well yet, is going to New Orleans. Marines drilled a short time on the quarter deck in the afternoon. Didn't do very well.

Sat Sep 3, 1864
Cleaned belts, musket and c. The steamer *Admiral* arrived from Pensacola. Has fresh beef, ice and c. Had the mid and 1st dog watches. Pork and beans and spuds for dinner.

Sun Sep 4, 1864
Had the morning and 2nd dog watches. Bullion and coffee for dinner. Marines in full uniform and white pants at quarters. Ships company in white. General muster after quarters. First Lieut. read articles of war. Crew mustered around the capstain, then piped down. We had just got below when we were ordered on deck again to receive a Brigadier General. He remained on board about half an hour and during that time we had to stay on the quarter deck. In the afternoon Pagnola–Mackin–Davoe (?) and Glynn went on shore on liberty. The *Tritonia* arrived from New Orleans. Received a letter from Mother. Davoe brought me a letter from shore. It is from Cap't John Little of Bath. He is in the 161st New York Volunteers and is on Cedar Point.

[Devoe could be Epamistus Devoe or possibly James B. Devoe, who was Acting Ensign on March 22 1864, then Acting Master on September 28, 1864, earning honorable discharged December 22, 1865. (Callahan, 1969); John F. Little was five years older than Brother and was studying law when the war broke out. His father, William, was an Irish farmer and his brother, also William, was the same age as Brother and probably a classmate. John Little married the daughter of Rev. Howard, rector of St. Thomas Episcopal Church and served as vestry alongside Henry Brother, Charley's father.]

Mon Sep 5, 1864
Wrote to Mother. The *Glasgow* left for New Orleans with the mail. Had the forenoon and 1st night watches. Fresh grub for dinner.

Drayton wrote to his friend Hamilton on September 5, 1864:

I have not heard from you very lately and am afraid that I have not myself written. The fact is that I was not in a very healthy condition and living on oatmeal and water, I should have been used up long ago as almost everyone else has been, even the admiral who prides himself on standing everything, but then he will drink a little wine and eat meat at breakfast. Throwing aside joking however, owning to a variety of causes many temporary other belonging unavoidably to my position, I feel that I am overworked, for from before breakfast until ten o'clock at night I am seldom unoccupied with squadron matters for five minutes at a time, and this is not exactly the climate for such devotion to business. I believe in all time and more so now than ever, the real hard work of military life is in the preparation for, not the actual fighting. . . . (Drayton, 1906)

Tue Sep 6, 1864
There is a report that the *Brooklyn's* guard is to be sent to Pensacola Navy Yard and the old stagers then are to be sent North on her. Had the afternoon watch. Fresh grub for dinner.

Wed Sep 7, 1864
Had the mid and 1st dog watches. Pork and beans for dinner. The *Glasgow* arrived from New Orleans in the forenoon, brought us a mail. Rec'd a letter and paper from Mary and a letter from Ellie.

Thu Sep 8, 1864
The *Glasgow* left for New Orleans with the mail. Had the morning and 2nd dog watches. Bullion and coffee for dinner.

Fri Sep 9, 1864
The *Onasco* arrived from Pensacola. Wrote to Ed Church. Had the forenoon and 1st night watches. Duff for dinner.

Sat Sep 10, 1864
Had the afternoon watch. Pork and beans for dinner. Cleaned belts brasses and c. for tomorrow's inspection. The *Glasgow* arrived from New Orleans in the forenoon. In the afternoon on the spar deck there was sold at auction, the clothing, bedding and c. of the men killed in battle. Most of the things brought good prices, but it didn't look just right to me to see them sold in that way. The *Circassian* arrived in the evening. She is bound North. The *Pinola* arrived in the afternoon from Pensacola.

Sun Sep 11, 1864
Had the mid and 1st dog watches. Bullion and coffee for dinner. In the morning several men who came on board from the *Park Royal* went on board the *Circassian*. Their times are not out and they are going North. Corporal O'Conner went as his time was out several days ago. In the afternoon some of our marines and sailors went on shore. Cole is made acting Corporal in place of O'Conner. Quarters for inspection in the forenoon at four bells, afterward general muster. Then general orders, then piped down. The *Circassian* left in the afternoon. The *Glasgow* left for New Orleans. Wrote to Mary and to Will Ingersoll. Some marines came on board from the *Richmond* in the afternoon. They say that all marines who enlisted between the months

of June and November 1862, are entitled to a discharge, on the grounds of having been enlisted under false pretenses, in that they were promised a bounty of one hundred dollars at the expiration of their term of enlistment, which offer was authorized and the bounty will not be paid. They say that some of the men are going North to be discharged on that account. As I enlisted at that time and upon those conditions I am as much entitled to a discharge as anyone else. Clean hammocks served out at evening quarters.

Mon Sep 12, 1864
Had the morning and 2nd dog watches. Pork and beans for dinner. Scrubbed hammocks in the morning, they were piped down just before dinner. A gang of men in charge of the First Lieut. and Boatswain went on board of one of the scows to the *Gaines*. They are going to take the guns and machinery out of her.

Tue Sep 13, 1864
The *Glasgow* due but did not arrive. I spoke to Captain Haywood about the discharge business. He says that if I will make out a disposition that I was promised the bounty, he will send it to Washington and see what can be done about it. Had the forenoon and 1st night watches. Duff for dinner.

Wed Sep 14, 1864
The *Glasgow* arrived about six AM. Brought a large mail. Received a letter and paper from Mary, a letter from Vep Darling. Had the afternoon watch. Pork and beans day.

Thu Sep 15, 1864
Wrote to Mary, to Ellie and to Vep Darling. The *Tritonia* left for New Orleans. Steamer *Tennessee* came in in the morning. Left in the afternoon. She reports chasing a blockade runner from Galveston but did not catch her. The blockage runner threw overboard a good deal of cotton which the *Tennessee* picked up. Had the mid and 1st dog watches. Bullion and coffee for dinner. Hunt is sick and McCristle is cook in his place.

Fri Sep 16, 1864

The steamer *Admiral* came in about seven o'clock in the morning. She is homeward bound. Her name has been changed to *Fort Morgan*. Sergeant Mark received a letter from her orderly Sergeant saying that Serg't Behrensen is in New York and getting well. That the pay of marines is and has been since the 1st of last May as follows: Orderly Sergeant $24.00 | Sergeant $20.00 | Corporal $18.00 | Music $17.00 | Private $16.00 Only one dollar per month is now kept back from the privates. Corporal Winters was today made Sergeant, and McSweeney a Corporal. Captain Haywood says that the ship is going home next month. Several sailors whose times are out went on board the *Ft Morgan* to go home. She left for the *North* in the afternoon. Sergeant Baird made Orderly Sergeant.

Wed Sep 17, 1864

Had the forenoon and 1st night watches. Fresh grub for dinner. Rained all day. Cleaned musket belts and c. on berth deck. Weather cool.

Sun Sep 18, 1864

Inspection at four bells in the forenoon. Marines in blouses, blue pants and white cap covers. Ships company in clean blue, with white caps. Had the afternoon watch. Bullion and coffee for dinner. Came off about five o'clock. McCrystle, Thompson, Brenan, Cole, and Hugnerin of the guard went on shore on liberty in the afternoon, also a number of sailors. Came off about five o'clock, McCrystle, Thompson, and Hugnerin very much under influence of strong tea. As Hugnerin reached the top of the gangway he fell inboard striking head first on deck, McCrystle about the same. Thompson managed to keep on his pins. Cole and Brenan all right. The *Tritonia* arrived from New Orleans in the afternoon. The *Seliago* left for Pensacola in the PM. Word passed for knapsack inspection tomorrow. Captain Haywood read order promoting Baird, Winters, and McSweeney.

Mon Sep 19, 1864
Had the mid and 1st dog watches. Pork and beans for dinner. Knapsack inspection in the morning. Got through it all right. Wrote to Father. The *Glasgow* left in the afternoon for New Orleans. Men at work painting ship inside.

Tue Sep 20, 1864
The *Mettacomet* came down from Dog River bar. Ft. Morgan fired a salute in honor of general Sherman's victory. Rained hard all day. Weather quite cool. It is said that we are going home next month. *Mettacomet* went up the river again. Had the morning and 2nd dog watches. Duff for dinner.

Wed Sep 21, 1864
Had the morning and 1st night watches. Pork and beans for dinner. The *Glasgow* arrived in the forenoon from New Orleans. Brought a large mail. Received a letter from Mary and wrote to her in the afternoon. The steamer *Connecticut* arrived with recruits for the squadron. Hoist flag at 9:00AM. The *Tritonia* left for New Orleans in the afternoon.

Thu Sep 22, 1864
The *Connecticut* left in the morning. A mail brought by her yesterday was distributed this morning. Rec'd a paper from Mary. Had the afternoon watch. The *Glasgow* left for New Orleans in the PM. Rained nearly all day. Bullion and coffee for dinner.

Fri Sep 23, 1864
Had the mid and 2nd dog watches. Duff for dinner. The *Tritonia* arrived from New Orleans, brought a small mail. Commodore Palmer and General Canby came on board in the forenoon. Marines had to be on deck nearly all the afternoon to be ready to give them a present when they went away at about four o'clock. It is reported that Commodore Palmer is to take command here and that Admiral Farragut is going home before long. The *Richmond* left for Pensacola in the forenoon. Weather damp and rainy.

Sat Sep 24, 1864

Had the afternoon and 2nd dog watches. Pork and beans for dinner. Cleaned belts and c. on berth deck. Weather showery.

Sun Sep 25, 1864

Marines in uniform and white cap covers, and ships company in clean blue and white caps at inspection in the forenoon. Had the forenoon and 1st watches. Bullion and coffee for dinner. Weather quite cool. Thermometer at 72. After retreat had general courts martial. Liberty men went on shore in the afternoon. Of the marines–Fenisy–Smith–O'Brian. . . Perley and Corporal Mason. When the boat came off at five o'clock the marines were not to be seen. The officer in charge of the boat reported that he could see nothing of them on shore. Another boat went off and came back after dark with the five marines all under the influence. All were put in the brig.

Mon Sep 26, 1864

Had the forenoon and 2nd dog watches. Pork and beans for dinner. Last night just after Langdon had relieved me at twelve o'clock, the officer on deck (Mr. Adams) told him to find the carpenter to sound the pumps. Langdon told him that he did not consider it his duty to hunt up the carpenter, and so refused to do it. Adams then had him relieved and confined. It is said that Langdon will be court martialed. Hope not. About nine o'clock in the forenoon a coal bark came alongside, and all hands went to work coaling ship. In the afternoon a sailor died in the sick bay. He belonged to the *Chickasaw* and came on board of us yesterday. The five marines were let out of the brig this morning. The *Glasgow* arrived from New Orleans, brought a mail. Received a paper from Mary and a letter from Tom Seymour.

Tue Sep 27, 1864

Wrote to Mother. The *Glasgow* left for New Orleans. Had the forenoon and 2nd dog watches. Duff for dinner. Weather warm. The *Winnebago* came down from up the bay. The man who died yesterday was taken ashore for burial at Pilot Town this morning. Finished coaling ship about five o'clock PM. Coal bark towed away by the *Narcissus*. I am getting this "moon blindness" pretty badly. Could see hardly anything for the last two nights.

[Moon blindness, a condition horses sometime get, caused vision trouble for sailors sometimes, especially in the tropics, if they slept on deck, "under the full light of the moon. It sometimes becomes so intense that the patient on awakening can scarcely recognize daylight and must be led about." (Stellwag Von Carion, 1873)]

Wed Sep 28, 1864
Had the mid and afternoon watches. Pork and beans for dinner. General exercise at quarters in the evening. After quarters went to Captain Haywood to ask to have another orderly put on in place of Langdon. Meaher was put on from 6:00 to 8:00. This morning Captain Haywood told the orderly sergeant to make out an affirmation for Sullivan and me to sign, stating that we were promised the one hundred dollars bounty, when we enlisted. There seems to be some chance of getting our discharge.

Thu Sep 29, 1864
Had the mid and 1st dog watches. Bullion and coffee for dinner. Men commenced painting on starboard side. Color will be light. Made out and signed affidavit today in regard to my enlistment and the promise of one hundred dollars bounty. Glynn–Wilcox–Tennesy–Sullivan–McSweeney and several others have done the same. Hope to be free before many months.

Fri Sep 30, 1864
Had the morning watch, have been feeling very unwell for some days. At 9:00 AM went to see the Doctor and was put upon the sick list. Took my application for discharge into the ward room in the forenoon but did not see Captain Haywood. Left it on his desk in his room. The *Glasgow* arrived from New Orleans, finished painting ship. Duff for dinner.

Sat Oct 1, 1864

Two years today since I left home to join the Navy. On the sick list. Pills. *The Glasgow* left with the mail. The *Richmond* arrived from Pensacola, has only top-masts up.

Sun Oct 2, 1864

Marines at quarters in uniform, white pants and cap covers. Ships company all white. Steamer *Kensington* came in with recruits from the North. Wrote to Mary. Still on the sick list, more pills. Bullion and coffee for dinner. Langdon released from confinement this morning. He will not be court-martialed. Adams wanted him to be but could not furnish proof. He is not going on the cabin door again, but will do regular guard duty. Liberty men on shore again. Of the marines–Ingram–Foley–Simonds and Mulvaney. All came off clean and sober. Clean hammocks served out.

Mon Oct 3, 1864

Still on the sick list, more pills. All hands scrubbed hammocks in the morning. Gave mine a sickly scrub and let it go at that. Pork and beans for dinner. The *Glasgow* arrived from new Orleans. Scrubbed hammocks piped down about four PM.

Tue Oct 4, 1864

Still on the sick list, more pills. Duff for dinner. Marines made application for money. I for ten dollars. Mail sent to Pensacola by the *Buckthorn* to go North by the *Kensington*.

Wed Oct 5, 1864

Still on the sick list. Pork and beans for dinner. Some rebel deserters came on board in the forenoon. The *Glasgow* left for New Orleans. Still taking pills.

Thu Oct 6, 1864
Still on the sick list, no more pills. Took something that tasted like camphor. A tug came alongside and brought us a lot of provisions, small stores and c. Bullion and coffee for dinner.

Fri Oct 7, 1864
Still on the sick list, more of the camphor medicine. A lot of recruits came on board in the morning, came from Pensacola on the *Cowslip*. Were all made to go to the head and give themselves a good washing, small stores served out in the afternoon. The *Selema* arrived from New Orleans, brought a mail. I received a *Waverly Magazine* from Mrs. Metcalf. *Glasgow* due but did not arrive. Duff for dinner.

Sat Oct 8, 1864
Weather quite cold, wind blowing a gale all day. We have two anchors down. Still on the sick list, medicine same as yesterday. The *Glasgow* arrived in the evening. Uniform hats served out to the guard once more. Pork and beans for dinner.

Sun Oct 9, 1864
Still on the sick list, medicine same as yesterday. Weather cold, but wind not so fresh. Marines at muster in full uniform, hats and all. Ships company in clean blue and mustering jackets. Bullion and coffee for dinner. Wrote to Mary, Marines ordered to wear fatigue coats instead of jumpers.

Mon Oct 10, 1864
Weather somewhat warmer. Still on the sick list. The *Glasgow* left for New Orleans. Purser served out clothes. Drew a pair of blankets and three pairs socks. Pork and beans for dinner.

Thu Oct 11, 1864
Still on the sick list. The supply steamer *Bermuda* arrived early in the morning. We got some fresh beef, vegetables and c. from her. She left in the afternoon. Received a *Waverly Magazine* from Mrs. Metcalf. Weather warm and pleasant. Duff day.

Wed Oct 12, 1864

Still on the sick list. Fresh grub for dinner. The *Glasgow* arrived from New Orleans, brought a good mail. Rec'd a letter from Mary.

Fri Oct 14, 1864

Still on the sick list and no better. The Paymaster served out money. I got ten dollars. There is a report that Petersburg is captured. Hope it is true. Fresh grub for dinner.

Sat Oct 15, 1864

Ten months today since the *Hartford* went into commission. Still on the sick list. Weather quite warm and very pleasant. Pork and beans day.

Sun Oct 16, 1864

Still on the sick list. Marines at quarters in full uniform. Ships company in clean blue and white caps. Wrote to Mary. Bullion and coffee for dinner. Weather cooler.

Mon Oct 17, 1864

Weather rather cool. Wind fresh. Still on the sick list, not much prospect of getting off soon. The *Seliago* came down from up the bay in the evening. Pork and beans for dinner.

Tue Oct 18, 1864

Still on the sick list. The *Glasgow* arrived about noon, brought a mail. Received a letter from Mary, Ed Church, and Mrs. Metcalf. Mason received a letter from Corporal O'Connor. He is in Boston and writes that all marines who enlisted from July '62 to August '63 are entitled to a discharge. So perhaps I will get mine.

Wed Oct 19, 1864

Still on the sick list. *Glasgow* left for New Orleans. In the afternoon General Granger and a Brigadier General came on board. Marines had to turn out to receive them. We were kept on the quarter deck all the afternoon at sunset and permitted to go below. Bullion and coffee for dinner.

Fri Oct 21, 1864
Weather quite cool. Still on the sick list, nothing new going on. Salt horse and soft tack for dinner.

Sat Oct 22, 1864
Still on the sick list. Marines cleaning up for tomorrow. *Glasgow* due but failed to arrive. Pork and beans day.

Sun Oct 23, 1864
Weather pleasant. Still on the sick list. Marines at muster in full uniform, ships company in clean blue. Bullion and coffee for dinner. The *Bermuda* arrived in the morning. She left in the afternoon and Hunt went on her. He is sick and going North, on the Doctor's orders. He is a good man and we are sorry to lose him.

Mon Oct 24, 1864
Still on the sick list but feeling a good deal better than for some days. Weather quite warm again. Pork and beans day.

Tue Oct 25, 1864
Duff for dinner. Still on the sick list. Steamer *Glasgow* arrived from New Orleans with the mail. Received a letter from Mary written on the 11th. Wrote to Mary. Also to the postmaster at New Orleans enclosing one dollar for postage stamps.

Wed Oct 26, 1864
Rain. Still on the binnacle list but think I will be off tomorrow as the doctor gives me no medicine today. The *Glasgow* left for New Orleans. News came today that Sheridan had whipped Early again and captured 41 pieces of artillery. Pork and beans for dinner.

Thu Oct 27, 1864

Off the sick list at last, have been on nearly four weeks, cleaned belts in the forenoon and donned a fatigue coat. The orderly Sergeant tells me to return to duty at the cabin door, taking Ingram's watch which is from four to six PM. Bullion and coffee for dinner.

Fri Oct 28, 1864

Had the morning and 2nd dog watches. Duff for dinner. Steamer *Glasgow* arrived in the forenoon from New Orleans. Supply steamer *Fort Morgan* came in about noon. We got some fresh provisions and ice from her.

Sat Oct 29, 1864

Cleaned belts muskets and c. for tomorrow's inspection. The *Glasgow* left for New Orleans. Steamer *Ft. Morgan* left in the afternoon. Mr. Munday went away with her. He is detached from this ship and ordered to the *Seminole*. Mr. Dickson the Boatswain has been sent to the hospital. Forenoon and 1st watches. Fresh grub for dinner.

Sun Oct 30, 1864

Had the forenoon watch. Fresh grub for dinner. Marines at muster in full uniform. Ships company in clean blue and white cap covers. Orderlyes in full uniform all day. Acting Master Dyer who was captain of the *Glasgow* is now attached to this ship.

Mon Oct 31, 1864

The *Monongahela* arrived in the afternoon from a cruise. Captain Strong her commanding officer now wears six stripes. Had the mid and 1st dog watches. Fresh grub for dinner.

Tue Nov 1, 1864

Had the morning and 2nd dog watches. Duff for dinner. The *Glasgow* arrived from New Orleans, brought a mail. Received a letter from Mary and one from Ed Smead. One from the postmaster at New Orleans enclosing the postage stamps I sent for. Rec'd a *Courier* from Mary and a *Waverly* from Mrs. Metcalf.

Wed Nov 2, 1864
Had the forenoon and 1st watches. Wrote to Mary. Small stores served out. I drew a bar of soap, blacking brush, and wisp broom. Pork and beans day.

Thu Nov 3, 1864
Had the afternoon watch. Bullion and coffee for dinner. The *Penguin* arrived from Galveston. At evening quarters the Guard mustered in watch coats for the first time this season. Weather quite cold. The *Glasgow* left.

Fri Nov 4, 1864
Weather still cold. Mustered at fore noon quarters with watch boats, waist belts and muskets. Had the mid and 1st dog watches. Duff for dinner. The *Port Royal* came down from up the bay in the evening.

Sat Nov 5, 1864
Weather somewhat warmer. Had the morning and 2nd dog watches. Pork and beans for dinner. Cleaned belts in forenoon. All hands aired bedding. The *Penguin* left for Pensacola. Captain Haywood showed us a copy of a letter he had rec'd from Colonel Zeilen, Commandant of the Marine Corps, stating that his letter of Oct 1, with the depositions made out by us had been received, and telling him to inform us that the order discharging marines who had enlisted between May '62 and July '63 had been revoked, and the President orders that we shall remain in the serve and receive the one hundred dollars bounty when it becomes due. So the prospect of getting a discharge before our time is out is rather slim. Guess I will have to put in the winter down here instead of at home. Clean hammocks served out at evening quarters, and word passed to sling them.

Sun Nov 6, 1864

Marines at quarters in full uniform. Ships company in clean blue and white caps. Had the forenoon and 1st watches. Bullion and coffee for dinner. Wrote to Mrs. Metcalf and Ed Smead.

Mon Nov 7, 1864

All hands scrubbed hammocks in the morning. Had the afternoon watch. Pork and beans for dinner. An army transport arrived from New Orleans loaded with troops. She brought the news that Pleasanton has defeated Price and captured 2000 prisoners.

Tue Nov 8, 1864

Wrote a letter to Mother, one to Ed Church and one to Tom Seymour. Had the mid and 1st dog watches. Duff for dinner. Several sailors whose times are out were transferred to the *Cornemangle*. She is going North for repairs.

Wed Nov 9, 1864

The *Glasgow* arrived from New Orleans with mail. Received a letter from Mary. Had the morning and 2nd dog watches. Pork and beans.

Thu Nov 10, 1864

Had the forenoon and 1st watches. Bullion and coffee for dinner. The *Circassian* arrived last evening. Breakfast at 4 bells this morning. We got a lot of fresh provisions (?) from the *Circassian*. In the evening the *Port Royal* went up the bay and the *Selma* came down. The *Glasgow* left for New Orleans with our mail. Wrote to Mary.

Fri Nov 11, 1864

Had the afternoon watch. Fresh grub for dinner. The *Lackawanna* left for Galveston in the morning. The *Kennebec* arrived from Pensacola in the afternoon. She brought some marines who came down on the *Union*. Some of them were sent on board the

Richmond, and nine brought on board of us. All are old soldiers except four. Among them is old Serg't Buckley, now a private. He was reduced for getting drunk while on guard. I did not know any of the others. The *Circassian* left in the morning.

Sat Nov 12, 1864

Cleaned belts, muskets and c. Had the mid and 1st dog watches, fresh grub for dinner. The admiral, Mr. Watson, Mr. McKinley, Captain Haywood and several other officers went on board the *Cowslip* in the morning and went up the bay. All returned about five o'clock PM.

Sun Nov 13, 1864

Had the morning and 2nd dog watches. Bullion, coffee and dandy funk for dinner. Inspection in forenoon at 4 bells. Marines in full uniform. Ships company in clean blue and white caps. Wrote to Rodney Harris.

Mon Nov 14, 1864

Had the forenoon and 1st watches. Pork and beans for dinner. The *Octorara* arrived from Pensacola in the evening. In the forenoon the admiral, Captain Drayton, Lieut. Watson, and several other officers went to Sand Island. I hear they are going to build a lighthouse there.

Tue Nov 15, 1864

Had the afternoon watch. Duff for dinner. Steamer *Fort Morgan* arrived in the morning. Also the *Glasgow* with mail. The *Mettacomet* came down from the bay. The rebels say that Lincoln is re-elected. Hope it is true.

Wed Nov 16, 1864

Had the mid and 1st dog watches. Pork and beans for dinner. The steamer *Mobile* arrived in the forenoon. Steamer *Admiral* left in the evening. In the afternoon a new monitor arrived from New Orleans. She is called the *Kickapoo*. Wrote to Mary.

Thu Nov 17, 1864

Had the morning and 2nd dog watches. Bullion and coffee for dinner. A short drill with muskets after quarters. Captain Haywood orders that hereafter we will fall in the box and waist belts only, using the frog in place of the bayonet belt. Steamer *Mobile* went out about 9:00 AM, the nine marines who came on board from the *Kennebec* went today on board the *Mettacomet* to go to New Orleans. One of them named Maher was a few months ago tried by court martial on board the *Monongahela* and sentenced to two years in prison. He was sent North but released on condition that he would re-enlist. He also got a large bounty. He has been making threats about killing the orderly Sergeant of the *Monongahela*, and saying that he could get out of the services by another court martial. He went on board the *Monongahela* and did some loud talking there. Captain Strong came on board of us to see the admiral about it and it is thought that Maher will be detained here and not sent to New Orleans. Had he kept quiet Cap't Strong would not have known he was out here again.

Fri Nov 18, 1864

Had the forenoon and 1st night watches. The *Glasgow* arrived from New Orleans and brought a mail. Received a letter from Mary, a bundle of papers from Mrs. Metcalf, and a *Ballon's Magazine* from Mother. In the magazine was a small flag with Lincoln and Johnson printed on it. News comes that Old Abe is re-elected beyond a doubt. The marine Maher was today brought on board here and then sent on board the *Cayuga* he is to be sent to some ship off Galveston. The *Mettacomet* left for New Orleans with the monitor *Manhattan* in tow. Wrote to Mary. Duff for dinner.

Sat Nov 19, 1864

Cleaned belts and c. in the afternoon. The admiral, Captain Drayton, Lieut. Watson, Mr. McKinley, and Capt. Haywood went to New Orleans on the *Glasgow*. The *Richmond* is flag ship here now. Had the afternoon watch. Pork and beans for dinner. Rain.

Sun Nov 20, 1864

Had the mid and 1st dog watches. Bullion and coffee for dinner. Marines at quarters in clean fatigues. Ships company in clean blue. Weather damp and rainy. Wrote to Mother. The *Ossippee* came in about noon but went out again.

Mon Nov 21, 1864

Had the morning and 2nd dog watches. Pork and beans for dinner. Weather cool.

Tue Nov 22, 1864

The *Tritonia* arrived from New Orleans, whether very cool. Duff for dinner. Had the forenoon and 1st night watches. The *Tritonia* brought some mail. I received a letter and *Harper's Magazine* and *Steuben Courier* from Mary, and a *Frank Leslies Monthly* from Mrs. Metcalf.

Wed Nov 23, 1864

Weather very cold. Ice on deck in the morning. The *Circassian* came in in the morning and left in the afternoon. Had the afternoon watch. Pork and beans day.

Thu Nov 24, 1864

Wrote to Mary. Had the mid and 1st dog watches. Bullion and coffee for dinner. Weather cold.

Fri Nov 25, 1864

Had the morning and 2nd dog watches. Salt horse for dinner but no duff, flour all gone. In the afternoon word passed to "bend sail," bent on our new sails. It is reported that Mr. Kimberly has received orders from Captain Drayton to get this ship ready as soon as possible to go North. He has been heard to say so.

Sat Nov 26, 1864

Had the forenoon and 2nd dog watches. Pork and beans for dinner. The admiral and staff arrived on the *Glasgow* at about half past seven AM. We are going North sure. A good many of our sailors and firemen are to be transferred to the *Richmond*. Twelve of our marines also are going there. In the afternoon the coal schooner *Wm Flint* came alongside and all hands commenced coaling ship. Finished at dark and the schooner was towed away. Maher is going on board the *Richmond* so we have only three orderlys now. The supply steamer *Bermuda* arrived in the afternoon.

Sun Nov 27, 1864
Had the morning and 1st dog watches. Bullion and coffee for dinner. In the afternoon a draft of sailors and firemen went from us to the *Richmond*. Also twelve of our guard as follows. Maher–Wilcox–Foley–Smith–Devoe–Knox–Brenan–Glynn–O'Brien–Mundell–Cavalier–and Bickford. They did not like the idea of going on the *Richmond* and went to Captain Drayton to see if they could stay with us, but it was of no avail, they had to go. Marines at quarters in fatigues with waist belts and muskets. We got in our 2nd cutter in the morning.

Mon Nov 28, 1864
Had the afternoon and 1st watch. Fresh grub for dinner. Our furnace fires started at 2:15 AM. We got under way at 6:15 and stood out to sea. The *Richmond* cheered us as we went out. At noon we were boarded by a Pensacola Pilot. At 2PM, just as we were abreast of Fort Pickens the *Constellation* laying inside the bay fired a salute of fifteen guns which we replied to with a salute of nine guns. We came to anchor off Pensacola Navy Yard about three o'clock. The *Potomac* cheered us as we passed. After we anchored, sent on shore and got our spars which were left here before the fight.

Tue Nov 29, 1864
In the forenoon we got up our top gallant masts and rigging. Got a lot of provisions on board. Expect we will leave tomorrow or next day. Had the forenoon and 2nd dog watches. Fresh grub for dinner.

Wed Nov 30, 1864

A coal vessel came alongside and all hands commenced coaling ship. Finished about 10:00 AM. Had the morning and 1st dog watches. Fresh grub for dinner. A pilot came on board about noon. We got under way at 1:00 PM and stood out to sea. The crews of the *Potomac* and *Constellation* and all the gun boats in the harbor maned their rigging and gave us three cheers as we passed. Fort Barrancus fired a salute which we returned. And now we are at last "Homeward bound."

Thu Dec 1, 1864

Had the mid, afternoon, and 1st watches. Bullion and coffee for dinner. Weather very pleasant. Nothing but salt water in sight.

Fri Dec 2, 1864

Warm and very pleasant. Had the afternoon and 2nd dog watches. Sea pie for dinner. In the forenoon a sail was discovered on our port bow. She was made out to be a fore and aft schooner standing North and east. Several sail in sight in the afternoon.

Sat Dec 3, 1864

Had the morning and 1st dog watches. Pork and beans for dinner. Cleaned belts brasses and c. Sighted the Tortugas lighthouse [Loggerhead Key, FL] about three o'clock PM. In the morning passed a side wheel steamer bound North.

Sun Dec 4, 1864

Had the mid, afternoon, and first watches. Bullion and coffee for dinner. Sighted Cedar Key light about two o'clock AM. A Key West Pilot came on board just after daylight. We came to anchor off the town about eight o'clock. The *San Jacinto* is alongside the dock taking coal. Acting Rear Admiral Stribling in command of the squadron here came on board about half past nine. The marines were ordered on deck in a hurry to receive him. Inspection at 10:00 AM. Marines in full uniform. Ships company in blue. Admiral Stribling left the ship about half past ten and Admiral Farragut went with him. At nine o'clock the *Dale* fired a salute of fifteen guns which we returned. About noon a coal schooner came alongside and our starboard watch commenced coaling ship at once. By four o'clock they had got in 40 tons and were relieved by the port watch. Finished coaling at ten PM. When hammocks were piped down.

Mon Dec 5, 1864
A pilot came on board at day light. We got under way at about seven o'clock and started for home. Fired a salute of thirteen guns. Had the forenoon and 2nd dog watches. Pork and beans for dinner. Ship making seven and eight knots.

Tue Dec 6, 1864
Had the morning and 1st dog watches. Sea pie for dinner. Weather very pleasant, light head winds. In the afternoon about three bells all hands were mustered on the quarter deck and First Lieut. read articles of war. Crew mustered around the Capstan. At six bells the guard fell in for drill on port side of quarter deck. Were drilled at manual of arms about an hour and a half by Sergeant Baird. Then inspected by Captain Haywood.

Wed Dec 7, 1864
Had the mid, afternoon and 1st watches. Pork and beans for dinner. In the afternoon sent up our fore, main and mizzen top-gallant yards and fore and main royal yards, wind right astern. Set all square sails in the afternoon. Sent up stern-sails forward. Ship making 8– 9– and 10 knots. Just before dark sent down stern sails on port side.

Thu Dec 8, 1864
Had the forenoon and 2nd dog watches. Bullion and coffee for dinner. Ship making 9 and 10 knots in the afternoon, with wind right astern and all sail set. In afternoon wind shifted and we had to take in all sail. Sent down top-gallant and royal yards

and housed top-gallant masts. At dark wind fresh from the North East.

Fri Dec 9, 1864
Had the morning and 1st dog watches. Duff for dinner. When I went on watch at 4:00 AM the wind was blowing a gale and sea running very high. Wind had lulled a little by eight o'clock but the sea continued to rise and at ten o'clock broke over us and put out some of the furnace fires. The Berth deck was all afloat, and pits, kettles, mess chests and c. flying about in grand confusion. Ship rolled and pitched very heavily. We sent down top-gallant masts. Stretched hawsers along the spar deck in rear (?) of the guns. Nearly all the boys sea sick. Some old sailors are sick and say this is the worst storm they ever saw.

Sat Dec 10, 1864
When I took the mid watch the storm was un-abated. Continued so during the whole watch. After I turned in at 4:00 AM the sea broke over us very heavily, carrying away two of our boats, the barge and dingy and our head bulwarks. At 8:00 AM the sea was considerable smoother and at noon we could get along quite steadily. Had the mid afternoon and 1st watches.

Sun Dec 11, 1864
Sea not so rough but a heavy swell on and the ship rolls badly. Had the forenoon and 2nd dog watches. Pork and beans for dinner. Weather cool. Suppose we are getting near New York.

Mon Dec 12, 1864
We sighted Barnegat Light about 4:00 AM. A pilot came on board about noon, but wind and tide were against us so strong that we could not get into New York, so about 4:00 PM we anchored off Sandy Hook. Let go both bow anchors. Had the morning and 1st dog watches. Weather very cold.

[New Jersey's "Old Barney" lighthouse]

USS *Hartford* New York Bay
Monday, Dec 12th, 1864 5:00 pm

Dear Father,
We arrived here this afternoon. The Ship is probably going out of commission and we Marines will probably be sent to barracks in a few days. You had better not write until you hear from me again. The mail leaves immediately so there's not time now to write more. Give my love to Mother & all the folks. Yours affectionately, Chas. Brother.

Tue Dec 13, 1864

Commenced getting up anchor about seven o'clock. They were foul and we did not get under way until noon, and stood in towards the Narrows. About one o'clock a revenue streamer met us and came alongside and a party of gentlemen came on board of us to accompany the admiral up to the city. Sent up top-gallant masts and set taut rigging. Arrived off the battery and anchored about 3:00 PM. Sent a letter to Father. The admiral and Captain Drayton immediately went ashore. Had the mid, afternoon, and 1st night watches. Duff for dinner. After we had anchored a Swedish frigate laying here fired a salute which we returned. An officer from her boarded us. Also the captain of a French gunboat here.

Wed Dec 14, 1864

Had the forenoon and 2nd dog watches. Pork and beans for dinner. The Swedish man of war left in the morning. As she passed us her crew manned the rigging and gave three cheers, which we returned.

Thu Dec 15, 1864

About one o'clock PM we got underway and went up to the Brooklyn Navy Yard, and anchored near the coal dock. We fired a salute and the coal dock battery returned it. The crews of the receiving ships *Vermont* and *North Carolina* manned their rigging and gave us three cheers which we returned. A number of sailors whose times are out went on shore in the evening. Had the morning and 2st dog watches. One year ago today this ship went into commission.

Fri Dec 16, 1864
Had the mid, afternoon, and 1st night watches. Pork and beans for dinner. Got out our shell and sent them into the Navy Yard. The admiral and Captain Drayton both on board for a few hours. The admiral gave orders for us to hoist the red pennant.

Sat Dec 17, 1864
Had the forenoon and 2nd dog watches. Duff for dinner. In the afternoon we got our powder out and about four o'clock hauled in alongside the dock. The men who went on shore Wednesday evening were today paid off and discharged.

Sun Dec 18, 1864
Had the morning and 2nd dog watches. Bullion beef for dinner. Nothing doing on the *Hartford*. Fleming from the *North Carolina* came on board. He says that Cameron was caught smuggling whisky on board and was transferred to the barracks and afterwards got his discharge. I can hardly believe that he had anything to do with that business.

Mon Dec 19, 1864
All hands at work all day getting out stores. Pork for dinner. Had the mid, afternoon, and 1st night watches.

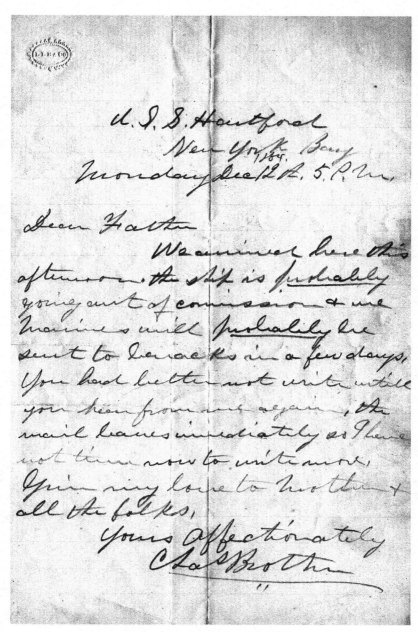

U. S. S. Hartford
New York Bay
Monday Dec 12th 5. P. M.

Dear Father

We arrived here this afternoon, the ship is probably going out of commission & we marines will probably be sent to barracks in a few days. You had better not write untill you hear from me again, the mail leaves immediatly so I have not time now to write more. Give my love to mother & all the folks,

Yours Affectionately
Chas Brother

45. Letter from Brother to his father, December 12, 1864

CHAPTER 7

Brooklyn Navy Yard in 1864

Tue Dec 20, 1864

Had the forenoon watch. Our ship put out of commission about 4:00 PM. Shortly after we left and were marched up to the barracks. Our baggage having been sent up ahead of us. We were put into room No. 17. For supper had tea and soft tack. The men here tell terrible stories about "Old Jack" (Colonel Jack Reynolds) who is in command here. Before leaving the ship I received two letters from Mary, one from Gregg, one from Ed Smead and one from Mary Becker. About nine o'clock in the evening we were marched over to the guard house where we saw Col. Jack. He is certainly a ferocious looking old chap. He made us a short speech. Told us we would probably get a furlough with permission to report for duty at any Navy Yard we might choose. Gave all of us a pass to go out, good until the 22nd (Thursday) at 9:00 AM. I went out in company with Sergeant Mark and Corporal Mason. We went to a restaurant corner of Broadway and Fulton Streets in New York, and had a good supper. As it was the first one of the kind for over a year, we fully enjoyed it. After supper we walked up Broadway and about town for a while. Stayed all night at "Harrison's," a hotel in Chatham Street.

Wed Dec 21, 1864

Turned out about eight o'clock. Had breakfast in the Bowery. Mason and I bought each a pair of boots for $8.50. Weather stormy and bad. Stayed at the hotel nearly all day. In the evening went up to see the Beckers at 626 6th Ave. They seemed glad to see me. Mrs. Mary Hotchkin of Prattsburgh was there. We had a good oyster supper about ten o'clock. Came back down town about eleven, and turned in.

Thu Dec 22, 1864

Turned out about seven o'clock. Mark and Mason came in during the night. We went to Crook's and had breakfast. Then started for Barracks where we arrived a few minutes before nine, just in time. We found that Taylor–McKiney–Langdon–Murtha–Mulvany–McCrystal–Huggot–Pagnello–Thompson–Graham–Whorton–Winters and Baird were also on time. McCrystle and Pagnello came in last night and were put in the guard house until morning. Huguenin—Mackin and Mullady were a few hours late and were put in the guard house. Wrote to Mother.

Fri Dec 23, 1864

All of our boys were let out of the guard house this morning. Lawrence–Ingram–Simons and McSweeney came in yesterday. Cole–Perley and Sullivan are still out. Weather very cold.

Sat Dec 24, 1864

Weather warmer. In the forenoon all hands sent out to shovel snow off the walks. I hear we are to be put on guard tomorrow, our accounts are not here yet. The Paymaster says they will not be ready before next Thursday. Cleaned belts and c. and packed knapsack, in preparation for going on guard tomorrow. Wrote to Mary.

Sun Dec 25, 1864

Christmas day. On guard at Barracks, Post No. 5, 1st relief. Countersign "Flag." Lieut. Mead officers of the day. We had fried fish for breakfast and chicken pot-pie for dinner. Pearly came in yesterday and is now locked up.

Mon Dec 26, 1864

As I did not care to go out, did not go for my pass. Weather damp and rainy.

Tue Dec 27, 1864

On guard at Barracks, post No. 6–1st relief, countersign "Ocean." Lieut. Mead officer of the day. Weather damp and foggy.

Wed Dec 28, 1864

Did not care to go out so did not go for a pass. Just after supper the police Sergeant came to see me and told me to go over to the guard house. The two men Henry 4th and Rooney 2nd who were on No 6 post with me yesterday were also there. It seems that there was some wrong doing in the vicinity of No 6 post last night and it was suspected that one of us knew something about it. So we were brought up before the officer of the day and questioned by him but each of us denied any knowledge of the affair. I certainly knew nothing about it. He said that the Colonel had ordered that we be confined and we were accordingly locked up in the guard house cells for the night.

Thu Dec 29, 1864

We three were taken before the Colonel in the morning after guard mount. He asked each of us, what we knew about the affair and each one declared he knew nothing about it, but he would not believe us, saying he was sure that one of use must know something about it. He let Rooney go but told the Sergeant of the guard to again lock up Henry and me. So we were put back into the cell. Were afterwards taken over to the barracks and put into No. 4 cell in the right wing. Sullivan and Cole came in and were locked up.

Mon Jan 2, 1865

Henry and I were released from the cells this morning. As the weather has been quite cold we have not suffered any on account of our confinement, as we had no duty to do and had full rations. But it seems rather hard to be punished when I don't

46. Maj. Henry A. Bartlett, USMC, NHHC NH 79181

---

deserve it. If I get a transfer furlough I will take good care to put myself out of reach of "Old Jack." Cleaned belts, musket and c. Wrote to Mary. Weather very cold.

Tue Jan 3, 1865
On guard at barracks, post No 4, 1st relief. Captain Collier officer of the day. Countersign "Dix." Weather not so cold. Received a letter from Father in the evening. He writes that Henry is at home but in very poor health. Am glad that he is home at last.

Wed Jan 4, 1865

A heavy snow storm last night. Came off guard at 9:00 AM. Cleaned belts, musket and c. All hands fell in for drill in the "Long room" at about eleven o'clock, were drilled about an hour by the officer of the day Lieut. Bartlett. Went to the Navy Yard with the patrol at 4:00 PM. The guard from the sloop of war *Saint Mary's* arrived at the barracks today.

[Henry Anthony Bartlett, USMC, was about age twenty-six in 1865. He had a long career at sea and attached to the Marine Barracks. (Powell and Shippen, 1892; D. Sullivan, 2019.)

Thu Jan 5, 1865

Sailed from New York on the Hartford one year ago today. Detailed in the morning for "Ready man." About half past ten AM was ordered to get ready for guard. Was put on No. 4 post, 1st relief. Did not have to stand the 1st tour. Lieut. Mead officer of the day. Countersign "Clear." A guard left for the double under *Muscosta* and one for the steamer *State of Georgia*. My cell mate Henry 4th went on the *Muskosta*.

Fri Jan 6, 1865

Weather very cold. Went to the Navy Yard with the patrol at 4:00 PM.

Sat Jan 7, 1865

Detailed in the morning for police work but had none to do. Went to the Navy Yard with the patrol at 4:00 PM. Drew a new pair of shoes.

Sun Jan 8, 1865

On guard at barracks. Post No 4, 2nd relief, countersign "Deserter." Lieut. Mead officer of the day. Mark Sergeant of the Guard. McSweeney was relieved on the evening for being intoxicated.

Mon Jan 9, 1865
Grand inspection in full uniform in the long room in the morning by Old Jack himself. Afterwards he visited and inspected all the rooms. Went to the Navy Yard with the patrol at 4:00 PM.

Tue Jan 10, 1865
On guard at barracks, post No 5, 2nd relief, countersign "Order." Lieut. Bartlett officer of the day. Winters, sergeant of the guard, weather damp and rainy. No liberty and no patrol to Navy Yard.

Wed Jan 11, 1865
Weather very cold. Wrote to Father. All hands at drill in the long room in the afternoon. Were drilled about an hour by the officer of the day, Lieut. Mead. Went to the Navy Yard with the patrol at 4:00 PM.

Thu Jan 12, 1865
Ready man today, went to the Navy Yard with the patrol at 4:00 PM. McSweeney was released yesterday and reduced to the ranks. All hands drilled about an hour in the forenoon by the officer of the day, Capt. Collin.

Fri Jan 13, 1865
On guard at barracks, post No. 2, 1st relief, countersign "Neglect." Lieut. Bartlett officer of the day, Winters sergeant of the guard.

Sat Jan 14, 1865
The Garrison signed accounts. I signed for $99.85. Went to the Navy Yard with the patrol at 4:00 PM.

Sun Jan 15, 1865
Detailed in the morning for police work, weather damp and rainy.

Mon Jan 16, 1865
On guard at barracks, post No 7, 2nd relief, countersign "Davis." Lieut. Bartlett officer of the day. Mark, sergeant of the guard. Garrison paid off. I received $99.85.

Tue Jan 17, 1865
Came off guard at 9:00 AM. Cleaned belts and musket and then went to see Old Jack to ask to have my name taken off the restrictive list, and to get a pass to go out in the evening. After some talk he agreed to do both. Went out at 5:30 PM. Went to a store in Myrtle Ave and bought some shirts, gloves, scarf and c. Went down to Fulton St. and bought a satchel. Went over to New York. Had several suppers then started for barracks where I arrived about half past ten.

Wed Jan 18, 1865
On guard at barracks, Post No 2, 1st relief, countersign "Assault." Lieut. Bartlett officer of the day. Mark, Sergeant of the guard. The guards of the *Mobile* and *Saint Mary's* got their furloughs today and yesterday. Received a letter from Henry. [Henry H. Brother, H.H., Charley's older brother by ten years.]

Thu Jan 19, 1865
Went to the Navy Yard with the Patrol at 4:00 PM. Went out on pass about five o'clock. Bought a fatigue cap at 210 Broadway. Had two or three suppers, a shave, shampoo and bath. Got back to barracks about 9:30.

Fri Jan 20, 1865
On guard at Navy Yard, Post No 4, 1st relief. Sergeant Alexander. It is said that the *Hartford* guard will get furloughs tomorrow.

Sat Jan 21, 1865
In the afternoon packed up and got ready for going on furlough. Got the furlough—seven days and to report for duty at Boston—about 2:00 PM. Send my bag and hammock over to

Adams express office in Broadway New York. Had them bill to Boston Navy Yard. Met Mallady, McKinet and Pagnello in New York. After exchanging with them the usual compliments I started for the Erie Depot. Bought a ticket for Bath, got on the cars and we were soon underway.

CHAPTER 8

Bath on Furlough

Sun Jan 22, 1865

Train arrived at Corning at 7:00 AM supposing that I could not go to Bath until evening I went to the Dickenson House, but Major Field told me a train would leave for Bath in a few minutes so I went back to the depot and caught the train.

[Both Maj. Almeron Field and his brother, Maj. Eliakim Field, were prominent and popular hotel operators. "He was formerly one of the most popular landlords in Southern New York, being in charge of the Dickinson House, at Corning for about ten years, then of the Brinerd House (now Rathbun) at Elmira, and afterwards of a hotel at Waverly. He was greatly esteemed as an honorable man and worthy citizen. His courtesy was proverbial, and he was ever vigilant to promote the comfort of his guests." —*Corning Journal*, Aug 27, 1885. "March 30, 1865— George W. Fuller succeeds Major Field as landlord of the Dickinson House." (Mulford, 1922)]

Arrived at Bath about eight o'clock. As I was going towards the house saw Mother at the west window in her room. She knew me and met me at the door. Soon saw Father, Val, and Mary, and Henry who I had not seen in twelve years. Went out to Deque's and up to Ellie's in the afternoon. Will Dutcher called and took me out for a sleigh ride.

[Brother was unsettled by the condition of his brother, Henry (H.H.) Oral history claimed that Henry's hair was white from the stress of his trip home from Australia.]

Mon Jan 23, 1865
Went up to the mills and saw the Wells's—Greek's, Johnson and the rest of them. Went down town and saw all the boys that are left, in the afternoon and evening. Mr. Sutherland and the folks at the store.

[According to the 1860 Census, the Greek Family lived two doors down from the Brother Family. William Greek was the same age as Charles Brother and later took over the family sawmill business with his brother.]

Tue Jan 24, 1865
Went to the mills in the forenoon. Went with Henry to call on Mrs. Mary Rice in the afternoon. Saw Mrs. Metcalf, went up to Ellies. Home in the evening.

[Brother paid a visit to Mary Fowler Rice, widow of Captain Burrage Rice (1823–1865), Brother's cousin. Rice was killed in action near Petersburg, VA on Jan 11, 1865 but he was not in uniform. Rice's body was embalmed and sent to Steuben County for burial on January 19,1865 with Masonic honors. He was with Co. C of the NY 189th Volunteers. He was a spy murdered while on a mission. It is unclear if the family knew all the details of his death at this time. The captain's adoptive father was married to Brother's aunt: Anna Pratt Rice. At the age of fourteen Burrage Rice came to Prattsburgh and later returned to Bath to clerk at the store of James R. Dudley, who was an old business partner of Henry Brother. Brother's sister Ellen married Jim Young, a land agent. Benjamin F. Young was a land agent for the Pulteney Land Office and an old friend of the Brother and Pratt families.]

Wed Feb 8, 1865
Was too busy visiting while at home and so neglected my diary. Went up to Prattsburgh with Henry Jan 26th and returned the next day.

On Sunday the 29th, Val, Henry and I were invited to Ellie's to dinner. Took tea with Deque on Monday the 30th.

Took tea at Mr. Sutherland's on Tuesday the 31st. We were all invited to a party at James Lyon's on the 1st inst., but none of us went. Mary and I called upon Mrs. Metcalf that evening.

Left Bath on the evening of Thursday Feb 2nd and 10:40. Val and Henry went to the depot with me. I found it harder to leave this time than before. Bought a through ticket to Boston for eleven dollars.

On arriving at Corning went over to the Dickenson house and saw Eliakim Field for a few minutes. Left Corning at about eleven o'clock. Took a bath in a sleeping car, never was in one before. Got breakfast at Port Jervis the next forenoon. The train was behind time so we did not reach Jersey City until four o'clock PM, of Friday the 3rd.

Was transferred by stage to the New York and New Haven RR Depot. I left my bundle there in the package office and went down town. Went to the "Belmont" and paid for a room. In the evening went up to Bryant's Minstrels. After it was out went to the Belmont and turned in. Turned out the next morning (4th) at five o'clock. Walked about town a while, had breakfast and then went up to the depot to take the eight o'clock train for Boston, got there in time but the package office was not open and I could not get my bundle, so I went down town again. Stayed at the Belmont all day.

Took the train for Boston at 8:00 PM. Arrived there about eight o'clock on the morning of the 5th. Found my way over to Charlestown without much trouble and reported to the Sergeant of the guard at the barracks. He took my furlough and sent me up into the right wing and leaving my things there I went down and got breakfast, then went into the right wing again.

About ten o'clock the Commanding officer, Captain Schemerhorn, sent for me. He was in his office. He asked me why I had not reported sooner. At the expiration of my furlough, and I told him that it was mostly my own fault, that I had not been able to finish my visit in time, and so had to stay a little longer. He asked me where I had been and I told him at my old home, he asked where that was and I told him. He said I was making a bad beginning to stay away seven days over my time, and told the officer of the day to confine me.

I was accordingly put up in No 1 cell. Wrote to Father informing him of my safe arrival. On the 7th received a letter from T. R. Harris. He and Gregg are in Brooklyn waiting for their furlough. They expect to report here. I was released this morning and assigned to the left wing. The room is so full I could get no bed so had to spread a mattress on the floor. Wrote to Harris. Sent the receipt for my baggage to the express office by the mail carrier. Got belts and musket of the quartermaster and cleaned them up.

[John Ingold Schermerhorn, USMC, may have known the Brother family. He was here about forty-one years old and from Middleburgh, NY, the son of a reverend. Even though he was commissioned second lieutenant from Indiana in 1858, he was part of the Schermerhorn family who settled in Geneva, NY, and befriended the Brother family when Brother's grandfather Valentine was developing the roads of Seneca, Geneva, and Hobart College. Valentine's niece Amia married a gentleman named Schermerhorn. (Johnson, 1884)]

CHAPTER 9

Boston Navy Yard

Thu Feb 9, 1865
On guard at barracks, Post No 1, 1st relief. Lieut. Lowry officer of the day. Tapley Serg't of the guard. Weather very cold. The *Wabash's* guard, about sixty men, came to barracks in the afternoon. Corporal Wharton was sent on board the receiving ship *Ohio*.

Mon Feb 13, 1865
My bag and hammock came from the express office this morning. Wrote to Henry and Mrs. Metcalf.

Tue Feb 14, 1865
On guard at barracks. Post No 4–1st relief. Lieut. Pope officer of the day. Young, Sergeant of the guard. Received a letter from Mary.

Wed Feb 15, 1865
Wrote to Mary. Weather much warmer.

Thu Feb 16, 1865
Wrote to Ed Church. About six o'clock in the evening I was ordered to get ready for guard duty at the Navy Yard. Got ready and went down to the yard. Was put on Post No 3–Paymasters office–1st relief, countersign "Stone" watch word "River." Liuet Lowry officer of the day.

Fri Feb 17, 1865
Came off guard at 9:00 AM. Weather pleasant. Perley and Murtha were sent on board the receiving ship *Ohio*.

Sat Feb 18, 1865
Second day off. Cleaned musket. Perley and Murtha came up from the *Ohio*. They like it there very well.

Mon Feb 20, 1865
On guard at barracks, Post No 4, 1st relief. Lieut. Pope officer of the day. Young Serg't of the guard.

Tue Feb 21, 1865
Came off guard at 9:00 AM went out on liberty about 12:30. Went over to Boston and wandered about until dark, meantime getting a few square meals. Got lost several times. Met McSweeney of the *Hartford's* guard in Sudberry Street. He was in citizen clothes and I think has deserted. He seemed glad to see me. Got back to barracks about seven o'clock. While in Boston bought *Dombey and Son* and *The Old Curiosity Shop*. Also a pair of shoes.

[*Dombey and Son*, a novel by Charles Dickens, includes themes about a town dependent upon a sea port economy adjusting to the competition of rail. Dickens' other book, *The Old Curiosity Shop*, is about the life of Nell Trent and her grandfather, both residents of a store in London.]

Wed Feb 22, 1865
George Washington and Henry Brother's Birthday. All work suspended in the Navy Yard. Bells ringing and guns fired off in town all day long. Weather pleasant.

Thu Feb 23, 1865
Third day off. Received a letter from Mary and one from Frank Smead. Answered both.

[The transcriber read this name as "Frank Swart," but it should be Frank Smead. Mary wrote to Brother about the visit to Bath by the Marines on furlough: Josiah C. Gregg and "Dora" Harris. "Life in the gallant Navy seems to agree with them." (*Steuben Courier*, Feb 15, 1865) Gen. William W. Averrell, another man from Bath who kept a diary of his military service, was in Bath at the same time.]

Fri Feb 24, 1865
On guard at barracks. Right wing and prisoners, 1st relief, Lieut. Daniels officer of the day. Young Sergeant of the guard. Weather pleasant.

[Charles Henry Daniels, age twenty-two, was born in Troy, NY. He was appointed acting midshipman at the United States Naval Academy in 1858 when he was fifteen. (D. Sullivan, 2019)]

Sat February 25, 1865
Came off guard at 9:00 AM. Went out on liberty about 6:00 PM. Went over to Boston, had a bath and supper. Got back to barracks about ten PM. The *Wabash's* guard paid off.

Mon Feb 27, 1865
Wabash's guard got seven days furlough. A good many of them are to report here. Wrote to Gregg. Third day off.

Tue Feb 28, 1865
On guard at barracks. Post No. 4, 3rd relief. Lieut. Daniels officer of the day. Fitzgerald sergeant of the guard. Lieut. Lowry left, bad and baggage.

Wed Mar 1, 1865
Came off guard at eleven AM. A guard of one Sergeant, two corporals and twelve privates left for the *Wachusett*. It is said she is going to China.

Thu Mar 2, 1865
Second day off. Went down to the *Ohio* in the forenoon with a party to escort some sailors to a steamer just gone into commission. Saw Perley. He tells me that Murtha is in the brig, upon bread and water, for attempting to smuggle whisky on board.

Fri Mar 3, 1865
On guard at barracks, Post No 2, 1st relief. Lieut. Daniels officer of the day. Sawyer Sergeant of the guard. Rec'd a letter from Gregg.

Sat Mar 4, 1865
Rain and cold. Came off guard at 9:00 AM. Bells ringing in honor of the inauguration of President Lincoln. Wrote to Gregg.

Sun Mar 5, 1865
On guard, 1st relief. Prisoners and night post at Navy Yard, Lieut. Pope officer of the day. Philbrook Sergeant at Barracks and Sawyer at Navy Yard.

Mon Mar 6, 1865
Came off guard at 9:00 AM. Went out in the afternoon with Leland. We went to the Boston Museum. In the evening went to see the "Nicolo" troupe of tumblers at the Tremont Temple on Fremont Street. Got back to barracks about 10:30 PM.

[Enlisted as a private in Boston, 14 August 1862, George R. Leland was severely wounded in the Battle of Mobile Bay while he was with Gregg, Smith, Oviatt, Angus, and others on the USS *Brooklyn*. He had "a bolt driven into left thigh, severe." (Department of the Navy, 1894–1922)]

Tue Mar 7, 1865
Second day off. Received a letter from Mary and one from Ed May. Answered both. Ed is on board the *North Carolina* at New York Yard.

Wed Mar 8, 1865
On guard at barracks, Post No 2, 3rd relief. Lieut. Pope officer of the day. Fitzgerald Serg't of the guard. Rec'd a letter from Ed Church.

Thu Mar 9, 1865
Came off guard at 9:00 AM. Wrote to Ed Church. Went over to Boston in the evening. Went to the "Howard Atheneum." The play was *The Workmen of Paris*. Got back to barracks at 10:30.

Sat Mar 11, 1865
On guard over prisoners and night post. Orderly Sergeant officer of the day. Sawyer Sergeant at Barracks. Philbrook at the yard. Received a letter from Gregg. He says that I am entitled to prize money from the capture of the blockade runner *Gertrude* by the *Vanderbilt*.

Sun Mar 12, 1865
Came off guard at 9:00 AM. Did not go down to inspection so of course was crossed off the liberty list. Wrote to Gregg.

Mon Mar 13, 1865
Second day off. In the afternoon went to the officer of the day for permission to go out after my boots which I had left at a shop for repairs. He gave me one hour. Went out and got a good dinner and the boots and was back on time.

Tue Mar 14, 1865
On guard at barracks, Post No 3, 2nd relief. Orderly Sergeant officer of the day. Taply Sergeant of the Guard.

Wed Mar 15, 1865
Did not go out. Wrote to Taylor–Pagnello and Huguenin.

Thu Mar 16, 1865
Second day off. Wash room orderly in the morning.

[Restrooms were not part of the interior of dwellings in those days. Water closets were installed in the Barracks for the first time in December, according to a report by Major McCawley to Major Slack, quartermaster of the Marine Corps. (Yates and Yates, 2015).]

Fri Mar 17, 1865
On guard at barracks. Post No 2, 1st relief. Orderly Sergeant officer of the day. Philbrook sergeant of the guard. As this is St. Patrick's day, all the Irish who are not on guard were allowed to go out on liberty.

Sat Mar 18, 1865
Came off guard at 9:00 AM. Did not go down to inspection so got no liberty. Wrote to Mother. At roll call at retreat the command fell in out on the parade ground.

Mon Mar 20, 1865
On guard at Navy Yard, Post No 1, 1st relief, Countersign "Chelsa." Watchword "Beach." Orderly Sergeant of the day. Corporal Mason acting Sergeant of the guard. The command out for inspection in full uniform.

Tue Mar 21, 1865
Came off guard at 9:00 AM. As I did not want to go out, did not go down for inspection. Dress parade in full uniform at barracks in the morning. Drill at 10:30. Went down into the yard in the afternoon. The *Kearsarge* is nearly ready. Will go into commission in about a week. Wrote to Ellie.

Wed Mar 22, 1865
Guard mount at 8:00 AM weather damp and foggy. No dress parade or drill. Second day off. Not much police work. Wrote to Tom Seymour and Will Brichard. Major McCawley arrived during the day. It is said he is to have command here.

Thu Mar 23, 1865
Third day off. Parade in the morning in fatigues.

Fri Mar 24, 1865
On guard at barracks, Post No 1, 1st relief, Lieut. Pope officer of the day. Fitzgerald sergeant of the guard. Parade in the morning fatigues. Major McCawly assumed command today. Drill at 10:00 AM.

Sat Mar 25, 1865
Came off guard at 8:00 AM. All hands aired bedding in the forenoon. Went out about one o'clock. Went to a photographer on Main Street on an errand for Leland. Went over to Boston and had dinner. Came back and went up to Bunker Hill monument. Returned to barracks about half past four. Went out again about six o'clock, went over to Boston and had supper. In the evening went to the Boston Theatre. Saw Lama Keene in the play *Our American Cousin*. On the way home stopped into Mose Pearson's in Hay Market Square and had supper. While there McClone came in and we went to barracks together arriving there at about 11:45.

[Pearson & Co. Eating House was a set of restaurants at 112, 114, & 118 Union Street "Lodging over each saloon." *An American Cousin* was the play President Lincoln was watching the night he was assassinated in April.]

Mon Mar 27, 1865
On guard at barracks. Post No. 2–3rd relief. Lieut. Pope officer of the day. Philbrook Sergeant of the Guard. Parade in fatigues at 8:00 AM. At half past ten knapsack inspection by Major McCawley. After that a short drill.

Tue Mar 28, 1865
Came off guard at 8:00 AM at half past twelve all hands fell in under arms, and went down to escort some sailors from the Brig *Sea Foam* to the receiving ship. When we got there we found there were not half as many sailors as there were marines who had been sent to guard them, so half of the marines were sent back to barracks. I went with the sailors to the receiving ship and then back to barracks. Wrote to Mary.

Wed Mar 29, 1865
Second day off. Dress parade in the morning. Received a letter from Mary. She writes that they have just had the greatest flood in Bath that they ever was known. Water was a foot deep in the cellar.

[That was "The Great Flood." (*Steuben Courier*, Mar 22, 1865)]

Thu Mar 30, 1865
Third day off. In the afternoon about twenty of us in charge of Serg't Phent went to escort some sailors from the gunboat *Stettin* to the *Ohio*. Last evening at retreat Corporals Mason and Wayland were read out as Sergents. Privates Wagnner and Gaul as Corporals.

Fri Mar 31, 1865
On guard at barracks, Post No. 2, last relief. Lieut. Pope officer of the day. Phent, Sergent of guard. Rain all day.

Sat Apr 1, 1865
At nine AM. All the ready and liberty men went down to escort some sailors from the *Ohio* to the *Paul Jones*. At 12:30 PM went down again to escort some sailors to the *Kearsarge*. Her guard went on board at the same time. They were Sergent Phent and two Corporals and twelve privates. In the evening went down to Charlestown bridge and got a lobster.

Sun Apr 2, 1865
On guard at barracks. Post No 5, Third relief, only three hours on duty. 1:00 to 2:00 and 12:00 to 2:00. Got a bed in the 2nd floor and moved down.

Mon Apr 3, 1865
Came off guard at 8:00 AM at 10:30 all hands fell in full uniform and packed knapsacks. Were inspected by Major McCawley. Told me to exchange my musket for one without a tape lock. Received a letter from Huguenin. He tells awful stories about

times in Brooklyn barracks with Old Jack Reynolds. Went out just after retreat. Went to Boston theatre. Saw Edwin Booth in *Macbeth*. Got back about eleven o'clock.

Tue Apr 4, 1865
Second day off. Last night about forty men came to barracks from the *Canandaigua*. A part of them were on the *St. Louis* and have been out over three years. They were put in the left wing, upper room.

Wed Apr 5, 1865
On guard at Navy Yard. Post No 1, 2nd relief. Lieut. Daniels officer of the day, countersign "Navy." Watch word "Gallant." Visiting day on the *Ohio* and a great many people going down there. Saw one [of the] old ships corporal, Tom Conner. He is going to work in the yard.

Thu Apr 6, 1865
Came off guard at 8:00 AM. Received a letter from Mary and one from Gregg. A *Courier* from Mother and *Ballon's Magazine* from Mrs. Metcalf. Went out in the evening at 6:15. Had a supper at Lane's. Went to the Boston Theatre. Saw Edwin Booth as Shylock in the *Merchant of Venice*. On the way home stopped into Mose Pearson's and had another supper. Got back to barracks about 11:30, wrote to Mary in the afternoon.

Fri Apr 7, 1865
Second day off. Dress parade and drill in the forenoon.

Sat Apr 8, 1865
On guard at Navy Yard. Post No. 2nd relief. Lieut. Pope officer of the day. Mason Sergeant of the guard. Countersign "Army." Watch word "Potomac." Weather very pleasant.

Sun Apr 9, 1865
Off guard at 8:00 AM. Did not go out. Wrote to Gregg and Huguenin.

Mon Apr 10, 1865
Second day off. In the morning we received the glorious news that Gen'l Lee and his army had surrendered to Gen'r Grant. Work was suspended in the Navy Yard. The admiral made a speech to the men and was loudly cheered. In Charlestown and Boston, bells were rung and guns fired all day. All the vessels in the harbor were dressed with flags. Everybody seems nearly crazy with joy. A salute of twenty-one guns was fired at the Navy Yard at noon.

Tue Apr 11, 1865
Third day off. Dress parade and drill in the afternoon. Wrote to Ed Smead.

Wed Apr 12, 1865
On guard at barracks, Post No 3, 2nd relief. Lieut. Daniels officer of the day. Mason Sergeant of the guard. Rec'd a letter from Father, one from Tom Seymour and one from W. J. Brichard. Weather damp and rainy. Father writes that he will try to get my discharge. Hope he may succeed.

Thu Apr 13, 1865
Came off guard at 8:00 AM. Received a letter from Mrs. Metcalf. Wrote to Father. Went out just after retreat. Had supper at "Lanes" and then went to the Boston Theatre. The house was decked with national flags and the orchestra played national airs at which the audience went wild and cheered until the house shook. Edwin Booth played *Richard 3rd*. Liked the best of anything of the kind ever saw. Got back to barracks at 11:30.

Fri Apr 14, 1865
Second day off. All hands paid off in the forenoon. I got $44.40. Went down into the yard in the PM and went on board the Monitor *Equando*.

Sat Apr 15, 1865
Third day off. A sad day for all. In the morning came the news of the shooting of President Lincoln. About nine o'clock report came that he had died. All the flags in the Navy Yard and on the vessels in the harbor are at half mast, bells were tolled throughout the cities and minute guns fired. About noon news came that Secretary Seward was dead, but it was contradicted in the evening papers.

Sun Apr 16, 1865
On guard. Prisoners and night post at Navy Yard, 3rd relief. Captain Butler officer of the day. Mason Sergeant at Navy Yard and Wayland at barracks. Received a letter from Mary.

[Capt. George Butler, USMC, was about age twenty-eight here. He was born in Washington, DC, and he served in the Battle of Fort Fisher while Commanding Marine Guard on the USS *Minnesota*. He died at the Marine Barracks at Portsmouth in 1884. (D. Sullivan, 2019)]

Mon Apr 17, 1865
Came off guard at 8:00 AM. All hands at knapsack inspection in full uniform at half past ten. Were inspected by Major McCawley. After inspection knapsacks were put away and we were drilled about an hour by the Major. Rec'd a letter from Gregg. Wrote to Mary and Mrs. Metcalf. Went out about six o'clock. All buildings draped in morning. All theatres closed.

Tue Apr 18, 1865
Second day off. About an hour drill in the morning. Received a *Courier* from Mother. Wrote to Gregg.

Wed Apr 19, 1865
Third day off. Wrote to Tom Seymour and Pagnello. Dress parade in the morning but no drill. Today is appointed for the funeral of the President at Washington. In Boston and Charlestown bells are tolling and guns fired. Work is suspended in the Navy Yard.

Thu Apr 20, 1865

On guard at barracks, Post No 3, 1st relief. Lieut. Pope officer of the day. Mason Sergeant of the guard.

Fri Apr 21, 1865

Came off guard at 8:00 AM. Went out about two o'clock. Met Leland at the depot in Haymarket square and we went to see a lawyer in Court Street in regard to getting our prize money. Left Leland at his cousin's. Had supper about six o'clock. Went to the Howard Atheneum. Miss Hellen Western the star. Got back to barracks about 11:30.

Sat Apr 22, 1865

Second day off. Camp and rainy. Received letters from Mother and Father. Wrote to Father and Ed Smead.

Sun Apr 23, 1865

On guard. Prisoners and night post, 1st relief. Lieut. Pope Officer of the day. Porter Sergeant at Navy Yard. Fitzgerald at barracks. A new arrangement at the Navy Yard now. None of the men on guard there can come to the barracks for meals or any other purpose. Their meals are taken down to the yard by the orderly detailed for that purpose.

Mon Apr 24, 1865

Came off guard at 8:00 AM. Received a letter from Gregg. The orderly Sergeant sent for me about nine o'clock and handed me a check on the Bunker Hill Bank for one hundred dollars. Said it was my bounty money, that he had been directed to pay me by Paymaster Cash. Went out about one o'clock. Went over to Boston and had dinner, bought a vest in Dock Square. Got back to barracks about four o'clock. Out again at 6:30. Had supper and went to the Boston Theatre. Saw Mr. and Mrs. Barney Williams in the *Fairy Circle* and *Yankee Courtship*. Got home at 11:30.

Tue Apr 25, 1865
Second day off. Weather very pleasant. Drill about an hour in the forenoon by Major McCawley.

Wed Apr 26, 1865
Third day off. Not much police work. No drill. Quarters inspected by the Major. Rec'd a letter from Tom Seymour and one from W. J. Brichard.

Thu Apr 27, 1865
On guard at barracks, Post No. 3, 2nd relief. Lieut. Pope officer of the day. Buckley Sergeant of the guard. Weather mild. Did not need watch coasts on post during the night.

Fri Apr 28, 1865
Came off guard at 8:00 AM. Drill in the forenoon from 10:00 to 11:00. Went out at six o'clock. Went over to Boston, had supper and went to Boston Theatre. Saw Barney Williams in *The Irish Tiger*, and *The Happy Man*, Mrs. Barney Williams in *An Hour in Seville*, in which she appeared in eight different characters. Got back about 11:30.

Sat Apr 29, 1865
Second day off. Dress parade in the morning but no drill. Rec'd a *Courier* from Mary.

Sun Apr 30, 1865
A big fire over in Sudbury Street this morning. On guard. Prisoners and night post, 3rd relief. Blake sergeant at barracks, Mason at the yard, Barney Sharpe was sent on board the *Ohio* in the forenoon. His term of imprisonment having expired. Lieut. Daniels officer of the day.

Mon May 1, 1865
Came off guard at 8:00 AM. Knapsack inspection at full uniform at 10:30. Drilled about half an hour by the Major. Received a letter from Mary. Went out about 5:30. Had supper at Lanes,

met Harris in Court Street and we went to hear Morris Brother's Minstrels. Got back about half past ten.

Tue Apr 2, 1865
Second day off. Received a letter from Pagnello, wrote to Mary and J. C. Gregg. Rec'd a *Courier* from Mary.

Wed Apr 3, 1865
On guard. Prisoners and night post at the Navy Yard. 3rd relief, Lieut. Daniels officer of the day. Fitzgerald sergeant at barracks and Porter at Navy Yard. The guards from the St. *Louis, The Canandaigua,* and the *Circassian* were paid off, and all who were not on guard got their furlough for seven days. At Navy Yard, Scotland went out at eleven o'clock PM. He threw away his belt and it was brought in by a watchman. Rec'd a letter from Mrs. Metcalf.

Thu Apr 4, 1865
Came off guard at 8:00 AM. Drilled about an hour by Captain Butler. Scotland was brought in about eleven o'clock. I went out about two o'clock. Went over to Boston, up to the common and public gardens. Bought a pair of boots in Charlestown square for $6.00. Came back to barracks about half past five. Went out again at 6:30. Went to the Howard Athenaeum in the evening. Saw Helen Western in *The Greek Corsair,* and *Paul the Pet of the Petticoats.* Got back to barracks at half past ten.

[Helen Western (1844–1868) was popular actress, native to New York, who got her starting role in *Uncle Tom's Cabin,* at the Boston Museum at age twenty-three. —*Daily Alta California,* Dec 30, 1868]

Fri May 5, 1865
On guard. Night post and prisoners, 2nd relief. Lieut. Pope officer of the day. Mason, sergeant at barracks and Blake at Navy Yard. Mason tells me that Serg't Mark has been reduced to the ranks by "Old Jack." The two Roche's were to day put on bread and water for smoking in the quarters.

Sat May 6, 1865
Came off guard at 8:00 AM. Went out at half past six. Had supper at "Lanes." Went to the Tremont Temple to see "Allyns" the wizard. Didn't amount to much. Got back to barracks at 10:30.

Sun May 7, 1865
Second day off. The two Roache's were let out in the morning. Wrote to Mother.

Mon May 8, 1865
On guard at barracks. Post No 4, 1st relief. Lieut. Pope officer of the day. Philbrook Sergeant of the guard received a letter from Gregg. Knapsack inspection in full uniform in the forenoon.

Tue May 9, 1865
Came off guard at 8:00 AM. Rain. No drill. Wrote to W.J. Brichard–Gregg, and Pegnello. Also to Captain Parker asking him to send me a statement that I was one of the *Vanderbilt* Guard when the *Peterhoff* was captured.

Wed May 10, 1865
On guard at barracks, Post No. 5, 2nd relief. Capt. Butler officer of the day, Wayland Sergeant of the guard. Mounted guard in full uniform for the first time this season. We wear it until six PM. Rec'd a *Waverly* from Mrs. Metcalf.

Tue May 11, 1865
Came off guard at 8:00 AM. Rain. No drill. Received a letter from Mary and answered it. Went out about half past five. Had supper at Lanes. Went to the Boston Museum. Got back about 12:30.

Fri May 12, 1865
Second day off. Most of the men who were on furlough reported yesterday. In the forenoon a company of about twenty of us went down into the yard to escort the *Oseola's* crew on board the *Ohio*. About noon her guard came up to the barracks. A Ser-

geant, two Corporals and twelve privates. They were assigned to the left wing, upper room.

Sat May 13, 1865
On guard at barracks, post No 6–1st relief. Capt Butler officer of the day. Fitzgerald Sergeant of the guard.

Sun May 14, 1865
Came off guard at 8:00 AM. Went out about half past five. Had supper at Lane's. Went up the common. A great many people there. Walked about until the evening.

Mon May 15, 1865
Second day off. Knapsack inspection in full uniform in the forenoon. The Mohican's men were paid off and got their furlough.

Tue May 16, 1865
On guard at Navy Yard, Post 1–3rd relief. Cap't Butler officer of the day. Ryan, Sergeant of the guard. Guard in uniform all day. Countersign "Italy." Watchword "Sicily."

Wed May 17, 1865
Came off guard at 8:00 AM. Went out about one o'clock. Went over to Boston and back, went over to Chelsea as far as the Hospital, then back to barracks. The warmest day we have had this spring. Went out again about half past six. Had supper and went to the Boston Theatre. Saw Mrs. D. P. Bowers in Elsie Venner. Got back about eleven o'clock. Rec'd a letter from Mary.

Thu May 18, 1865
Second day off. Cold and Cloudy. No drill nor dress parade. Rec'd a letter from J.C. Gregg.

Fri May 19, 1865
On guard at barracks, Post No 2, 1st relief. Capt. Butler officer of the day. Gilliand Sergeant of the guard. Cold and damp. No uniform, no drill.

Sat May 20, 1865
Came off guard at 8:00 AM. Did not go on liberty. Wrote to Mrs. Metcalf. Follet got his discharge and left.

Sun May 21, 1865
On guard at barracks. Post No 6–3rd relief. Lieut. Daniels officer of the day. Ryan Sergeant of the guard. Full uniform all day. Weather warm and pleasant.

Mon May 22, 1865
Came off guard at 8:00 AM at 9:30 went with a party to escort some sailors from the ship *National Guard* to the receiving ship *Ohio*. It rained a part of the time and we got pretty well wet. Wrote to Mary, J.C. Gregg and Tom Seymour. Went out in the evening just before tattoo. Went to Mose Pearson's and had supper. Got back about ten o'clock. Rec'd a letter from Pagnello.

Tue May 23, 1865
Second day off. Received a letter from Captain Parker enclosing a certificate that I was on the *Vanderbilt* when she captured the *Peterhoff*. He asked if the *Peterhoff*'s prize money was yet ready for distribution.

Wed May 24, 1865
On guard at barracks, Post No 4. 1st relief. Lieut. Daniels officer of the day. Wayland Sergeant of the guard.

Thu May 25, 1865
Came off guard at 8:00 AM. Drill from 10:00 to 11:00. Went out about half past one. Went up to Boston common with Huggins. Got back about four o'clock. Went out again about half past six. Had supper and went to Tremont Temple. The play was *The Streets of New York*. Didn't amount to much. Got back to barracks about eleven o'clock.

Fri May 26, 1865
Second day off. Drill from 10:00 to 11:00 AM. Wrote to the 4th
Auditor of the US Treasury asking him to pay me my share of
prize money from the *Gertrude*. Took it to the Major and he endorsed it.

Sat May 27, 1865
Third day off. Neither drill nor uniform. Rec'd a *Waverly* and
Courier from Mrs. Metcalf. L. Roach time out.

Sun May 28, 1865
On guard at barracks. Post No. 4, 1st relief. Capt. Butler officer
of the day. Ryan Sergeant of the guard. My old Shipmate Wilcox
reported here this morning. He was invalided to Philadelphia.
Got a furlough and reported here. A draft of sailors came on
from New York and went on board the *Ohio*. They came in the
North Carolina, in charge of Lieut. Bartlett. Among them were
Sergeant Sullivan, Corporal Fleming and private Melcrone.
Rain.

[Private Rufus E. Wilcox, USMC, was deemed insane. The hospital records from October 20, 1865, in Boston report "Patient broken down in
health great nervous prostration cause it is supposed by masturbation."
Along with his fighting in the Battle of Mobile Bay, Wilcox had gonor-
rhea and typhoid fever in 1863. In January 1865 Wilcox was reporting
that he couldn't breathe and that he had palpitations in his chest. Dillon
J. Carroll wrote about Wilcox's mental illness. His scholarship is part of
The Journal of the Civil War Era, part of the George and Ann Richards Civil
War Era Center/UNC Press.]

Mon May 29, 1865
Came off guard at 8:00 AM. Did not have our usual knapsack
inspection. Were drilled about an hour by the Major. Sergeant
Miller, two Corporals and twelve privates were sent on board
the gun boat *Dacotah* about one o'clock. Wrote to Pagnola. Went
out in the evening. Had supper at Lane's. Went to the Boston
Museum. The plays were *Married Life* and *His Last Legs*. Got back

to Barracks about half past eleven. Perley and McGreevy discharged. Time out.

Tue May 30, 1865
Second day off. At nine o'clock went down into the yard with a party to escort the crew of the *Tuscarora* to the *Ohio*. Got back to barracks at half past one. The guard from the *Tuscarora* arrived before us. Tom Roach discharged. Time out.

Wed May 31, 1865
Detailed for post at Paymaster's office but did not have to go down as we were not needed. Third day off. In the forenoon about twenty five men from the *Ohio* came up and fell in with us from drill. We were drilled about an hour and a quarter by Major McCawley, preparatory for parade tomorrow. Received a letter from Father and one from Tom Seymour. Father writes that he went to Washington to see the grand parade of our army, and while there went to see the Secretary of the Navy and asked to have me discharged, but the Sec'y said that so many Marines were being discharged now because their times are out, that they can't give any special discharges.

[Dates of parades were May 22 and May 23, 1865. (Welles and Welles, 1911)]

Navy Secretary Gideon Welles wrote about the parades in his diary.

[May] On the 22d and 23d, the great review of the returning armies of the Potomac, the Tennessee, and Georgia took place in Washington. I delayed my proposed Southern trip in order to witness this magnificent and imposing spectacle. I shall not attempt at this time and here to speak of those gallant men and their distinguished leaders. It was computed that about 150,000 passed in review, and it seemed as if there were as many spectators. For several days the railroads and all communications were *overcrowded with the incoming people who wished to see and welcome the victorious soldiers of the Union. The public offices were closed for two days. On the spacious stand in front of the Executive Mansion the President, Cabinet, generals, and high naval officers, with hundreds of our first citizens and statemen, and ladies, were assembled. But Abraham Lincoln was not there. All felt this.* (Welles and Welles, 1911)

Brother's father wrote to Charles, letter dated May 28, 1865.

I obtained through R.B. Van Valkenburgh an introduction to Assistant Secretary Fox and stated your case to him accompanied with a request for your discharge on the grounds first that you had not been paid your bounty & secondly that the war being over I supposed the Govt could dispense with your services.

His reply was that insted [sic] of having too many Marines they had too few and were enlisting more all the time, that they had not discharged any Marines except for other causes & he could do nothing for me in the matter. (U.S. Navy, 1971)

Thu Jun 1, 1865

Fourth day off. The Garrison fell in at nine o'clock. Marched over to Boston proceeded by the Ohio's brass band, and followed by about four hundred sailors from the Ohio. We marched to Market Street where we halted. Stayed there until about twelve o'clock when the procession came along and we fell in, taking the right. Don't know all the streets we went through but we kept up a steady march until three o'clock PM. Then we halted at the corner of Washington and Winter streets. About four o'clock we started for barracks, were pretty well tired out when we got home.

47. Gen. R.B. Van Valkenburg. Library of Congress

Fri Jun 2, 1865
On guard at barracks, post No. 1–1st relief. Sergeant Groll officer of the day. Blake sergeant of the guard. Received a letter from Mary.

Sat Jun 3, 1865
Came off guard at 8:00 AM. Went out about 1:30. Went to 140½ Main Street and sat for some photographs. Went over to Boston and up on the common. Came back to barracks and out half past four. Went out again in about an hour. Went to the Boston Theatre. The plays were *Paul Pry*, and *My Young Wife and Old Umbrella*. Saw Miss Carrie Augusta Moore the great lady skater.

Sun Jun 4, 1865
Second day off. Received a *Waverly* from Mrs. Metcalf. Wrote to Mary and J. C. Gregg. Sent a paper to Father with an account of the parade on Thursday.

Mon Jun 5, 1865
On guard at barracks. Post No. 2 Third relief. Lieut. Pope officer of the day. Gilliard sergeant of the guard. At 10:30 all hands in full uniform for knapsack inspection. Inspected by Major Mc-Cawley. We put away knapsacks and fell in again, marched out on the parade ground and listened to Lieut. Daniels read "Articles for Government of the Navy."

Tue Jun 6, 1865
Came off guard at 8:00 AM. Drill from 10:00 to 11:00 by Capt. Butler. We made a mess of it as usual when he tried to drill us. Went out about two o'clock. Went over to Boston and up on the common. Got back about half past four. Went out again after supper.

Wed Jun 7, 1865
Second day off. Was asleep at noon and lost my dinner. Received a letter from the 4th Auditor of the treasury saying that I am entitled to $64.25 prize money from the *Gertrude*. The or-

derly sergeant tells me to send it to Paymaster Cash, and he will pay it. The guard from the *Tacony* came to barracks yesterday.

Thu Jun 8, 1865

Third day off. Wrote a letter to Paymaster Cash and the Major endorsed it for me. Guard mount and dress parade in fatigue costs and caps and white pants. That is to be the dress for summer. It will be much more comfortable than the full uniforms. Drill about an hour in the forenoon by Captain Butler. Leland went out in the afternoon and got my photographs. Weather very warm. Sergeant Mason discharged.

Fri Jun 9, 1865

On guard at barracks, post No 3, 1st relief. Serg't Groll officer of the day. Gillard Sergeant of the guard. Sergeant Smith, two Corporals, and twelve privates left in the afternoon for the *Winnipec* a new side wheeler.

Sun Jun 11, 1865

Second day off. In the evening at retreat an order was read to the effect that in future, until further notice, the drill will be in the morning from six to seven o'clock, on the same days as heretofore.

Mon Jun 12, 1865

On guard. Prisoners and night post. Gillard Sergeant at barracks. Lieut. Pope officer of the day. Countersign "Kentucky." Watch word "Indiana." At 10:00 AM the command fell in in full uniform for knapsack inspection. As I was on post I got rid of it for the 1st time this season.

Tue Jun 13, 1865

Came off guard at 8:00 AM. Did not go out. Sixteen months more before I'm free. Weather very pleasant.

Wed Jun 14, 1865

Second day off. The orderly sergeant paid me my prize money from the *Gertrude*. Went down into the yard in the afternoon with Whitcomb. Went on board the *Ohio*. Saw Joe Wharton and Murtha. Joe is on extra duty for overstaying his liberty. Saw boy Gill who was on the *Hartford*. Went to the Museum and through the rope walk. Rec'd a letter from Mrs. Metcalf.

Thu Jun 15, 1865

Third day off. Drill from 6:00 to 7:00 AM. Wrote to Mrs. Metcalf.

Fri Jun 16, 1865

On guard at barracks, post No 3, 1st relief. Lieut. Daniels officer of the day. Porter Sergeant of the guard. No drill in the morning because of rain.

Sat Jun 17, 1865

Drill in the morning from 6:00 to 7:00, not the regular day for it, but as we missed it yesterday we had to make it up today. Came off guard at 8:00 AM. "Bunker Hill Day," and about as big a day here as the 4th of July. Went out at eleven o'clock with Leland and Whitcomb. We went up to Bunker Hill and then over to Boston and up on the common where there were a great many people. About noon Leland and I had dinner and then went on the common again. There was a temperance meeting there and we heard several speakers. Among them were John B. Gough, and a negro preacher named Grimes who seemed to be very popular. Afterwards we walked out to Cambridge. Saw Fort Washington, said to be built by General Washington. It is a breast work about four feet high and mounts three old 32-pound cannon. Went back to Boston on the street car. Had supper at Copeland's, the best place in town. Got back to barracks at tattoo, received a letter and *Courier* from Mary.

[John Bartholomew Gough, about age fifty in 1865, was a motivator for temperance. He was from Massachusetts. Leonard A. Grimes (1815–1875)

48. Leonard A. Grimes. Library of Congress

was the pastor of the Twelfth Baptist Church in Boston, which harbored fugitive slaves. Grimes was born free in Loudoun County, Virginia. (Simmons, Turner and Haven, 1887)]

Sun Jun 18, 1865
Second day off. Wrote to Mary and John Sutherland. Guard detail for tomorrow read out at retreat. Word passed for inspection in full uniform in the morning.

[John Sutherland (1841–1883) was the son of James Sutherland, Charley's old boss in Bath.]

Mon Jun 19, 1865
On guard. Prisoners and night post. Lieut. Pope officer of the day. Knapsack inspection in full uniform at 10:00 AM.

Wed Jun 21, 1865
Longest day in the year. I was called about one o'clock in the morning by Corporal Curtis who told me I was to relieve him. I got ready, went down to the guard room and relieved him. Corporal McCarthy who was on and was the regular relief had been taken off and placed under arrest for failing to take a bottle of whisky away from Hall when he came in from liberty. The officer of the day asked Curtis to recommend someone for acting corporal and he named me so I was roused out accordingly. Got through with the business of the morning very well. Came off guard at 8:00 AM. Did not go on liberty.

Thu Jun 22, 1865
Second day off. Went down into the yard with a party on escort duty in the afternoon. Went to the lower wharf and escorted the crew of a small steamer on board the Ohio. Then took a crew from another steamer near the dry dock. Drill 6:00 to 7:00 AM.

Fri Jun 23, 1865
Third day off. Drill in the morning from 6:00 to 7:00. Rec'd a letter from John Sutherland.

Sat Jun 24, 1865
On guard at barracks, post No. 5, 1st relief. Lieut. Daniels officer of the day. Philbrook serg't of the Guard.

Sun Jun 25, 1865
Came off guard at 8:00 AM. Rec'd a letter from Tom Seymour. Went out about three PM. Went over to Boston Common. Had supper at Hunter's. Strolled about Boston a while and then home.

Mon Jun 26, 1865
Second day off. Knapsack inspection in full uniform and white pants. Wrote to Tom Seymour and John Sutherland. Weather very warm.

Tue Jun 27, 1865
Third day off. Drill from 6:00 to 7:00 AM. Posting sentinels, receiving and c. Received a letter from Ellie with a photograph of her Charley. Received a letter from Gregg.

Wed Jun 28, 1865
On guard at barracks, Post No 2, 1st relief. Lieut. Daniels officer of the day. Philbrook sergeant of the guard.

Thu Jun 29, 1865
Came off guard at 8:00 AM. Went out about noon with Whitcomb, went over to Boston and up on the common. Went to Tony Pastor's in the evening.

Fri Jun 30, 1865
Second day off, weather very warm. No drill in the morning. It is to be on Saturday here after instead of Friday. Wrote to Mary and J. C. Gregg.

Sat Jul 1, 1865
On guard at barracks, Post No.6 , 2nd relief, Lieut. Pope officer of the day. Drill from 6:00 to 7:00 AM by Captain Butler.

Mon Jul 3, 1865

Second day off. Knapsack inspection in full uniform. Leland and Whitcomb got passes until tomorrow at 12:00 PM. There is to be a big dinner here tomorrow. For once the Marines are to have something extra.

Tue Jul 4, 1865

On guard. Prisoners and night post at Navy Yard. Cap't Butler officer of the day. The arcade decorated with bunting. Had dinner under the arcade at one o'clock. Ham and mutton, green peas, string beans, potatoes, pickles, beets, and apple, custard and Washington pies. Ale to wash it down. Pretty good dinner for marines.

Wed Jul 5, 1865

Came off guard at 8:00 AM. Word was passed at half past ten to receive Admiral Farragut. Got ready and with Leland, Petty and several others was in our room waiting for orders to fall in when the corporal of the guard came up and asked why we were there. The rest of the men had gone down and we knew nothing about it. We then went down and the orderly Sergeant was of course very wroth because on our account he had to form the company over again. Threatened to have us blacklisted. We were marched down into the yard and halted on the walk opposite the Commodore's office. In a short time some carriages came along in one of which were Admiral Farragut and his wife. They drive up to Admiral Stringham's residence.

There they got out of the carriage and after a while came down to the office on foot. As they passed us we presented arms. The drummer gave three rolls and band struck up "Hail to the Chief." We then went back to barracks and broke ranks with the warning that we would have to fall in again after dinner. We fell in again about half past one and marched down to the Ohio's landing and halted. In a short time Admiral Farragut and his wife, Admiral Stringham and wife, and other officers and ladies came along to go on board the Ohio. As they passed us we presented arms and the crew of the Ohio maned the rigging and gave three cheers. The admiral is looking well. This is his birthday. He was born in 1801. We marched back to barracks and got out uniform. I went out about two o'clock. Went over to Boston and up on the common. Got back about half past six.

Fri Jul 7, 1865
Third day off. Received a letter from W.J. Brichard. In the afternoon went with a party to escort some blue jackets from the *Ohio* to the ship *National Guard*.

Sat Jul 8, 1865
On guard at barracks, Post No 2, 1st relief. Cap't Butler officer of the day. Received a letter from John Sutherland and Ed May.

Sun Jul 9, 1865
Came off guard at 8:00 AM. At 10:30 attended church in chapel in the yard.

Mon Jul 10, 1865
Second day off. No knapsack inspection. Wrote to W. J. Brichard and Ed May.

Tue Jul 11, 1865
On guard at barracks, post No 2, 2nd relief. Rain in the morning so no drill. Lieut. Biglow officer of the day.

[Horatio Ripley Bigelow, USMC. Born in 1844, Bigelow was a few months older than Brother. He attended the US Naval Academy, reaching the rank of midshipman at age seventeen. He was one of the Marines guarding the Lincoln assassination conspirators at the Marine Barracks in Washington. (D. Sullivan, 2019)]

Wed Jul 12, 1865
Came off guard at 8:00 AM. Did not go out. Rec'd letters from Gregg and Tom Seymour. Wrote to Mother and John Sutherland.

Thu Jul 13, 1865
Second day off. In the afternoon a corporal from the *Powhatan* told me that Darling was on board of her. I tried to get down to see him but the officer of the day would not let me go. Received a letter from Mary and Mrs. Metcalf. Too damp in the morning for drill.

Fri Jul 14, 1865
On guard at barracks, Post No 5, 3rd relief. The *Richmond's* guard arrived. Lowden among them. Paymaster Cash arrived. Weather very warm.

Sat Jul 15, 1865
The garrison paid off. I received $44.40. On Liberty until retreat. Went out about 12:30. Had dinner at Hunter's. Went up on the common. Returned about half past six.

Sun Jul 16, 1865
Second day off. Attended church in the Navy Yard chapel. Wrote to Mary and to J. C. Gregg. Weather very warm.

Mon Jul 17, 1865
On guard at Navy Yard, Post No. 22nd relief. Counter sign "Herald." Watch word "Times." Lieut. Pope officer of the day. Porter Sergeant of the guard. Very hard rain in the morning so we had no knapsack inspection. A marine from the *Santiago DeCuba* tells me that Charley Kimmerle is on furlough and will report for duty here.

Tue Jul 18, 1865
Came off guard at 8:00 AM. Received a letter from John Sutherland. Knapsack inspection in full uniform at 10:00 AM. Went down into the yard in the afternoon. Asked an officer who came in a boat from the *Powhatan* to let me go on board in his boat, but he declined the honor saying it was the wardroom boat, so I suppose common people are not allowed in it. Sent word to

Darling that I could not get on board. Went on liberty in the evening, back at 10:30.

Wed Jul 19, 1865
On guard at barracks, Post no. 6–3rd relief. Lieut. Biglow officer of the day. Rec'd a letter from Joe Faulkner.

[Faulkner was wounded in action on May 25, 1864 and mustered out on June 5, 1865. A corporal in Company D of the 107th, Joseph P. Faulkner, from Bath, NY, was a printer before the war. As mentioned earlier, just as his pals were enlisting for the war, in a thirty-foot fall at work, he had significant injuries, but he'd rallied in time to enlist on August 15, 1862, and followed Sherman's March to the Sea.]

Thu Jul 20, 1865
Came off guard at 8:00 AM. Did not go out. Charley Kimmerle reported for duty in the morning. He says he got a good deal of prize money on his last cruise and was paid off with nine hundred dollars.

Fri Jul 21, 1865
Was not detailed for guard but went in Ashton's place to accommodate him. Navy Yard night post, 1st relief. Lieut. Pope officer of the day. Sent a letter to Darling and received one from him.

Sat Jul 22, 1865
Came off guard at 8:00 AM. Feeling very unwell on guard last night and today. Chills and fever. Did not go out.

Mon Jul 24, 1865
Was detailed for guard but told the orderly sergeant that I was not able to go so he put Whitcomb in my place. Have been feeling very unwell since Saturday. Went to see the doctor this forenoon and he put me on the sick list and gave me a dose of medicine.

Tue Jul 25, 1865
On the sick list. Saw Doctor Jackson in the morning and he told the steward to give me some quinine. [Used to treat malaria.]

Thu Jul 27, 1865
On the sick list. Received a letter from Mary. Wm Kimmerle came to barracks in the morning. He is a corporal now. Is on furlough and will report here for duty.

Fri Jul 28, 1865
Still on the sick list. Wrote to Mary. A letter from Gregg tells that T.R. Harris has been given a discharge. He is quite sick, supposed to be consumption. Rec'd a letter from W.J. Birchard.

Sun Jul 30, 1865
On the sick list. At 9:30 AM the command fell out in full uniform to receive Lieut. Gen'l Grant. I wanted to fall out with the rest to see the General but as I am on the sick list they would not have me. Marines marched down to and formed in line in front of the admiral's office. The Gen'l came along about ten o'clock and the workmen in the yard gave three cheers. He afterwards went into the admiral's house. The marines formed to give him a salute when he should come out, but he stole a march on them and went out at the front door, before anyone knew about it. I should think he would get tired of so much cheering and saluting.

Tue Aug 1, 1865
Came off the sick list. Leland's brother came to see him in the forenoon. A fine looking young man. Wrote to John Sutherland.

Wed Aug 2, 1865
On guard at barracks, Post No 1, 1st relief. Lieut. Daniels officer of the day. Porter sergeant of the guard.

Thu Aug 3, 1865
Came off guard at 8:00 AM. Drill in the morning from 6:00 to 7:00. Went down into the yard about 10:30 with Leland's brother. Went to the machine shop and ships houses. Saw the old ship *Virginia*. She has been on the stocks over forty years. She will probably never be launched. She is old fashioned and out of date. Returned to barracks about noon. Went up on the common. Bought a cap at Bent and Bushes. Had supper at Lane's. Went to Boston Museum in the evening.

Fri Aug 4, 1865
Second day off. Police work in the forenoon. Weather very warm.

Sat Aug 5, 1865
Anniversary of the battle of Mobile Bay. On guard at barracks, post No. 1, 2nd relief. Lieut. Daniels officer of the day. Rec'd a letter from Mary. All hands aired bedding in the forenoon.

Sun Aug 6, 1865
Came off guard at 8:00 AM. Did not go out on liberty. Wrote to Mary.

Mon Aug 7, 1865
Second day off. At one PM went on escort duty down in the yard, to take the crew of the *Kennebec* to the *Ohio*. Knapsack inspection in the AM.

Tue Aug 8, 1865
On guard at Navy Yard, Post No. 1, 1st relief. Lieut. Daniels officer of the day. Countersign "Quebec." Watchword "Montreal."

Wed Aug 9, 1865
Came off guard at 8:00 AM. Went down into the yard and on board the *Powhatan* with Corp'l Kimmerle, we soon found Darling, went out about one o'clock. Went over to Boston. Came in about five and out again at half past six, in again at ten. Received letters from Tom Seymour and Joe Faulkner.

Thu Aug 10, 1865

Twenty-one years old today. Don't feel very old, nor much more like a man than I did yesterday. On guard at barracks, post No. 6, 2nd relief. Lieut. Pope officer of the day. Rec'd a letter from John Sutherland.

Fri Aug 11, 1865

Came off guard at 8:00 AM. Wrote to the 4th Auditor of the Treasury, inquiring about my prize money from the *Peterhoff*. Wrote to Mother. Went down on board the *Powhatan* in the afternoon. Saw Darling. Went over to Boston in the evening and to hear "Brickley's Serenaders," back at 11:00.

Sat Aug 12, 1865

Second day off. Drill in the morning from 6:00 to 7:00. Received a letter from Gregg. He says there is no use trying to get a discharge before our times are out. Colonel Zeilen won't listen to it. Wrote to Gregg.

Sun Aug 13, 1865

On guard at barracks, post No 2, 1st relief. Cap't Butler officer of the day.

Mon Aug 14, 1865

Came off guard at 8:00 AM. Knapsack inspection in full uniform in the forenoon. Went out about three o'clock PM. Went over to Boston. Met Mrs. May and Whitcomb's sister. They invited me to go up there in the evening. Went up there about half past seven and stayed until ten.

Tue Aug 15, 1865

On guard at barracks, post No 6, 1st relief. Lieut. Daniels officer of the day. Drill from 6:00 to 7:00 AM.

Wed Aug 16, 1865

Came off guard at [?] AM. Went out with Whitcomb at half past eleven. We went to Mrs. May's and had dinner. Then with Mrs.

M. and Whitcomb's sister we went over to Boston. Went up to the Common and in the evening to the Boston museum. The plays were *Still Waters Run Deep* and *The Quiet Family*. After it was out we had supper at the May's and went home.

Thu Aug 17, 1865

Second day off. Drill in the morning from 6:00 to 7:00. Went down on board the *Powhatan* in the forenoon and saw Darling. Received a letter from Mary. Wrote to Mary. W.J. Brichard and J. Sutherland.

Fri Aug 18, 1865

On guard at Navy Yard, Post No 1, 2nd relief. Lieut. Pope officer of the day. Meehan sergeant of the guard. Countersign "Ontario," watchword "Huron," Received a letter from Gregg, visiting day at the yard and a great many people going in.

Sat Aug 19, 1865

Came off guard at 8:00 AM. Wrote to Gregg, T.R. Harris and Tom Seymour. Did not go out.

Sun Aug 20, 1865

Second day off. Room orderly with Bone.

Mon Aug 21, 1865

Third day off. Room orderly again. Knapsack inspection in full uniform in the afternoon. The Major not out. Capt Butler in his stead. Fenton 1st died at hospital last night of brain fever, caused it is said by having his head shaved. The guard from the *Sacramento* came up in the afternoon.

Tue Aug 22, 1865

Weather damp and rainy in the morning so we had no drill. On guard at barracks, post No 2–1st relief. Lieut. Pope officer of the day. Ryan sergeant of the guard.

Wed Aug 23, 1865
Drill in the morning from 6:00 to 7:00. Lieut. Saltmarsh joined the command. Came off guard at 8:00 AM. Rec'd letters from Mary, John Sutherland, and Ed May. Wrote to Mary and Ed May. Did not go on liberty.

[This is First Lieutenant Edward Channing Saltmarsh, USMC. He is twenty-five years old here. Born in Philadelphia, he was commissioned captain with Co. E of the 12th Regiment out of Massachusetts before his commission with the Marines in June 1862. (D. Sullivan, 2019)]

Thu Aug 24, 1865
Second day off. Drill in the morning from 6 to 7. Received a letter from Gregg. A *Courier* from Mother.

Fri Aug 25, 1865
Major McCawley's wife presented him with a boy, last night or this morning. Drum and fife laid aside for the present so as not to disturb her. On guard at barracks, post No. 4–2nd relief, Lieut. Biglow officer of the day. Rec'd a letter from Gregg.

Sat Aug 26, 1865
Came off guard at 8:00 AM. All hands aired bedding. Drill from 6:00 to 7:00 AM. Did not go out.

Sun Aug 27, 1865
Second day off. Weather warm. White pants in order again. Rec'd a letter from T.R. Harris. Wrote to John Sutherland and Joe Faulkner. At three o'clock PM an alarm of fire was given in the yard. All hands fell out under arms and started for the fire which was in the rope walk. Before we had gone far, word came that the fire was out. So back we came.

Mon Aug 28, 1865
Third day off. Knapsack inspection in the forenoon by the Major. Mrs. Major must be better for we are using the drum and fife again as noisy as ever. Two recruits enlisted in the forenoon.

Tue Aug 29, 1865
On guard at Navy Yard. Post No 1, 3rd relief, Countersign "Concord," watchword "Lexington." Lieut. Biglow officer of the day. Drill from 6:00 to 7:00 AM.

Wed Aug 30, 1865
Came off guard at 8:00 AM. Did not go on liberty. In the afternoon received a letter from Mary Becker in which she said that Ed Smead is soon to be married to a Baltimore girl, a sister of Jim's wife.

[James Smead's wife was Laura Aylor of Baltimore. The Smead Family was connected to the Becker Family through the marriage of Cornelia Dodge to Vroman Becker, a land speculator and developer. (*Manchester Democrat-Radio*, May 14, 1913)]

Thu Aug 31, 1865
Second day off. Drill with packed knapsacks in the morning from 6:00 to 7:00. Carter and I room orderlies for the day. Wrote to Ed Smead.

[Carter (1843–1929) died in Shelby Co., Alabama. But in 1922 he was living in Syracuse, New York, and listed City Directory as "William J. USMC Carter."]

Fri Sep 1, 1865
On guard at barracks, post No. 3, 3rd relief. Drill in the forenoon from 10:00 to 11:00. No more drill in the morning for this year, white pants laid away. Lieut. Daniels officer of the day. Porter Sergeant of the guard.

Sat Sep 2, 1865
Came off guard at 8:00 AM. Went out after dinner with Carter and Corporal Dayton. We went out to Mount Auburn. A very beautiful place but did not seem to me as nice as Greenwood Cemetery. On the way we saw the old elm tree under which Washington first took command of the Continental Army. Went back to Boston and had supper at Lane's. Got home at half past nine.

Sun Sep 3, 1865
Second day off. White pants once more for men on guard. Weather very warm. Received letters from Gregg and Whitcomb. Wrote to T.R. Harris.

Mon Sep 4, 1865
Third day off. Supernumerary. Received letters from Mary and Tom Seymour. Knapsack inspection in full uniform in the forenoon. Asked the Major for special liberty but did not get it. Wrote to Mary. Went down to see Darling.

Tue Sep 5, 1865
On guard at barracks, Post No 1, 1st relief. Lieut. Daniels officer of the day. Drill in the forenoon from 10:00 to 11:00.

Wed Sep 6, 1865
Came off guard at 8:00 AM. A guard of twelve privates came from Washington in charge of Sergeant Buckly, are going on board the *Powhatan*. Two Corporals and two privates go from here with them, and fourteen privates and two Corporals come here from the *Powhatan*. Vep Darling among them. Went out at two o'clock PM and over to Boston. Back at half past four. Out again at 5:30. Went with Leland to see some friends of his at Winter Hill, went out on street car. Arrived there at night and was introduced to his friends Mr. and Mrs. Whitton, daughter Emely and son George. Spent a very pleasant evening. Emely played and sang for us. We were given a cordial invitation to call

again. Walked home. Got there at 12:30. Received letters from Joe Faulkner and Ed Smead.

Thu Sep 7, 1865
Second day off. Drill in the forenoon from 10:00 to 11:00. Wrote to Gregg, Whitcomb, Tom Seymour and Ed Smead. In the afternoon went down into the yard with Darling. We went on board the *Ammonsoosuc*. She is a fine ship. 355 feet long.

Fri Sep 8, 1865
On guard at barracks. Post No 6, 2nd relief. Received a letter from Gregg.

Sat Sep 9, 1865
Came off guard at 8:00 AM. Went out with Darling about 12:30. Went over to Boston, up on the common and all around to show Vep the City. In the evening went to the Boston Theatre. The play was *The Streets of New York*. Got back to barracks at twelve.

[The popular play was written by Dion Boucicault.]

Sun Sep 10, 1865
Second day off. Room orderly with Bone. Received a letter from Mary with the news of the death of little Henry Lyon, on the 2nd inst. Wrote a letter to Mary and Mrs. Metcalf.

Mon Sep 11, 1865
Third day off. Room orderly with Bone again. Knapsack inspection in full uniform in the forenoon. Inspected by Capt Butler. The Major not out. Got special liberty until retreat, went out with Darling at 12:30. We went down on board the *Powhatan*, went over to Boston, up on the common and into the state house. Had a fine view of the city from the dome of the state house. Got back to barracks at 5:15 PM. Some prisoners came from Philadelphia to serve their sentence here. A great many men reporting here from furlough. Rec'd a letter from Ed May.

Tue Sep 12, 1865
On guard at Navy Yard, Post No 1, 1st relief. Countersign "Savannah" watch word "Georgia." Saw our old quartermaster Joe Perry and quarter gunner Harrington. Also Lieut. Jones.

Wed Sep 13, 1865
Thirteen more months to serve before I am a free man. Came off guard at 8:00 AM. Went out about six o'clock with Darling. Went over to Boston and to Morris Brother's Minstrels. Got back about 11:30.

Thu Sep 14, 1865
Second day off. Barracks are crowded because so many men are reporting here from furlough. Drill in the forenoon from 10:00 to 11:00. Big Carey reported here for duty, he has been reduced to the ranks.

Fri Sep 15, 1865
Third day off. Went to the Major and got special liberty until retreat. No drill because of warm weather. Went over to Boston. Had supper at the New England Dimsy (?) Rooms. Got back about six o'clock.

Sat Sep 16, 1865
On guard at barracks, post No. 6, 2nd relief. Lieut. Saltmarsh officer of the day. Rec'd a letter from J.C. Gregg.

Sun Sep 17, 1865
Came off guard at 8:00 AM. Went out with Darling about half past one. Walked about Charlestown a while and up to the Monument. Went over to Boston on the Cambridge bridge. Met ex Serg't Philbrook and he took us down to his place of business at 105 Blackstone Street. Had supper at Wrights. Philbrook came over to barracks with us. Went out again in the evening with Leland. We went on the street cars to Summerville and went to church with Miss Emely Whitton and her friend Fanny Ellis. Got back to barracks at half past eleven.

Mon Sep 18, 1865

Second day off. Room orderly with Bone. No knapsack inspection. Corporal Stopher on the *Powhatan* fell down a hatchway this morning about three o'clock and was almost instantly killed.

Tue Sep 19, 1865

Third day off. Weather quite cool. Corporal Stopher buried. The funeral party consisted of twelve privates as firing party, and six as pall bearers from the *Powhatan*, and twenty-six marines from the barracks with side arms. We left here about half past nine and went to the *Powhatan*. Left the ship about ten o'clock and went to the cemetery at the Chelsea Naval Hospital. There the burial service was read by the Chaplain and the body was lowered into the grave. Three volleys were fired over the grave by the firing squad and we returned to barracks, arriving there about half past eleven. No drill today. The quarters all cleaned thoroughly. Colonel Zeilen is expected here tomorrow on a tour of inspection. Rec'd a letter from Tom Seymour.

Wed Sep 20, 1865

On guard at barracks. Post No 2, 1st relief. Lieut. Saltmarch officer of the day. Dress parade and guard mount in full uniform. Colonel Zeilen, Commandant, arrived about noon. He reviewed us and inspected the garrison. Rec'd letters from Father, Mrs. Metcalf and Joe Whitcomb. Weather very pleasant.

Thu Sep 21, 1865

Came off guard at 9:00 AM. The hour for dress parade and guard mount changes from 8 to 9 o'clock today. Wrote to Father. Went out about half past five with Corporal Kimmerle and Darling. Went over to Boston. Returned in the evening. Leland's Father and Mother visited him in the afternoon. Drill in the forenoon from 10:30 to 11:30.

Fri Sep 22, 1865
Second day off. Room orderly with Wolf. No drill. Wrote to
Whitcomb and John Sutherland. Went down into the yard with
Darling in the afternoon. Went on board the *Powhatan* and *Ohio*.

Sat Sep 23, 1865
Third day off. Received a letter from Mary. All hands aired bedding in the forenoon. Wrote to Mary and Mrs. Metacalf.

Sun Sep 24, 1865
On guard at barracks, post No 2, 3rd relief. Lieut. Daniels officer of the day.

Tue Sep 26, 1865
Second day off. Rec'd a *Courier* from Mary. Knapsack inspection
in full uniform by the Major. Room orderly with Bone. Rec'd a
letter from Gregg. Wrote to W.J. Birchard.

[Gregg may have shared the news about his sister Sarah Eugenia's wedding in Bath to Capt. H. C. Plumb, who built the firm Plumb Brothers
in Des Moines, Iowa. In the 1869 Des Moines city directory, the Plumb
Brothers operated a jewelry store. (History and Business Directory of
Madison County, IA, 1869)]

Wed Sep 27, 1865
Third day off. Room orderly again with Bone. The *Powhatan*
hauled out into the stream and the *Franklin* took her place at
the dock.

Thu Sep 28, 1865
On guard. Prisoners and night post at Navy Yard. Countersign
"Pensacola", watchword "Mobile." Lieut. Daniels officer of
the day. The *Niagara* hauled in alongside the dock. Chas Kimmerle fell down stairs and was thought to be badly injured. Was
picked up insensible and the doctor sent for. Drill from 10:00
to 11:00 AM.

Fri Sep 29, 1865
Came off guard at 9:00 AM. Received a letter from Mary. Niagara's Guard came up about half past eleven. Drill from 10:00 to 11:00 AM. Went out at five and in again at 6:15. Out again at 6:30 with Leland. Went up to Winter Hill and called on the Whitton's. Had a very pleasant evening, played chess and euchre. Got back to barracks at half past eleven. Wrote to Mary in the afternoon.

[Euchre was a game invented by the Germans; it spread in popularity through America from Pennsylvania. His ancestors played this.]

Sat Sep 30, 1865
Second day off. A guard of one Sergeant, two corporals and twelve privates was detailed for the Tuscarora.

Sun Oct 1, 1865
Third day off, detailed as first Supernumerary. Three years ago today since I left home. Rec'd a letter from Gregg in the forenoon in which he says the commandant at Washington has promised to give us our discharge if we will furnish each a substitute for four years. Gregg says that he can get substitutes there so I need have no further trouble in the matter. About half past eight in the evening, Healy 1st ran out past No 3 post. The sentry was relieved and I put on in his place, 3rd relief.

[A supernumerary is assigned to be a stand-in watchman; "on call." Brother's sisters married Robert Moses Lyon and James Young. These men both hired substitutes when called to service in the August and October 1864.]

Mon Oct 2, 1865
Came off guard at 9:00 AM. Knapsack inspection in full uniform by Capt Butler. One sergeant and thirteen men sent on the Powehatan. Went out about 5:30, walked about Boston until 7:30 and then came back to barracks.

Tue Oct 3, 1865

Second day off. No drill. Went to the Major to get special liberty from retreat until 12:00 PM. Got it after a good deal of talk. Went out at about half past five. At half past six met Leland at the gate and we took a horse car for Winter hill. Got back about 10:30. Room orderly today with Stoeckle.

Wed Oct 4, 1865

Third day off. Room orderly with Boyd 2, Rec'd letters from Joe Whitcomb, W. J. Birchard and John Sutherland. John writes that sister Ellie's little boy Charley is dead.

[Ellie's son, Charles Hobart Young, died at age two on Oct 1, 1865.]

Thu Oct 5, 1865

On guard at barracks, Post No 2, 1st relief. Lieut. Biglow officer of the day.

Fri Oct 6, 1865

Came off guard at 9:00 AM. Received a letter from Mary. She writes that Ellie's little Charley is dead. Went out about half past twelve. Got measured for a suit of clothes at 765 Washington St., came in about half past three, went out again after supper. Met Leland at the B & M Depot at seven o'clock wand we went to the Mechanics fair in Faneuil and Quincy Hall's. There was a large display of manufacturers, machinery, pictures and c. and c. All well worth seeing. Got back to barracks at eleven o'clock.

Sat Oct 7, 1865

Second day off. Room orderly with Stoeckle. Wrote to Ellie, Mary, and Gregg. In the evening Marines, prisoners under sentence of court martial, came from New York under guard. They are to serve out their sentences here.

Sun Oct 8, 1865
Weather damp and rainy and so no full uniform. Orderly Sergeant Groll tells me that the Colonel Commandant has ordered that my clothing accounts be sent to Washington, as soon as I furnish acceptable substitutes for four years. The Sergeant says his own time will be out in four days and he will enlist as my substitute for four hundred dollars, but that is rather too high priced for me. A Sub can be had for less money.

Mon Oct 9, 1865
On guard at barracks, Post No 1–2nd relief. Lieut. Biglow officer of the day. Knapsack inspection in full uniform at 10:30 AM by the Major. Lieut. Bartlett joined command today.

Tue Oct 10, 1865
Came off guard at 9:00 AM. Drill from 10:00 to 11:00 AM. Wrote to Gregg, went out with C. Kimmerly at 1:30 and over to Boston. At a lodging house in Eliot Street we found two men who said they wanted to enlist and we proposed to one of them he go as my substitute, for a consideration. He seemed well pleased with the idea and promised to come over to the barracks in the morning and see about it. Got back to barracks at five PM.

Wed Oct 11, 1865
Second day off. Rec'd a *Courier* from Mary, a letter from Gregg in which he tells me that he will provide substitutes for both of us. The men who promised yesterday to come over this morning, failed to put in an appearance.

Thu Oct 12, 1865
Third day off. Room orderly with Carey. Drill from 10:00 to 11:00 AM.

Fri Oct 13, 1865
The third anniversary of my enlistment. On guard at Navy Yard, post No 1, 1st relief. Lieut. Biglow officer of the day. Countersign "Shiloh," watchword "Vicksburg." Sergeant of the guard Meehan got drunk, was asleep on watch when the officer of the day came down at 9:30 PM. Sergeant Jones was ordered out to relieve him. Drill from 10:00 to 11:00 AM. Received a letter from Mary.

Sat Oct 14, 1865
Came off guard at 9:00 AM. The garrison paid off and *Powhatan* and *Niagara*. Guards got their furlough. I received $44.40. Went out at 1:30 PM. Met Bone in Haymarket Square and we went to the Providence Depot, then to the Old Colony depot. Several of the *Niagara*'s men were there and left for New York.

Sun Oct 15, 1865
Received a letter from Gregg informing me that he has found a substitute for me, that he is enlisting and my accounts have been sent for. The orderly Sergeant tells me that an order has come for my accounts. On guard at barracks, post No 6, 2nd relief, Lieut. Pope officer of the day.

Mon Oct 16, 1865
Came off guard at 9:00 AM. Wrote to Mary and Gregg. Went out about noon. Bought a pair of boots in Hanover Street. Bought an overcoat in Salem Street. Got back to barracks at seven o'clock PM. No Knapsack inspection because of the weather being bad.

Tue Oct 17, 1865
On guard at barracks, Post No. 2, 1st relief, Lieut. Bartlett officer of the day. Drill from 10:00 to 11:00 AM but being on 1st relief I got clear of it.

Wed Oct 18, 1865

Came off guard at 9:00 AM. Went out at half past one with Kimmerle, walked about Charletown a while and then came in, went out again about five o'clock. Bought a pair of boots in Sudbury Street. Met Huggins at Scollay's building and we went to the Howard Athenaeum, got home about eleven o'clock.

Thu Oct 19, 1865

On guard at barracks, post No 1, 3rd relief, Lieut. Saltmarsh officer of the day. No drill because of the bad weather.

Fri Oct 20, 1865

Came off guard at 9:00 AM Drill from 10:00 to 11:00 AM. Went out in the afternoon and bought some shirts, collars and c. In the evening went up to 765 Washington Street and got my clothes. Got back to barracks at 7:30.

Sat Oct 21, 1865

On guard at Navy Yard, Post No. 1, 1st relief. After I had been about half an hour on post, a man was sent down from barracks to relieve me. I concluded at once that my discharge had come, and when I got to barracks found that to be the case. I was ordered to turn in my belts, musket and epaulets. Got my discharge and was paid off about noon. I packed up and left the barracks at about two o'clock, went back about six o'clock to bid the boys good bye. Leland and Huggins went to the Depot with me. I bought a ticket for New York and left on the 8:30 train.

CHAPTER 10

Bath After Discharge

Sun Oct 22, 1865

Got into New York about half past seven in the morning. Went down to the Day Street House. After breakfast took a walk over to the Brooklyn barracks. Went up to see the Becker's in the afternoon. Mrs. Mary Hotchkiss of Prattsburgh was there. Mary Becker and I went up to Central Park, took tea with the B's, leaving there about eight o'clock.

[Mary Becker was still teaching at School No. 49, located at 37th Street near 2nd Avenue, under the leadership of Frances E. A. Gutch in the 21st Ward. If Mary was inspired by Gutch, then she was attached to the National Education Association and a suffragette. The 1860 Census shows the Becker Brothers: Frank, Jacob, Adam, and their young families living in Ward 20, District 4, New York, New York. Mena Becker, Frank's wife, who became a naturalized citizen on September 27, 1865. Her declaration papers lists Jacob Becker as a witness. His address was 330 W. 36th Street. (Index to Petitions for Naturalizations Filed in Federal, State, and local Courts in New York City, 1792–1906.)]

Mon Oct 23, 1865

Went over to the Navy Yard in the morning. Got in without any trouble and went down to where the scow used to come in. She comes in now in the same place and Fitzgerald was sentry on her. The old *North Carolina* had gone out of commission and the scow now runs over to the coal dock. The marines live in a wooden building on the coal dock. I did not know many of them there as only a few of the guard left who were there when I was. Went up to see the Becker's in the afternoon. Left New York on the 6 o'clock PM train.

Tue Oct 24, 1865
Arrived at Corning about seven o'clock in the morning. Went to the Dickinson House [hotel] and had breakfast. Saw Will Whiting and a number of other boys who used to live in Bath. Left Corning at 6:46 PM and arrived at Bath in due time. Mother and Father were at home. Mary was at the Court House attending the teacher's institute. I went downtown. Saw Gregg and some of the other boys, Mr. Sutherland and John. Saw P.S. Towle and John Little at the Court House. I went there after Mary and went home with her. Gregg got his discharge a few days before I did so got home ahead of me.

[John Sutherland was three years older than Charley. He served in the 107th, Company D. Lieutenant Little wrote to Charley in August or September 1864. Little's brother William was the same age as Charley.]

Wed Oct 25, 1865
Went downtown in the morning, saw nearly all the boys. At twelve o'clock went to the Episcopal church where Carrie Bull and John Wilson were married. In the afternoon went out to Deque's with Mary and Jennie Young. In the evening went to the teachers institute with Mary.

[Ellie's daughter Jennie was four years old. John Wilson/Willson was the brother of Warren W. Willson. Warren married Susan Metcalf. John and Warren were the sons of John A. Wilson and Rebecca Minott. John and Warren also had a sister, Ellen, who may be the mysterious "Ella W." Brother mentions. She married Alonzo Hadley and, by 1883, was settled in Springville, New York. (Briggs, 1883)]

49. Mary Brother, 1867

Thu Oct 26, 1865
Met Towle downtown in the forenoon and brought him home with me to dinner. Went to the teachers institute in the evening with Mary.

Mon Oct 30, 1865
As Jim Young has gone to Ontario I stayed at Ellie's last night and had breakfast there this morning. In the afternoon went to see Will Ingersoll but he was not at home. Met him afterwards in the street, looking very badly and coughing terribly.

Sun Nov 12, 1865
Being busy visiting have not attended to my diary lately. Attended a dance at the Park Hotel Hall the evening of Nov 2nd. Had a fine time. On the afternoon of the 3rd started for Prattsburgh with Mary. Roads were very bad, arrived there about five PM. Went to see Aunt Rice in the evening. Saw many old acquaintances at Prattsburgh. Came back home on Tuesday the 7th. I cast my first vote in the afternoon, voting the straight Republican ticket. Republicans carried the state by about 27,000 majority.

Went to work at Gansevoort & Barron's store on the 8th. Am to work a month on trial. Like it very well so far. Attended church this forenoon. Went out to Deque's with Mary in the afternoon.

[Park Hotel (Bath). H.H. & J. Sahler, proprietors. (H. Child, 1867). While on liberty on September 4, 1863, Brother visited with Mr. C.H. Barron of Bath, his future employer. Banks was a merchant who lived near Mr. George Knight. Charles Haydon Barron, age thirty-eight, was the same age as Brother's sibling, Val and was with Val, actively involved as a Freemason. Mr. Barron was busy with young children in his household. "Mr. Barron was a genial and kindhearted man and especially thoughtful regarding children having a good time, and though having five of his own, he always found room for other children when there was a picnic or anything for children's amusements going on."

50. Park Hotel in Bath, NY, courtesy Steuben County Historical Society

A list of members of the Freemason Lodge "Steuben Lodge No. 112" in April 1861: "Anthony L. Underhill, L.P. Hard, C.H. Barron, Reuben Robie, James Sutherland, Timothy L. Whiting, Charles H. Barron, William W. Allen, Paul C. Cook, George H. Knight, Lewis D. Fay, Oscar J. Averill, and others. (*Steuben Farmer's Advocate*, May 17, 1916)]

~

The transcript of Brother's last diary held by Indiana University's Lilly Library stops here. The remaining chronology known and inferred allowed me to understand Fannie's poetry and affection for her father as well as her silence.

Working at Gansevoort & Barron's hardware store on Liberty Street, he was able to stand watch and visit with his old boss's tailor shop, which was next door. Brother must have felt the death of Sutherland's son in the war, but of course not as fully as Mr. Sutherland did, especially as he struggled to compete with a new tailor in town, who sold readymade clothing at cheaper prices in greater varieties.

Sutherland's store was located at 16 Liberty Street in the 1868–69 gazetteer. The W.W. Willson (Warren W. Willison) general store was located at 13 Liberty Street. (H. Child, 1868) According to the 1865 New York Census, the Brother family lived next to the James Gansevoort family.

The energetic Brother family, as always, had plenty to talk about at the supper table at 22 West Morris Street. Val, now thirty-eight, and H.H., age thirty-one, ran the mills. Cornelia (Mrs. W. B. Pratt) and Rebecca (Mrs. Robert Lyon) were still in Steuben County, raising their young families. Ellen (Mrs. James Young), Mary, and Charles were thinking about Iowa. In 1854 congress passed the Iowa Land Bill to help build the railroads. In 1855 their father purchased 400 acres in Fairfield Township, Grundy County while other friends in Bath were making connections in Clinton, Iowa, 170 miles east. While Henry Brother's sibling, Charles S. Brother, and their friends in the state assembly and back in Geneva (including the Beckers) were buying forest land for lumber in the Michigan-Toledo strip, Henry was buying land in Iowa. (*Farmers Advocate*, Jul 31, 1852; H. Child, 1868)

Charley Brother and his friends learned that their school burned down on January 29, 1866. A month later, Brother attended the funeral for his shipmate, Will Ingersoll, who died of lung disease. Ten days later, Charley's uncle, Charles S. Brother, a former state assemblyman, died in Seneca, Ontario County. Two days later, his wife died. The couple, who did not have children, were buried in the same grave. With the fever spreading, his father took some time for the bug to pass before heading back to his childhood farm to settle the estate.

Disease Prevalent

. . . but it is only lately that it may be said to have become epidemic. What was called the 'spotted fever' some years ago, of which. . . Charles S. Brother and his wife, of this town, died so suddenly about 7 years since, was undoubtedly the same disease which medical men now denominate 'cerebro-spinal meningitis.' There were a number of other cases about the same time, and the sudden fatality. . . excited wide-spread alarm.

—*Geneva Gazette*, Apr 26, 1872

In January 1867, Val and H.H. promoted their improvements at Belfast Mills, now providing custom grinding and flouring grist mill. They continued with the saw and plaster mills and announced that they accepted goods for grinding now at their feed store. This same year, Charley Brother attended the wedding and reception of his childhood friend, John Sutherland. Sutherland's brother, James Jr., later moved to Clinton, Iowa. Soon Charley's fellow Marine, P.S. Towle, was heading that way also, but he would be going with Charley's sister Mary. By December, Mary and Towle were married at St. Thomas Church and started packing for Clinton, Iowa. (Ellen's girl was born in 1867 in New York, but they were in Iowa by 1870.)

In April, someone set fire to the Brother Flour Store, next to Ed Smead's bakery.

Destructive Fire in Bath

That portion of Steuben Street (north side) lying between the Barber brick store and the Old Cemetery, was destroyed by fire early on Tuesday morning last. There were three frame buildings destroyed - The Union Hotel, Warner Cook, Proprietor, the Carter building, occupied by Van Wic Bros, Grocers, and the Flour Store and Bakery owned by Henry Brother, jointly occupied by V. & H. H. Brother, Flour Store, and E. S. Smead, Bakery. Over Van Wie's Grocery, Geo. Quackenbush had a Harness Shop, and Mr. Joseph Carter has stored there a large quantity of Wool. The fire was discovered in a portion of the Hotel buildings (formerly known as the "Star Bakery") not now used, and was doubtless the work of an incendiary.

— *Angelica Reporter*, Apr 29, 1868

Charley Brother hung around long enough to establish the Rescue Hook and Ladder Company with the boys: John Sutherland, Moses H. Tharp, T.W. Seymour, William Howell, Jr, Charles H. Lindsay, Casin Obert, and Will Dutcher joining in later. (Thomas W. Seymour was the son of a former Bath sheriff, Orange S. Seymour, who died in 1903.) But soon the boys were restless and not interested in waiting for the next fire to be put out.

CHAPTER 11

Iowa

Brother settled in Fairfield Township, Grundy County, Iowa, in May 1868. Grundy Center was the county seat and a stark contrast to Bath.

Tired of the cold and isolation, someone in Charley's same predicament, in February 1870, may have sent word to *The Corning Journal* of Steuben County, New York, calling attention to the serious lack of women. The newspaper was owned by his distant cousin, George Pratt, who was the editor from 1851 to 1906.

> *A Clergyman in Grundy County, Iowa, objects to the practice prevalent among his flock, of holding meetings and charging a quarter to kiss the girls, to raise money to pay his salary. There are some grumblers who are never satisfied.*
>
> —George W. Pratt, *Corning Journal*, Feb 24, 1870

The deprivation was amplified in March when Brother witnessed a winter storm that swept across the Dakotas through Iowa. The March 14, 1870, storm was so harsh that the German immigrants in Estherville, Iowa, 180 miles northwest of Grundy, used the word "blizzard" for the first time in print in their newspaper, *Vindicator*. The origin of the name is attributed to the early German settlers, who called the storms blizartig (lightning-like). "The lightning-like fury of these most de-

51. Charles Brother

structive and perilous winter storms are chronicled throughout Iowa history." (Waite, 1970)

That June Charley Brother, now twenty-five, worked his 400-acre farm with his partner, Ebenezer Wright Hurlbut. Already in Iowa when Charley arrived, Hurlbut may have known the Brother family through its connection to the Pratt family or through Hurlbut's ancestors from Clinton, New York. The Hurlbut children eventually became active in the Baptist church and headed further west, but for November of this year in Grundy, Brother, the Hurlbuts, and their neighbors, especially their daughters, were excited to get out of the house, and the new church was an appropriate place to congregate, even if they were motivated to flirt. According to the United States Census, 1870: Rosina Hurlbut was in the household of Ebenezer Harlbut, Iowa. (E.W. Hurlbut, 1819–1877). His son Enoch married Trilla Pratt, who became the organist for the Baptist church. Hurlbut also had a brother, Enoch, and his wife (A. Riley Pratt) were in the area before Brother, having buried two daughters in 1864 and 1865. From the Grundy County grave records for Fairfield Township Census Records: Ebenezer Hurlbut was fifty-one, born in Vermont. His wife Mary age forty-six was born in Canada. Rosina, a schoolteacher, was twenty, born in NY. Enoch was eighteen. Carissa was sixteen, born in Wisconsin. James Century Hurlbut was born in Franklin, Ohio, in 1846 and also lived in Grundy County, Iowa. There were several Hurlbut's living in Bath, NY in the 1830s but moved west in the early 1840s. (Hurlbut, 1888)

If Charley Brother was still the serious correspondent he proved to be in the war, at least the new church was something to write about to the boys in Bath. Meanwhile, Brother started 1873 in a blizzard.

> [The storm] . . .came swooping down on the city and adjacent country yesterday afternoon, about 4 o'clock. The wind blew a regular hurricane, and the air was filled with fine snow that blinded travelers and almost shut down our eyesight. . . Trains were stalled, and roofs were blown from one or two small houses on Capitol Hill. Snow was a foot or two deep and greatly drifted. (Waite, 1970)

Brother continued to hear from Bath, which was not immune to the national financial panic of 1873. He was concerned, rightly so, about its impact on the mills and how the boys were getting along–or not. Writing to Val, Charley might have taken care to joke about how the men in Grundy Center were busy establishing a bachelors' club. Val worked hard and was still unmarried.

At this time, the Hurlbut family, still living on Brother's farm, celebrated the marriage of Rosina, their daughter. Methodist minister Rev. Borroughs presided. Charley Brother must have attended this wedding and visited with one of the biggest supporters of the Methodist Church, the confident Mr. Henry Spawn. Although he lived just across the township line, Spawn had a good-sized property and family. His brothers, Lewis and William J., were also nearby, about eight miles west of Cedar Falls. All three Spawn brothers were veterans of the Civil War and members of the Grand Army of the Republic (GAR), with Henry Spawn a Freemason, like Charley Brother.

Spawn came to town after Brother, by way of Winnebago County, Illinois, but he was born in Albany County, New York. He was attached to the cavalry and was well known for breeding horses. The size of his estate, family, resources, farm, and confident personality could not be missed.

If there was nothing happening in the winter of 1874, Charley Brother would have turned to watch the February fundraiser by Mr. Spawn to bring in more support for the Methodist church. Spawn held a social at his home, south of New Hartford,. Rev. Burroughs, short on cash, was much obliged for donations to build the congregation. ("Our New Hartford Letter. New Hartford, Iowa, Feb 4, 1874" appeared in the *Cedar Falls Gazette* on Feb 6, 1874.)

About this time someone in Grundy Center sent another flare to the New York papers, crying about the poor supply of females. Sympathetic or merely entertained, *The New York Express* printed on April 14, 1864, about the sad situation, writing that the town "has 492 more male than female inhabitants. One Miss Grundy is equal to a dozen men, however."

Apparently, a lady was aware of the sad situation in Grundy County, but was not about to budge. The reply from the more progressive parts of New York, including the Finger Lakes, triggered the guy in Grundy County to vent when he got his reply: "Elizabeth Cady Stanton has a sister in Grundy County, Iowa, who is living in a state of abject married slavery, actually loves the tyrant whose name she bears, has no 'mission,' and does not want to vote." (Official Democratic County Paper, *Eastern State Journal*, May 23, 1874)

Brother gave up and turned his interests to rail. With a keen interest in any and all plans for improvements, Brother monitored any movement to begin building the line through Grundy Center. The Chicago, Rock Island, & Pacific Railroad arrived about 1877, so Brother was surely observing the surveying underway. The railroad line was first known as the Cedar Rapids, Iowa Falls & Northwestern Railway, and later as Burlington Cedar Rapids & Northern. He still had to make occasional trips to Cedar Falls, about five miles to the east, for supplies and entertainment.

GRUNDY CENTER, IOWA
Pop: 330

51 dwelling houses	1 tailor shop
2 churches	1 harness shop
3 grocery stores	1 shoemaker shop
2 drug stores	1 meat market
1 hardware store	2 restaurants
3 blacksmith shops	1 billiard salon
1 wagon shop	1 Freemason Lodge
2 hotels	1 Odd Fellow Lodge

(Beckman, 1876)

In August 1875 Charley Brother and the residents of Grundy Center prepared for the first annual county fair. Everyone knew about Mr. Spawn's good fortune with his cucumber seed sales in April, but cucumbers were not as refreshing as beer. That September the newspaper sent a message to the do-gooder temperance group:

> The proprietor of a beer saloon and billiard hall in that heretofore more than temperate town, Grundy Center, comes out in a card in the Atlas requesting all ladies who do not wish their husbands to drink beer in his saloon to notify him in writing and he will refrain from selling them 'nose paint.'
>
> —*Sioux City Journal*, Sep 1, 1875

Brother, now thirty-one years old, acknowledged in December the birth of his sister Ellie's new baby in Clinton. He accepted the reality that his brothers in Bath had to sell the mills, including 128 acres near the Kanona Depot.

But something else, and not just Christmas, was on his mind: Mr. Spawn's nineteen-year-old daughter, Esther. Born in Schoharie County, New York, Esther was living with her sister Julia and her grandparents William and Temperance in Albany, New York. Esther Spawn was now carrying Charley Brother's child.

Charley felt a nudge in his back to get married, fast. He also felt the urge to move. They announced the wedding. One newspaper got her name wrong, and different references were made to the marriage date, changed to hide the pregnancy. In pension records completed by Brother, the marriage year was 1875.

Won and Wedded

Charley Brother has sold his farm, south of here, to John Donahue, and has taken to himself a wife, Miss Esther Sharon, of Grundy Co. May success attend them is the wish of the many friends of Charley in New Hartford.

—*Cedar Falls Gazette*, Apr 4, 1876

While the newspaper stated that the couple was headed to New Hartford, they eventually made their way to Cedar Falls. In a few weeks, his brother Val would also have a simple, quiet wedding, nothing like his sisters'. Val married one of Brother's old schoolmates, the former Mary Scarvell, who was now divorced from the town drunk, Civil War veteran John Cunningham. This act meant that Val, almost fifty years old, attached himself to one of Bath's pioneer settlers, marrying someone who was Charley Brother's age. Val and his bride went with a Baptist minister

52. Esther Louise Spawn Brother

and not to St. Thomas Church. But everyone knew Mary's unique situation. She was the daughter of Thomas Scarvell, another miller in town, and the sister of Val's friend, Henry H. Scarvall, who died in 1863 in his service with the Company of the 1st NY Regiment. Due to Cunningham's erratic behavior and frequent trouble with the law, the Brother family watched her ex-husband's rants, bracing themselves.

Brother found the money he needed to relocate with Esther by selling his farm. After purchasing Brother's Grundy County farm, John Donahue of Butler County promoted his expansion of land, adding another quarter to his already numerous parcels, just over the county line, for $20 per acre, as noted in the *Cedar Falls Gazette* on April 7, 1876. That July Esther gave birth to a son. They named him Henry.

Charley Brother stayed in Cedar Falls with Esther, possibly working the county fair while his siblings traveled to Bath to celebrate their parents' fiftieth wedding anniversary. In September 1876, friends and family gathered at the same fireplace built by Ira Pratt. This was the same fireplace where Henry Brother married Ira's daughter, Mary Ann.

On this happy occasion, Charley Brother's sister Mary was pregnant but happily showing off her babes, including a toddler, named Charles Brother. Her husband, P.S. Towle, visited with his old boss from Olean, Mr. R.O. Smith, asking about the health of fellow Marine Miles Oviatt and Willard Moon Smith.

The anniversary celebration for Brother's parents was on September 20, 1876, and was noted in the *Prattsburgh News* as "The Golden Wedding" on October 12, 1876.

By May 1877, Charley Brother received word that Val and H.H. were now deemed insolvent debtors with the Belfast Mills. The Supreme Court ordered them to foreclose. About the same time, construction began on the Soldier's Home on the same grounds as their mill. Rev. Henry Beecher Stowe was there to bless the placement of the cornerstone according to the *Courier* on May 17, 1877.

That fall, Charley got news of the death of his sister Ellie's girl, Jenny, in September. Ellie was now living 70 miles north of Grundy Center. His seventeen-year-old niece was lost to typhoid fever. Family correspondence included other troubles. In October H.H. moved to Kanona, about seven miles north of Bath along the Cohocton River, operating a steam saw, this time without Val. Both were in hot water for their debts.

53. Soldiers and Sailors Home in Bath, NY, courtesy of Steuben County Historical Society

Charley and Esther Brother started off 1878 with a new baby girl. The record of Mary being born in January was noted in Brother's Invalid Pension Application, Department of Interior, Form 3-173.

AT IT AGAIN !

Having purchased the Steuben Mills in this village and resumed the Milling Business in conjunction with the sale of FLOUR AND FEED. . . At my old stand, on Steuben Street. . .I hereby invite my old customers, as well as new ones, to give me a call, promising that no pains shall be spared to do their business promptly and in the very best manner. ~H. Brother

—*Farmer's Advocate*, Jan 17, 1879

In March 1879, Henry Brother tried to sell the Bath mill operation to find cash, even improving the Steuben Mills, putting in a new saw and stronger power, making it more attractive. Val and H.H. were still restructuring their debt, sending notice to the paper for their creditors in May. In August, the Belfast Mill was razed for the new Soldier's Home.

Against these dramatic scenes, Brother reviewed the results of the Steuben County elections. His sister Cornelia's husband, William B. Pratt, was running for state senator with the Democrat Party. That November Henry Brother had to stifle his political views to keep the family "getting along." There was nothing Charley could do about it in Iowa, and Esther was pregnant.

That winter Charley Brother welcomed another daughter: Frances, born on February 22. The little girl deserved an extra special kiss as she joined the ranks of those sharing her birthday: his father, Henry Brother, and George Washington. They called her "Fannie."

A month later Brother accepted the news about sale of the Steuben Mills flour mill to L.B. Joy of Buffalo for $8,000. Other than Jenny's death, things were looking good enough in Iowa that Charley's sister Ellen determined to stay in Clinton for good. Ellen M. Brother Young and her husband, James Young, moved to Clinton Iowa in 1880, according to his obituary.

That summer H.H. was moving on too, but still in Steuben County. Living at Orlando Martin's National Hotel and tavern in Kanona, he boarded next door to the infamous Carrie Dawson, whose brother-in-law ran the joint. H.H. was growing fond of her.

Once a well-known teacher, Carrie was a better-known victim. In 1870, while living with a family as a private tutor, she was too pretty for the matron of the home. In the middle of the night, men in sheets came for her and pulled her out of the house. They ripped of her clothing, tarred, and feathered her for being shapely. Carrie testified that she was only tutoring the children and not crossing any lines. The trial was written about in detail in the *New York Express*, July 28, 1870: "Mob attacked Carrie, 'a well-shaped woman' in Cohocton at the home of Mr. John Curtis."

Carrie believed that she would finally be safe in Kanona, surrounded by her sister and travelers, more or less. But she knew that she could be even more safe with a Brother boy, the son of a sheriff. All the Brother boys married late in life to women who needed protection of some sort. According to his obituary, hotel owner Orlando Martin (1858–1907) was "for many years" the proprietor of the National Hotel at Kanona and "removed" to Rochester, NY, in 1897.

54. National Hotel in Kanona, NY, courtesy Steuben County Historical Society

Charley's friend Casin B. Obert announced his marriage on June 9, 1880, to Charley's niece, Anna Pratt Lyon, in Bath. The couple would someday update their plans to move to Iowa—and Charley was thrilled to have another level of support.

The boys in Iowa were doing well. Towle, still in Clinton with Charley's sister Mary, was having success with gold and silver mining ventures. Towle's investors included the old Brother family friend, Moses H. Lyon, and Jim Young, who married sister Ellen. The Youngs now lived in Clinton at 836 6th Ave., just a few houses down from the Towles. The 1880 Census reported that P.S. Towle and family were living at 792 6th Avenue with twenty-five-year-old Irish servant, Rose Maloy.

Meanwhile, Charley and Esther Brother farmed sixty-seven acres in Cedar Falls.

Charley stayed in touch with the boys from Bath. His good friend W.W. Willson became county clerk in January 1881, having sold his store to Brother's friends, Ed Church and Casin Obert. If Brother wanted to get back home, wear a suit and vest, get off the farm, he had friends in the know. Something else was doing for Charley Brother. The *Steuben Advocate* reported on January 5, 1881: "Business Changes: Bath is to have several business changes during the coming month. Mr. W.W. Willson goes out of the dry goods business and Messrs. Church & Obert will occupy the Willson store." By 1890 W.W. Willson was in Washington, DC, after his time in the late 1880s as clerk of the Steuben County Court.

That March, Charley and his young family watched a blizzard shut down the railroads, blocking fuel and food.

March 1881 Blizzard report by Dr. Gustavus Hinrichs, Iowa Weather Service

...high winds caused immense snow drifts which 'completely blocked even the oldest and best east and west railroads for a day or two and stopping all traffic on the other lines for a much longer time.' He further states that continuous snow cover 'till the latter half of the closing decade of March gave us over one hundred days of good sleighing, but also much anxiety in regard to the final breakup.' (Waite, 1970)

The Robert Jolley Family, who tried farming in the region about this time, described Woodbury, Blackhawk County, Iowa. Jolley's son Sidney was just starting out. His father urged him to head further west to better conditions, writing, "There is not enough grass to bury and cover a bird Ass." The area was not to be farmed and he would not even take it as a gift. (Jolley Family Papers, Special Collections and Archives, The University of Iowa Libraries)

The situation called for a change in scenery. Charley took off for Bath in September, visiting in time for the county fair, catching up with all the goings-on: Mary was already there when he arrived, arriving weeks before. Val pushed a bakery booth: "He will give you good eating and plenty of it." H.H. was occupied with his own mill in Kanona. He called the business Excelsior Mills and planned to make cider, promoting his place as the "Cleanest mills in the county" according to the *Prattsburgh News* and other local papers in 1881.

While in Bath, Charley Brother called on Ed Church, now thirty-six and overwhelmed with grief over the death of his wife, the former Augusta Bull, leaving him with three small children. The funeral was at St. Thomas. Ed could use a real friend for sure, but what he needed now was a business partner. In March 1882 he tied himself up with their good friend Casin Obert, who was "a character of unusual force and eminence." They promptly promoted their fresh merchandise, selling new stock of carpets. (Wolfe, 1911)

About this time, Brother heard of the death of his cousin, Peter Schuyler. Pete was fifty years old and had become an express messenger attached to the Erie railroad, assigned to the line between New York City and Hornellsville in Steuben County. Pete was also related to Brother's former shipmate, William G. Johnson, who was an express agent before the war like fellow Marine John K. Murdoch in Ithaca, New York. When Brother learned of Schuyler's death, it stirred in him the thought of a new career, another prize or better gig, something other than the pace of things on the farm.

In 1882 Brother learned more about the whirling of the fates. Valentine was reaching for a more predictable situation, taking a cashier job in April, working at the Bath store of J. & J. C. Robie. Right after the Civil War, Robie had been a competitor of Brother's pal W.W. Willson. Then in September, Brother got the news about the death 95 miles south of him in Iowa City. His friend George P. Hess, the brother of his late shipmate, William Hess, and the son of Charley's godfather Hiram R. Hess, killed himself, unable to cope with the grief after the drowning of his sixteen-year-old son.

When Brother returned to Bath that October, I wondered if he mentioned it to his folks. His father was good friends with George's father. It would have been something else to talk about other than his own unraveling domestic situation, which he kept to himself along with the stress with the farm, the blizzards, the kids, and Esther, who was becoming more and more strange. She was probably just exhausted.

In February 1883, back in Cedar Falls, Iowa, the Brother house caught on fire. Charley ran through the house to save what he could, including his Civil War diary. Fannie, only three years old at the time, survived to tell her grandchildren, many years later, that her earliest memory was being thrown out a window. Fannie's grandchildren knew so little about her childhood, but this snippet of her being tossed from a window was so rare that it was successfully passed down in oral history.

FARM HOUSE BURNED

The dwelling house of Charles Brother, 5 miles east of town, caught fire from the kitchen stove pipe on Wednesday morning of this week and burned to the ground in one hour and fifteen minutes. Through the efforts of Mr. Brother, and the timely arrival of near neighbors most of the furniture and contents of the house were saved. Mr. Brother had no insurance on the house at the time of the fire, his policy having expired some two weeks previous

—Quad-City Times, Feb **13, 1883**

Charley Brother's mother Mary Ann died in April. He stayed in Iowa; Esther was pregnant. Later in April, Brother would have also learned of the death of his godfather, Hiram R. Hess (and father of his shipmate William Hess).

The next month Brother heard of the death of Bath boy, John Sutherland, who was only forty-two. He had helped Brother and the other boys of Bath establish the Grand Army of the Republic (GAR) post and the fire company in Bath after the Civil War.

Closing out one of the worst years of his life, Brother kissed his new baby girl. They named her Cornelia.

In February 1884 Val was elected a Justice of the Peace in Bath. From his position, Val monitored the situation with his wife's ex-husband, John Cunningham, who had been arrested at least four times the previous year for drunk and disorderly conduct.

In April H.H. married Carrie Dawson in Kanona—one full year after his mother's death. He was forty-eight years old.

Newspaper articles do not mention his bride's name or his residence at the saloon:

"Local News: Mr. H.H. Brother is no longer a bachelor." (*Steuben Advocate*, Apr 30, 1884) and "Orlando Martin of Kanona pleaded guilty to indictment for violation of excise law. Fined $50." (*Corning Journal*, Oct 14, 1880) The obituary for Carrie Dawson Brother shows that Mr. Martin was her brother-in-law, so Carrie was living with her family at the hotel.

Brother's family would have read in the papers about a bigamist who was caught while keeping a room at this hotel in Kanona and other colorful characters. The way of life for H.H. was not as polished or programmed as that of his siblings. (*Steuben Advocate*, Apr 12, 1882).

With his children settled and his strength and color coming back after the death of his wife, Henry Brother, now eighty-three, took off for Iowa. This was when Charley Brother applied for employment as a railway postal clerk on the Cedar Falls & Des Moines Line. The position offered adventure, travel, respect, and nice benefits. A political appointment, the job was competitive, required quality references and rigorous testing.

In June of 1884, while trying to focus on this new prospect, run the farm with young, crying children, and monitor the moods of an overwhelmed wife, Charley Brother and his father took on long conversations on the porch. They also read urgent news from Bath: H.H. was dead.

We are pained to record the death of Henry H. Brother, of Kanona, on Saturday last. But a few days ago he made us a visit, and complained of being seriously afflicted with rheumatism, so much so that it was difficult for him to walk. On Saturday last he attempted to step over the moving carriage in his sawmill, stumbled, and by some manner was thrown against the rapidly moving circular saw. In less time it takes to pen this paragraph his body was severed in twain. He leaves a wife to whom he was but recently married, the sad news of her husband's untimely death almost driving her frantic. The funeral was on Monday last. Mr. Brother was the son of Henry Brother, of Bath, his aged father being now on a visit to other children of his family in a western state.

—*Steuben Advocate*, Jun 25, 1884

Brother put his father on a train back to Bath. Charles could not go. He was locked in his farm and ongoing fight for an exit from the hell he was going through at home.

More than overdue, Charley Brother got some good news. He won the prize—he landed the job as a railway postal clerk. US Senator William Bremmer Allison and US Congressman David B. Henderson signed off on a recommendation for his route on the Cedar Falls & Des Moines

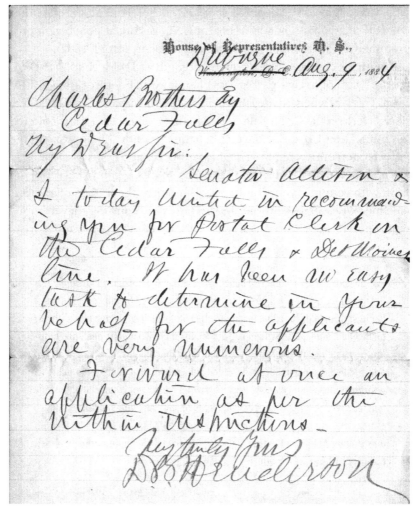

55. Postal clerk recommendation letter, August 1884

Line, stating, "It has been no easy task to determine in your behalf for the applicants are very numerous."

This letter of recommendation for postal clerk remains in the family archives, dated August 9th.

In Iowa, Charley Brother threw himself into work, committing to memory the fine and frequently changing details of postal schemes:

shorthand, codes, symbols, jargon, and regulations. Brother learned to multitask with great speed, while learning the order of small towns, reading faint letters in cursive handwriting in poor light, always adjusting for changes to arrival times due to weather, mechanical failures, and human errors or illnesses. Charley Brother stood like this for years, moving rigorously, in all weather, with all the grime and rackety noise of the rail. He worked the Dubuque-Sioux City railway route with salary of $1,000. (United States, 1885)

Years later, in better conditions, the job of a nineteenth century rail mail clerk was described:

> There is no position in the Government more exacting than that of a postal clerk, and no one that has so many requirements. He must not only be sound 'in wind and limb,' but possessed of more than ordinary intelligence, and a retentive memory. His work is constant, and his only recreation, study. He must not only be proficient in his own immediate work, but he must have a general knowledge of the entire country, so that the correspondence he handles shall reach its destination at the earliest possible moment. He must know no night and no day. He must be impervious to heat and cold. Rushing along at a rate of forty or fifty miles an hour, in charge of that which is sacred-the correspondence of the people. . . .
> (Cooley and Clarke, 1890)

The working conditions for Charley Brother and his rail mates were more dangerous, including reaching out to a moving train to grab the fresh mail bag. The worker's shock absorbers being built in and organic: the knees, hips, and sense of humor. The boys felt it in their bones and lower back when anyone failed to perform as a team. Work was loud and busy. One wonders if there was much opportunity for conversation. Brother made good impressions and steadied on, still with no sign of motion sickness.

In the *Common Book of Prayer*, handed to Charley Brother by his mother before his departure from Bath on his way to join the Marines in October 1862, and something that survived the fire in 1883, I found an undated newspaper clipping about the Diagonal line: "Chas. Brothers is working into his new position as postal clerk on the Diagonal route in good style, and if hard study and close application to business will win, Charlie will be sure to hold his end with the best of them in a short time." (I found a road named "Diagonal Road" in Grundy Country on a modern map of Fairfield Township.)

In June, Val was dead. He was fifty-eight years old with a wife and two young girls, living at his childhood home on Morris Street with his father. The newspapers varied the details slightly. The *Steuben Courier* on June 12, 1885, said Val died at midnight Tuesday from typhoid fever, which triggered pneumonia. Another newspaper wrote that Val died from pneumonia at age fifty (*Bath Plaindealer*, June 13, 1885). With Val's death, Charley Brother was aware that such an ending closed a paternal line, leaving him as the only living male Brother descendant, and the only one with a boy child.

Soon after this news, Charley took off. Something was going on in Dubuque, perhaps training for testing or work, a veteran's reunion, or some much needed rest. Maybe he was getting treatment for Esther. He booked a room at the Lorimer Hotel for a week. Charley Brother's stay at a hotel was printed in the *Daily Times* on June 14.

In August that year when a state census worker took down the names for the household, they listed the name of the lady of the house as not Esther but "Charlotte."

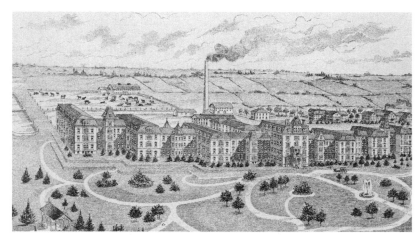

56. Hospital for the Insane, Independence, IA. Library of Congress

In early December, Charley Brother took Esther to the board of commissioners. They labeled her insane and ordered her to the state hospital in Independence. Hospital admission records noted that Charley Brother reported that his wife used to be a good woman and housekeeper. He said her decline began in 1880. He added that Esther's mother was also insane. And his in-laws, by the way, were "intolerable."

Esther L. Brother, a R.R. Postal Clerk's wife. Born in NY. Age 30

Has had five children. Age of youngest 2 yrs. [Esther had only four children survive to adulthood. Brother never indicated having more than four kids.]

Five years ago, began to have spells of being crass, unreasonable, and irritable.

For more than a year has had delusions that her husband was not the man she married but his twin brother. (He has no brother). That a waif found the door step by a neighbor was a child of hers, believing that she had twins at her last confinement & the Dr. attending her had taken one to this neighbor.

In the last 6 mos. She has lost her interest in her children & household affairs. No adequate cause assigned & case tending towards dementia.

Father badly balanced. Mother hysterical. (Hospital records Dec 2, 1885)

[New Entry, no date:]
Has behaved very nicely since admission. Says her husband has no brothers living, has never had twins. That her health was not good and she could not do as much work as formerly but all she needed was change and rest.

A week after Brother left Esther in the hands of these strangers, the railroad mail service published a change in clerk assignments. He was transferred to Sioux City. Going into the career, Brother understood the

57. Main Building, Iowa Hospital for the Insane. Independence, IA. Library of Congress

political nature of the job: administrative turnovers were common after elections.

It is impossible to know if Charley committed Esther because he was being transferred and it's doubtful that he had any influence to request the transfer, unless perhaps to get further away from the situation or closer to people who could help him watch the children, now ages nine, seven, five, and two.

Winter was coming, and Charley Brother had a new situation, a new route, and a new schema that he had to commit to memory very quickly to keep his job and hold it together. The work, even the agitation of it, hitting him from the other side of life, and of course the boys helped him hang on. Details of the typical demanding workday of a railroad postal clerk are described well in the article "Railway Mail Service: A Review of the Workings of This Important Branch of the Postal Department." Someone like Charles Brother could have written it.

> The routes centering at Sioux City are nine in number and to do the work thereon thirty-two men are employed. Of these, seventeen are appointed from Iowa, ten from Minnesota, three from Nebraska and two from Dakota, and since the new administration came into power there has been at least a dozen changes from various causes, the first removal being that of C.B. McHendy, of Dubuque, whose place was filled by the transfer of Chas. Brother from Cedar Falls and Des Moines railway post office.
>
> —*Sioux City Journal*, Dec 12, 1885

A blizzard came in January 1886, suffering the greatest loss of life of any storm in Iowa's history, killing twenty people. (Waite, 1970)

The nurses reported on January 30: "Esther was very despondent, countenance dejected, doing little or nothing. Said cared nothing for husband for he does not care for her but will live for her children."

By February 28, the hospital logs were updated. Esther had "cheered by again, is jubilant and industrious."

In March, Brother headed to Independence to bring Esther home. She promised the nurses that she would come back, and she was back by the end of the month. The hospital log for March 8, 1886: "Went home with husband on visit promising to return." And on March 31, 1886: "Returned."

But the trip caused a disturbance. The nurses reported that Esther "has tried to keep up but today is melancholy, talking to herself."

In May, Brother checked on Esther again. Hospital log for May 31, 1886: "About two weeks ago gave Black cohosh which did not seem to agree with her and was in bed several days, is better now; visited by her husband today." (Black cohosh is an herbal option for those low of estrogen.)

Exhausted, Brother let the housework slide. In October he was sick with typhoid fever. Bath was put on notice to send prayers: Brother was "seriously ill." Word reached Clinton too, and his brother-in-law and fellow Marine P.S. Towle rushed to Brother's side. Towle must have seen quite a sight. The situation in the Brother home had seen better days. Towle stayed until Brother turned a corner, perhaps doing a load of dishes himself. The *Clinton Morning News* on October 20, 1886 reported, "A few days since Mr. P.S. Towle received a telegram from Cedar Falls this State, announcing the dangerous illness of Mr. Charles Brothers [sic], brother of Mrs. Towle. Mr. Towle went at once to Cedar Falls and remained until Monday, when he returned home, Mr. Brothers [sic] being greatly improved and in a fair way to recover."

As Charley recovered his strength and coloring in early November, perhaps well enough to cut some wood or clean up the place, he had to tell the children: Esther was dead. Brother's pension records specify Esther's date of death was November 6, 1886. She died from complications from Bright's disease and pneumonia.

Details of the next order of events remain a mystery. Brother arranged for his boy Henry, now ten years old, to live with relatives close to home, but it is unclear which relatives. Because the boy was experienced with the farm and because he later in life became a successful livestock trader, Brother most likely sent his son to live with Esther's family in Pomeroy, Iowa, or near the region of Brant Lake, South Dakota. (Family oral history instructs that Henry was sent to Esther's family farm.)

Concerning the girls, Charley, now forty-one, had to pull some strings, which were in Bath. Capt. John F. Little, about forty-six years old, was the Bath town supervisor and would have been a friend to Brother in such circumstances. Five years older than Brother, he was

58. Sarah Lyon Davenport, courtesy Steuben County Historical Society

studying law when the war broke out. Brother's diary mentions Little on September 5, 1864. Little's father, William, was an Irish farmer and John's brother, William Little, Jr., was the same age as Charley. Capt. John Little married the daughter of Rev. Howard, rector of St. Thomas

59. Davenport Home for Orphaned Girls, courtesy Steuben County Historical Society

Episcopal Church, and served as vestry alongside Charley's father, Henry Brother. Capt. Little was Bath's Town supervisor 1883–1885. He eventually served the state of Florida during reconstruction, treating the residents well and helping to establish the first school for African Americans. (Weinfeld, 2012)

News about Brother's situation reached Sarah Lyon Davenport. Three years behind him in school, she was an old family friend, attending St. Thomas. Her older brother was Robert Moses Lyon (1823–1903), who married Charley's sister Rebecca. Charley spent time on the Lyon farm as a child and knew Sarah. She married into the wealthy Davenport family and became Trustee of Davenport Home for Girls, the family's orphanage. In 1884, she was appointed to NYS Charities Aid Association.

Charley Brother's girls were soon enrolled at Davenport Home for Orphans, where they could and would receive a quality education and trade. These arrangements were against the rules, for the orphanage was meant only for those who lived in the region. Brother was grateful for the accommodations. He likely paid for the arrangement. This allowed him to focus on getting the girls ready to travel to Bath. They had a lot on their minds. *What will it be like? What will happen? Did you pack my dolls? Will we ever see this place again? Will we ever go back?*

In the spring of 1887, Mary was nine, Fannie seven, and Cornelia was three and a half years old. The orphanage required new girls to be at least five years old. Relatives in Bath looked in on the girls. They would be alright and Brother assured them that his girls would benefit from the situation: Fannie and Cornelia could learn dressmaking; Mary could learn how to be a schoolteacher.

MY MOTHER
by Frances "Fannie" Brother Toyne

Who made my first pair of pants
'Twas not my cousins nor my aunts,
'Twas she who tucked me into bed
After my answering prayer was said
Lulled me to sleep the while she read.
'Twas Mother

Who always saw some good in me
'Twas not my Dad or sisters three
'Twas she who washed my hands and face,
So Dad could go right on with "Grace"
And I'd not be sent from my place
'Twas Mother.

And who was there as I older grew
And thought I knew a thing or two,
Would be awake most half the night
In order to turn out the light
Who prayed that I would go alright
'Twas Mother.

And who when all the world went mad
Sent forth the only son she had:
But I could see her mouth tight set

And I fight for her—you bet
I've not grown weary of fighting yet
'Twas Mother.

And as I cross the Great Divide
With awe approaching the other side
Who think you there will welcome me
And stand aside that I might see
Who blazed that upward trail for me
'Twas Mother.

Brother returned to work in February, taking on the mail route between Sioux City and Dubuque, accommodating the new administration and their political preferences alongside people he could trust. People like Comstock. He and other clerks learned about Brother's status in the paper: "Chas. Brother, mail clerk on the Sioux City & Dubuque line has so far recovered from his illness as to be able to resume his run." (*Waterloo Courier*, Feb 9, 1887.)

George Erwin Comstock, forty-seven, who also kept a diary of his Civil War experience, served with the Iowa 12th Volunteer Infantry, Company C. A prisoner of war, Comstock wrote beautifully about his love for his fellow soldier, knowing he survived starvation and near death only for the sacrifices made by his fellow brothers and the grace of God. They knew how to stick together then and now. (Genoways and Genoways, 2001)

By April, Charley Brother was in trouble: "The postal clerks on the Dubuque & Sioux City day run who were invited to resign a short time ago are W.E. Harriman, G.E. Comstock and Charles Brothers. All are old clerks and they express the determination to stay in the service until their pay is stopped, which will probably be in a short time. The Democrats are just as hungry now for the places as they were two years ago."

Charley's friends at the newspaper reported the situation with a twist:

> It is reported that G. E. Comstock and Chas. Brothers, two of the 'offensive partisans,' left in the mail service on the Illinois Central, have been relieved. These were among the best men on the road and Mr. Brothers has been sick nearly all winter.
>
> —*Fort Dodge Messenger* via *Daily Times*, Dubuque, IA, Apr 28, 1887

In May Charley's father Henry Brother died. Five days later, working the day shift on the Illinois Central line, he was on the drop list again. While his siblings headed to Bath for the funeral, Brother kept plodding in Iowa. (*Steuben Courier*, May 27, 1887).

In June 1887, Brother felt the change in political appointments in Dubuque. Mail clerks were reassigned. He was on the list.

> . . .Charles Brothers, one of the few remaining "offensive partisans" in the mail service, has received notice that his salary has been stopped and his future services would be dispensed with. . .
>
> —*Waterloo Courier*, Jun 15, 1887

In July, Brother finally headed to Bath, staying with his friend Obert (In late 1882, Obert bought the old three-acre Van Housen property). Obert had been a witness to Charley's father's will. Here he learned of a scandal at the soldier's home in Bath, which infuriated him. He monitored the drama with strong opinions about the failed quartermaster. Surely he could do a better job for his brothers.

Charley Brother was likely still in Steuben County for his birthday in August. He was in Prattsburgh that September, visiting his sister Cornelia, who was planning another wedding. He told her of his recent land purchase in Pomeroy, located about 100 miles west of Grundy. Perhaps he was using some of his inheritance to do something nice for Henry, who was about the same age, eleven, that Charley was when his father bought all that land in Grundy. Maybe the point of buying land in Pomeroy was to give his boy something to focus on and aim for, something to do to cheer him up—maybe it could do the same for him.

Esther was from Pomeroy and her grandfather William still there, although old and dying. Platted in 1870, folks in Pomeroy thought the rail would come through. The land was originally part of a contract with the Iowa Railroad Land Company. Pomeroy was in Butler County, Iowa. The Steuben county newspaper wrote that Brother was still living in Cedar Falls, Iowa. Perhaps it was hard to keep up with him. "Chas. Brother of Cedar Falls, IA., is visiting his sister, Mrs. W. B. Pratt." (*Prattsburgh News*, Sep 1, 1887)

Concerning his next move, Brother must have been reviewing his inheritance and aware of the Spawn family estate in Pomeroy. In February 1888 Lewis Spawn, Esther's uncle, announced that he was on his way from his home in Sioux Falls, South Dakota, to say goodbye to his dying father, William Spawn, in Pomeroy, Iowa. (Sedgwick Brothers and Stilson, 1887)

Still in Steuben County for his niece's wedding that October, Charley Brother enjoyed seeing old friends and spending time with his girls, who probably enjoyed their cousin's wedding and festivities. Mary Brother Pratt was a very pretty bride.

The scene was laid at the old time homestead which dates from 1817 and was built by Capt. Joel Pratt, who gave the town its name. It has been held in the family ever since - at this time in the third generation. The wedding Wednesday was the first one occurring in the house and happened to be on the 66th anniversary of the first birth therein.

Out from the laden and leaky clouds of several preceding days came bright sunshine during the festivities, making yet more lustrous the glistening, gorgeous hues of autumn with which groves and forests were decked.

—Steuben Courier, Oct 7, 1887

Charley also attended the wedding of his niece, Helen Gansevoort Brother Lyon, and said hello to the Davenports who also attended. Helen was Rebecca's daughter. She married the son of a long-time Brother family friend: Mr. William W. Allen, who was the cashier at the First National Bank of Bath. Besides visiting his girls in the orphanage, Charley visited the GAR chapter in Bath. He was still a member and of course saw all the boys, renewing friendships and catching up on all the changes. He enjoyed seeing the improved facilities and their beautiful grounds of the Soldiers Home, which overlay on the site of the old Brother family mill and scenic views of his childhood. (J. Sullivan, et al., 1927)

Back to Iowa by April 1888, Brother headed to Dubuque and booked a room at the Merchant's hotel. Perhaps to win back his job?

In September 1888, Brother visited Bath, picking up five-year-old Cornelia from the orphanage, taking her to Prattsburgh, and showing her the county fair. He waited for his father's estate to be settled.

The *Prattsburgh News* on September 28, 1888, noted: "Steuben County Fair: The 35th annual Exhibition of the Steuben County Agricultural Society, opens at Bath on the 25th inst., and continuing for four days, bids fair to be the grandest show this society has ever given."

In October the Brother estate sale was postponed by thirty days. And by May of 1889 he got his old job back.

> J.E. O'Brien, of Williams, has been appointed postal clerk on the Dubuque and Sioux City line, in place of D.B. Conway, of Fort Dodge; and Charles Brothers, of Cedar Falls, has been appointed in place of J.J. Pentony, of Manchester. Mr. Brothers [sic] was an old clerk on the same line, and has been out about two years. All the appointments now made are dated back to April 29th.
>
> — *Prattsburgh News*, Sep 28, 1888

Charley was in Bath for Memorial Day and he made sure that the newspapers shared the good news that his old position as chief railway mail clerk had been restored: he would be working again along the

Dubuque & Sioux City, Iowa, route. *The Steuben Courier* in May 24, 1889 wrote, "He has been spending a number of months in Bath, his former home."

Charley Brother wrestled with his situation. Admission procedures for girls in the orphanage required guardians to surrender custody, but it is unclear if an exception was made for his case. But he was tiring of the political nature of his railway job. In August he applied for the quartermaster job at the soldiers' home. A week later his railway superiors gave him a new assignment.

Cedar Falls Items

Chas. Brothers has been transferred from his former run as postal clerk on the Illinois Central and now runs from Sioux City to Egan, Dakota. . .

—Steuben Courier, Aug 16, 1889

In November, Brother headed to Clinton, Iowa, to visit his sisters Mary and Ellen. Mary was occupied with her application for membership with the Daughters of the American Revolution just a few months after the organization was established. (DAR, 1899)

The following spring, Brother entertained himself with the GAR in Sioux City. He would not have missed the perfectly timed death of Captain Lidick. The veteran and railway foreman died in time for his body was wrapped in the American flag and incorporated as part of Memorial Day ceremonies. The GAR provided a special send-off with local railway men attending to the body. The Knights of Pythias band led the procession to the church. The beautiful and rising star, Rev. Mary A. Safford, presided over the funeral. Lidick's popular and outgoing widow, Frances Julia Whiting Garlock Lidick, who liked to be called "Frank," accepted the casket flag, surrounded by many supporters. Frank's marriage to Lidick was her second. Weeks before Lidick's death, pharmaceutical inventor and multi-millionaire E.C. DeWitt visited Frank, his mother-in-law, to render aid, bringing his pain medicines. Dewitt came in from Chicago with his wife Cora. An elaborate, emotional obituary for Lidick was printed in the *Sioux City Journal* on June 1, 1895.

For his birthday in August 1890, Charley Brother returned to Bath to visit the girls at the orphanage and see the boys. He probably visited the family of Mrs. Metcalf and with her son-in-law, his old friend W.W. Willson, in town from Washington, DC, for her funeral. Perhaps he thought of his mother, who was taken care of by the Metcalfs as she was left an orphan all those years ago.

The newspapers tracked the details:

"Charles Brother, of Dubuque, Iowa, is visiting relatives in town." —*Plaindealer*, August 23, 1880, which also included the obituary for Mrs. Mary A. Hess Metcalf.

"Charles Brother of Sioux City, Iowa, is visiting his sister, Mrs. W. B. Pratt." —*Prattsburgh News*, August 21, 1890.

Brother returned to Sioux City and checked in with the GAR, periodically running into Frank, the pretty and outgoing widow of Captain Lidick, who was now their junior vice-president of the Women's Relief Corp, the auxiliary club. One of their top priorities was to prepare for Memorial Day services and teach patriotism and instill a love of George Washington. Brother lit up with the idea.

In September 1891, Brother headed to New York, this time making it to Elmira to visit his sister Rebecca for a couple of weeks as noted in the *Elmira Daily Gazette and Free Press* on September 16, 1891.

Another birthday on the 10th and Charles Brother turned forty-seven. A few weeks later his former in-law, Lewis Spawn, was in Sioux City, visiting from Sioux Falls, perhaps to return Brother's son Henry, now sixteen. Soon after Spawn showed up, Brother took off for Bath, this time with his sister Mary, suggesting that it was an extra special visit or reunion.

The papers continued to record Brother's whereabouts: "Charles Brother, of Sioux City, Iowa, has been spending the week with his sister's family, Mrs. W. B. Pratt." "Mr. and Mrs. P.S. Towle of Clinton, Iowa, are guests at Mr. R. M. Lyon's." (*Advocate*, Sep 15, 1891)

Charley and his son Henry returned to Iowa, leaving the girls in Bath. Henry was now living with Charley. The all-grown-up-now boy gave a speech at school in October 1891 on the topic of the value of an education in commerce. Brother and his son talked about the boy's future in the farming industry. Unlike Brother, his boy had grown attached to the way of life. They had thought about land in Pomeroy, where Esther had family. While they mulled that over, Henry took work at a local candy manufacturer and occasionally noted the parties going on down the street to one of the most popular girls, Minnie Garlock. Minnie's mother was Frank—the widow of Captain Frank Lidick—and she wanted everyone to know about her daughter's prospects and drive to "marry up." She did a fine job with her older daughter, Cora, who married a multi-millionaire, pharmaceutical wiz, E.C. DeWitt. (*Sioux City Journal*, Nov 15, 1891). A week later Mrs. E.C. DeWitt of Chicago was the guest of her mother at 722 Jones Street. (*Sioux City Journal*, Nov 22, 1891)

In November 1892, Frank mailed invitations to the marriage of her daughter, Minola, to a young banker, F.M. Wilson. The wedding was held in December. Rev. M.W. Darling, of the First Congregational Church conducted the ceremony. Minola was "a pronounced blonde" according to the *Sioux City Journal* on November 20, 1892. Minola or "Minnie" Garlock married Fleming McCormick, "a decided brunette." The wedding took place at Frank's home, located at the corner of Jones and Eighth streets per the *Sioux City Journal* on December 4, 1892.

The following winter, Brother, still in Sioux City, ran into Minnie's brother, George Garlock, who landed a job at the post office. He seemed to keep running into Frank, and probably on purpose.

That same month, February 1892, Brother entered for taxation a warranty deed based on a contract lot. He paid the Railroad Land Company for land in Pomeroy. Esther's family still had relatives living in Pomeroy by July 1897 when the *Pomeroy Herald* printed news that he desired to move back to Pomeroy.

In June 1892 Brother was still living at 211 W. 6th Street and with his son Henry. About this time Brother's friend Casin Obert announced his plans to end his business partnership with Ed Church, who was now engaged to be married. Obert was leaving Bath and joining the firm of P.S. Towle in Clinton, Iowa.

Brother and his son visited the orphanage in Bath that September. Mary was fourteen years old, Fannie twelve, and Cornelia eight. Brother most likely attended the wedding of Susan Church, the daughter of Ed Church, held at St. Thomas.

Back in Iowa, he followed the news of the annual ball for letter carriers in April 1893. Over 400 tickets were sold for the Sioux City event. The various planning committees receiving applause were listed in the

60. Davenport Orphanage in Bath, 1892. Mary (14), Fannie (12), and Cornelia (9), courtesy Steuben County Historical Society

newspaper; one of the helpers was Frank Lidick's son, George Garlock. The praise did not last long; George was fired in May.

On July 6, 1893, a tornado hit Pomeroy, destroying 80 percent of the town. This blow changed the stress level with the Spawn family.

Pomeroy Swept out of Existence

As far as heard from the calamity took the most frightful form at the village of Pomeroy, a town of about 900 population. Reports received are to the effect that the entire town, except thirty houses, was swept from the face of the earth.

—*Gazette*, Jul 7, 1893

Charley visited Bath in September, staying with his sister Rebecca. He visited the girls and went to the fair, listening to stories about the town's centennial celebration held in June.

With each visit to Bath, Brother checked in with the GAR, then shared with the boys in Iowa what was going on in both regions, keeping a pulse on politics while he completed pension forms and tried to stay in touch with the boys who could validate his claims of service. On December 28, 1893, the GAR newspaper, *The National Tribune*, printed out of Washington, DC, listed new officers for the Marine Battalion, citing the previous eighteen commissioners, including Charles Brother.

In 1894 Charley's son Henry married a second cousin, Lena Spawn: both eighteen years old, and set sights on leaving Iowa for South Dakota. Brother was on his own, but by 1895 the state census enumerator stopped by the Forth Ward in Sioux City, where he found Charles Brother living with Frank Lidick and her family: thirty-five-year-old son, George Garlock (with his occupation noted as "letter carrier") and his new wife Elizabeth or "Lizzie," age twenty, and her niece, Mabel Whiting, age nineteen. Mrs. Lidick may have been running a boarding house. Brother would have known Mrs. Lidick's older brother, Charles A. Whiting, who ran a grocery store on 4th Street. He was also a partner in a broom factory that operated on the second floor of the old Hunt School.

Charley Brother turned fifty-one in August 1895 and visited Bath, bringing his daughter Mary home. In May she graduated from Haverling School. She had good grades and a reputation of being, like her father, "brisk." She established her teacher training in Iowa, starting at the normal school that September with the top score on the entrance exam.

Brother became a grandfather in April 1896 when his son Henry and the former Lena Spawn welcomed a baby girl in South Dakota. They named her Esther.

Having moved away from the Garlock-Lidick household, Charley Brother celebrated with daughter Mary at their home at 212 9th Street. By November, Mary landed a trial as a teacher. Mrs. Frances J. Lidick still lived in town, boarding a room at 1334 Jennings with her son George H. Garlock, "a broom maker," according to the Census.

In 1897, Mary landed a permanent teaching position. Brother worked the postal route between Egan, South Dakota and Manilla, Iowa, giving him closer proximity to his granddaughter. In September, the boys in Bath told him that John Cunningham was dead. He was a brave soldier under Major Stocum's first NY Regiment and laid to rest by their mutual friends at the GAR. Known as a "character" who could not stay sober, his wife divorced him and later married Val Brother. In the end, the only one who took pity on him was Val's widow and her elderly mother.

61. Mary Brother, daughter of Charles Brother

In November Brother's childhood friend, Ed Church, died from typhoid fever. Church's daughter later married into the family of the Brother's former business partner, Parkhurst Fish, who was attached to the Belfast Mill.

In 1898 Mary landed a teaching contract. At the same meeting, the board of education set a rule that no teachers could be married, a common arrangement for the times.

That July, Brother coped with the death of friend, brother-in-law,

and former Marine, Phineas S. Towle. Age sixty-two, Towle died in Elmira, New York, having gone there with Mary for the graduation of their
son, Charles Brother Towle, who had just finished his degree with Troy
Polytechnic School. Towle died suddenly on his sister's porch while
reading the newspaper. The girls in Bath—Brother's sister Rebecca and
Towle's sister Sarah—rushed to Mary. Brother's daughter Mary headed
that way too, to stay with Rebecca for the rest of the summer.

Brother certainly recalled the kindness Towle had shown him on
the USS *Vanderbilt* when he was sick, and that same nature as he attended
to Brother when he was sick with typhoid fever when Esther was in the
asylum. Towle was a good companion. These events were on Brother's
mind when a blizzard came into town that November. "A norther raged
all day of the 21st, the high northwest gales continued until evening of
the 22nd. Snow drifted greatly and in places was five or six feet deep. It
was one of the severest blizzards in this section for many years. A cold
wave followed which continued nearly all week." (Waite, 1970)

In 1899 Brother checked in with his daughter Mary, now a teacher
at Everett School and sharing an apartment with Henry. This must have
been the time Henry and his wife Lena were not getting along.

In January the boys in Bath told Brother about the death of their old
friend, Joe Faulkner, who never woke up after a drunken binge.

Joseph P. Faulkner, of Bath, dropped dead on the street in Geneva last
Thursday. He was a printer by trade, having learned the business at Bath,
where he worked for many years. He had traveled considerably. He spent
several years on whaling vessels, where he lost his eye sight, being almost
totally blind. . . His body was sent to Bath for burial.

—*Herald*, Jan 30, 1889.

More Trouble—About the 21st January 1889, one Joseph P. Faulkner of
Bath came to Geneva, and as alleged in complaint drank to excess of one
or more of the various brands of liquor sold here. . .

—*Geneva Advertiser*, Feb 11, 1890

If Brother was still reading the Sioux City newspapers, he followed the Garlock-Lidick sagas, aware of the stress Frank was under. Despite her girls having married very well, Frank couldn't seem to help her son. In April she was mortified when George was being sued for divorce by his wife Lizzie, claiming George was abusive, drunk most of the time, and that he deserted her and their child. The divorce was reported in the *Sioux City Journal*, April 28, 1899.

In May 1899, Brother headed to Bath to participate in the Memorial Day parade. He was back with the boys at the GAR. "The line of march will be down Morris Street to Grove Cemetery to the Court House, where the address and other exercises as follows will take place."

About this time, Brother got his rail job assignment and was headed to Des Moines. I believe this is when he pulled his girls out of the orphanage. Fannie had turned nineteen in February, and Cornelia was sixteen.

"Mr. Charles Brother of Des Moines, who has spent several months in Bath, has been given his old position as chief railway mail clerk between Dubuque and Sioux City, Iowa." (*Steuben Farmer's Advocate*, May 22, 1889) In walking by Grove Cemetery, Brother may have noted the fresh dirt on the grave of Mrs. Polly Metcalf, who died in January—"the daughter of the late John Metcalf, was born and has always lived in this town. Her husband was landlord of the "Eagle" hotel 40 years ago." The tavern was on the site of the old Metcalf Tavern. (*Steuben Farmers Advocate*, Jan 28, 1889)

In December Charles Brother collected a pension of $6.00 a month based on the Act of June 27, 1890. The certificate was signed by a Civil War veteran from New Hampshire and Illinois, James L. Davenport.

From the boys in Bath, Charley was happy to hear about the congressional appointment for his old friend, W.W. Willson, who was now going to be Bath's assistant postmaster. Meanwhile Brother hosted a coming out party for his daughters Fannie and Cornelia at his home on the corner of 9th and School Street (1008 9th Street).

Brother set off the next century properly with his GAR assignment to visit the Forest Home School for George Washington's birthday. Brother's assignment for George Washington's birthday was published in the *Des Moines Daily News*.

From time to time Brother checked in with his son Henry, who was working in Sioux City and living at 816 W. 5th Street. His daughter Mary was still teaching in Sioux City and boarding at 719 Otoe. His kids updated him on the well-publicized troubles of George Garlock.

If Brother visited his children in Sioux City, he may well have stopped by to comfort Frank, who lived just a few blocks from Henry. Frances J. Lidick (Frank) was living at 214 9th Street , Sioux City, Iowa with her stepdaughter, Helen Lidick. Despite her daughters' prospects and wealth, Frank was increasingly frustrated by her son's scandals: bankruptcy, bad check writing, drunkenness, etc., but, throwing herself into girly affairs, she occupied herself with Helen's education and ambition, and turned the other way.

In July 1898 George Garlock was in trouble for forgery. When police went looking for Garlock, an officer "found Garlock secreted under a bed in the sitting room and immediately placed him under arrest and brought him to the station. He refused to talk about the matter to a *Tribune* reporter this morning. Garlock was for four years a small mail carrier in Sioux City and it is understood that he has wealthy relatives in New York." (*Gazette*, Jul 22, 1898).

In 1901 Charles Brother was still living at 1008 9th Street with Cornelia, Frances, and Mary, who was a nurse at the Des Moines Home for Friendless Children, possibly for the summers when school was not in session.

He started off the year in Des Moines with the Republican meeting and dinner at the Victoria Hotel, enjoying a bit of the spotlight on him. Showing off a prize from his family archives, Brother provided some entertainment for the night.

> The *magnificent prize banner*, which is to be presented by A.B. Cummins to Monana County Republicans Friday evening at the Victoria hotel, on behalf of the Veterans Tippecanoe Club, is on exhibition in the Harris-Emery window. It is announced that the celebrated red bandanna flag, which was carried in the campaign of 1840, has been loaned to the Tippecanoe Club by Charles Brother, of 1008 Ninth street, for exhibition at the banquet Friday night.

This flag was owned by Ira R. Pratt of Prattsburg, Steuben County, New York, and carried by him in the campaign of 1840. After the death of Mr. Pratt the flag was owned by his aunt and foster-mother, Mrs. Anna Rice, of Prattsburg, until her death in 1876. Mrs. Henry Brother, of Bath, NY, a niece of Mrs. Rice and a sister of the original owner, fell heir to the flag at that time, and kept it till her death in 1883. Her husband, Henry Brother, then kept it until his death, when his son, Charles Brother, of Des Moines, came into possession of the historic banner.

—*Des Moines Register*, Feb 7, 1901

Ira Rice Pratt, C.E., B.N.S, son of Ira and Rebecca Turner Pratt, was born at Bath, Steuben County, NY., January 10, 1822. Prepared at Franklin Academy, Prattsburgh, NY., which was in charge of Rev. Flavel S. Gaylord. His parents died when he was quite young, and he was adopted by his uncle and aunt, Burrage and Anna P. Rice, of Prattsburgh. He was always delicate, and a cold taken while on a geological excursion with his class, after his graduation, developed into consumption, of which disease he died suddenly from a hemorrhage, at his home, January 16, 1843. His father, Ira Pratt, was a prosperous merchant in Bath at an early day. His grandfather, Capt. Joel Pratt, of Spencertown, NY, near the beginning of the century settled in Prattsburgh and gave the town its name. (Rensselaer Polytechnic Institute 1887)

For George Washington's birthday lesson, Brother was assigned to visit Summit School, which was noted in the local papers.

That July, Brother and Fannie headed to Bath. She was going to spend the summer with friends in Batavia and attend the fiftieth wedding anniversary in August of Robert Moses Lyon and Rebecca Brother. The happy occasion agitated Brother, who was soon turning fifty-seven and lonely. Meanwhile, back in Sioux City, Frank Lidick rushed to her engagement party.

62. Charles Brother

Charley Brother married Frank Lidick in October in Des Moines. The newspaper printed the wrong age for the bride, hiding the fact that she was five years older. Witnesses were the couple's daughters: Fannie and Minnie.

"On Tuesday evening at 8:00 p.m., Charles Brother married Mrs. Frances Lidick at his home at 1008 Ninth Street. The Reverend Mary A.

Safford officiated. It was a quiet home wedding," stated the *Des Moines Leader* on October 24, 1901.

The following summer, Brother's wife announced that her million-aire son-in-law was planning a visit to them in Des Moines. But by November the new Mrs. Brother was upset, still getting used to Charley's daughters, who were living with them, and taking on more bad news about her son George.

Husband a Forger. Mrs. Lizzie Garlock is Granted a Divorce in the District Court.

In giving her testimony before Judge Wakefield in an action for divorce in the district court yesterday afternoon Lizzie Garlock, of this city, stated that her husband, George Garlock, was now a fugitive from authorities of the city of Racine, Wis., where he had committed forgery.

"I was asked not long ago," she said, "If I knew where he was, so that the officers might get him. He left here on account of similar trouble."

Mrs. Garlock charged her husband with extreme cruelty toward her. She said that he was an inveterate drinker and that he had taken the Keeley cure. He was a great deal worse after he took this treatment than he was before, she said. The woman said he frequently came home intoxicated and used indecent language toward her, and that the last six weeks before he deserted her he did not breath a sober breath. She said he had struck her over the head with a chair once and another time he struck her with a heavy tin dipper. She wanted the custody of their little daughter. They were married in Sioux City in 1890.

Judge Wakefield made an order granting the decree of divorce and giving the custody of the child to the plaintiff.

—Sioux City Journal, Nov 7, 1902

Charley could not comfort Frank for long because a month later he was in a wreck, injured in a train accident on Christmas Day. While parked in Keokuk on the Chicago, Rock Island, and Pacific line, Brother's mail car was struck by the Great Western Great Western freight train. Thrown back against the rear of the car, he suffered a concussion

63. Cornelia Brother, daughter of Charles Brother

to his spine. The headline in the *Des Moines Register* on December 26, 1902, read: "Serious Wreck was Imminent: Fates Were Kind and No One Was Badly Injured in Accident. Crossing Collision. Great Western Switch Engine Backs into Rock Island Passenger Engine."

During 1903, Brother experienced many days like the old hash-mark days he spent in service. People in his life came and went. In April, Frank left town for her birthday party with her friends in Sioux City. About twenty women enjoyed a three-course meal and entertaining games. Frank's daughter Minnie made the arrangements, even though she was living in Templeton. When she returned, Frank showed Charley her present: a black silk dress, trimmed in white.

On June 13, 1903, Rebecca's husband Robert Moses Lyon died in Bath at age seventy-seven. Next Brother said farewell to his son Henry, who moved to South Dakota. Fannie moved to Glidden. Charley turned to nineteen-year-old Cornelia, who was still "at home," but not for long.

In July, Fannie married John Toyne, a civil engineer in Glidden. A month later, Mary eloped with Arthur Hunt, risking her job as a teacher. In September Brother sued Chicago Great Western.

Claims $2,000 for Injuries. Charles Brother Commences and Action Against Chicago Great Western. For injuries he claims to have received as a result of the negligence of Chicago Great Western railroad employees. Chas. Brother has commenced a suit in the district court against that company to recover $2,000.

He was a mail clerk on the Rock Island road and while the train was crossing the Great Western tracks in East Des Moines he claims the Great Western train collided with his train, throwing him against the car and seriously injuring him as he has since been compelled to employ two helpers, after he recovered from his injuries. He claims to have been totally incapable for work for over a year.

—Des Moines Register, Sep 10, 1904

Brother filed an injury lawsuit against the Chicago, Rock Island & Pacific Railroad Company, seeking $15,000.

He claims that on December 25, 1902, he was a railway clerk and was traveling in a mail car pulled by the defendant company. By a violent stop he claims he was hurled to the floor, striking the end of his spinal column upon the hard wood. He claims to have sustained such injuries as will permanently injure him.

—Evening Times-Republican, Dec 17, 1904

On Wednesday, October 26, 1904, Cornelia married a young lawyer, Norman Huyck. And in November, Frank came home sick after two weeks at Minnie's. Charley went to the doctor. Despite three years after the railway accident, he was not recovered.

A blizzard struck on Christmas and shut down their household for days. (Waite, 1970)

Something had to happen to lift Brother's spirits, if only he could get out of the house. In February 1905 he accepted his assignment for educating schoolchildren on George Washington's birthday, but was distracted by his stepson George, who was arrested.

George Garlock Arrested: Former Sioux Cityan Wanted at Aurora, ILL; Passed Bad Checks Here. Broommaker admits doing so several years ago, but claims he has done nothing wrong since - Divorced wife lives in Sioux City.

—Sioux City Journal, Feb **19, 1905**

George Garlock Arrested: Man Wanted in Des Moines for Forgery is Caught in Sioux City and Will Be Brought Back. . . . His mother, Mrs. Brothers, lives at 837 W. 19th Street. Garlock worked for a time for Harrah and Stewart, and it is the firm's name which is appended to the questioned checks.

—Des Moines Register, Feb **22, 1905**

Garlock must go to Aurora first. George Garlock, Arrested in Sioux City and Wanted Here, Must Answer for Other Crimes."

—Des Moines Register, Feb **23, 1905**

> Garlock Balks a Little but Accompanies Illinois Officer After All. Didn't
> Want to be 'Cuffed' Chief Michels Sooths Him by Admitting that No One
> Could Tell Which of Them Was Culprit—What he is Wanted For.
>
> —*Sioux City Journal*, Feb 23, 1905

> Garlock is Much Wanted. Former Mail Carrier Has Charge to Answer in
> Des Moines.
>
> —*Sioux City Journal*, Feb 24, 1905

In March 1905, Brother obtained a hearing date for his case against the C.R. I. & P. Railway Company. That spring, the boys in Bath let him know about the death of his old friend, Will Dutcher. Age sixty, Dutcher had been a teller for the Farmers and Mechanics Bank and "had long been prominent in the Fire Department and also in social matters. . . For over thirty years had been one of the best-liked residents of Bath." (Corning Journal, May 31, 1905)

In Sioux City, Mary was in trouble. Someone had ratted to the school district that her real name was Mrs. Arthur Hunt. Soon, the list of lies from Arthur Hunt was coming to light, even some new to Mary. In the court case to settle bills in Sioux City and other locations, they reported that Hunt was on his third marriage. Although he eventually divorced his second wife, he was still married when he and Miss Brother tied the knot in 1904. He was also a father and being pursued for child support. When hauled into court, Mr. Hunt stated that the couple was planning a honeymoon trip to Portland, Oregon. The authorities laughed. Where was he going to get the money? Hunt filed bankruptcy. Mary skipped the interview at court and buried her face. (Corning Journal, May 31, 1905)

Brother's wife returned from a visit at her daughter's place in Templeton a week before the scandal broke. They had a new apartment by 1906, still in Des Moines. He continued to monitor his daughter Mary's troubles with the Sioux City courts: this time for an unpaid hotel bill. A judge ordered Mary to pay $33.25. When the bill collector found the couple in Seattle, Washington, the overdue invoice was returned with the words "You are a liar!" The document, supposedly written by Mary's hand, was admitted as evidence. (*Sioux City Journal*, Apr 1, 1906)

On February 17, 1907, the *Des Moines Register* reported that Brother accepted a GAR assignment to visit the Olive McHenry school to promote the memory of George Washington.

On March 22, 1907, Brother held his tongue as his wife hosted a dinner for two state senators (Democrats) and their wives. Robert C. Stirton was from Monticello, Jones County, Iowa, where Frank lived with her first husband. Brother, now sixty-two, understood what was required to have a nice dinner with politicians, talking about people of influence, letting them know they were clever. So tiresome. Shortly after the pretentious occasion, Brother sat down for an imaginary, but more real conversation with his sister Rebecca. It was her birthday.

April 1, 1907

Dear Sister,

I think it is Mark Twain who said that this is the day that reminds us of what we are every other day of the year.

But I am thinking of this particular date seventy-seven years ago — that seems a long time. Of course you cannot remember about events that happened so long ago. & you may be surprised that my memory is so much better than yours, that I can distinctly remember of going from our old home down to the old green store on the morning of April 2, 1830 —

It was a very pleasant morning, spring had come on rather earlier than usual, & Captain Smead & Deacon Fowler were working in their gardens. As I passed the Metcalfe house, Polly sang out to me, "How do you like your new sister," & I replied that she was fine & dandy (that was quite a common expression in those days) & that Aunt Julia had said that she would be the flower of the family.

Aunt Nancy McCarly [McCalla] was sweeping off her door step as I passed, & Uncle John was just going over to the hat factory on Steuben St. Mr. Bridwell was hammering away in the old blacksmith's shop, & as I neared the corner I saw [unintelligible] Benton putting on his apron preparing to begin his days work in the harness shop.

Just then I heard Mrs. Gansevoort call out across the street to Mrs. Lyon, that Mrs. Fowler had just sent word that Mrs. Brother had another girl baby, to which Mrs. Lyon replied, "O Well, I have some boys that are just about the right age for her. Ha! Ha! Ha!" & so I went on to the store.

Well, the baby grew a face (that is the way the story books run) & in the short space of two years we see her running about the house & as she steps on some fresh paint on the parlor threshold, she skips into the parlor leaving her foot print on the floor. Where I have often seen it, & where it no doubt is to this day & then in about another year we hear her say, "I'm three, Neely's four, & Dolly's five" at which we laugh. & her mother feels like shaking her.

I will have to skip a few years, not being able to remember all the details, but I know she used to scare her good little brother almost into fits by making faces at him, & also she used to catch him by the dome of his pants & carry him screaming around the room – Then on that eventful 20th of May 1851, I saw her attire for her wedding journey, as she tripped down the front stairs, & that is about all I can remember about the bride on that day. But I know the picture was vividly recalled when just 37 years afterwards I saw her youngest daughter on the, to her, equally important occasion & attired for her wedding journey, trip down the stairs in that other old home where has dwelt the mother with the boys who were "just about the right age."

That was nearly twenty years ago & since then we have gathered at the same old home (the Lyon home) to celebrate the golden anniversary of the event of May 20, 1851–

And still the time is flying. & the little girl baby has lived to see her own babies, & her baby's baby's, & her baby's baby's baby. & we have seen Aunt Julia's prediction more than verified.

Your good little brother,
Charles

A copy of this letter to Rebecca Brother Lyon was given to me by Marjorie (nee Brother) Peterson in 2013. Mrs. Gansevoort was the wife of Ten Eyck Gansevoort, who with Brother's father, Mr. Smead, and Moses H. Lyon, were among the first officers of the village. Fowler was related to Mary Beach Fowler, the wife of Capt. Joel Pratt, Brother's great grandfather. Charley Brother's sister Rebecca married Robert Moses Lyon in Bath. Captain Smead is Benjamin Smead, one of the founders of Bath and a newspaper publisher. Charles Brother was friends with his grandson, Ed Smead, a baker. Among the first dwellings of Bath were Metcalf's Tavern and the homes of McCalla, Cruger, and Ira Pratt, Charley's grandfather's home, which would later become the Brother House. Polly Metcalf Finch was Mary Metcalf, who later married Ralph Knickerbocker Finch, the well-loved teacher of the Bath Classical School who inspired Val and H.H. Brother with his sea voyage stories. Ralph K. Finch drowned in 1845. John McCalla on Morris Street was a local character and founder of the "Bachelors of Bath," who entertained everyone with his dry wit, particularly the boys who liked to hear his stories of challenging the older, family set politicians, which included Charley's father. (Ansel J. McCall, "History of Bath for the First Fifty Years," Hull, 1893)

Brother welcomed a visit from his daughter Mary that August, perhaps for his sixty-third birthday. She was coming into town from Seattle, Washington, still going by Mrs. A. M. Hunt. Soon after her stop, Charley took off for Bath.

While walking through Bath, memories of his childhood started to fall out. When he was eight years old, in 1852, he was entertained by John Stocum, who was nineteen years older than Charley, but just two years older than his brother Val. Stocum was a cabinetmaker and later became the undertaker for the soldier's home. He was attached to the Metcalf family too, marrying their girl Elizabeth. To the veterans of Bath, he offered good times on Keuke Lake with his yacht. Charles Brother sat down to write.

He submitted this story to the *Steuben Advocate*, but it was also printed in *The Plaindealer*, August 17, 1907, and *Farmer's Advocate*, August 14, 1907.

Reminiscences

Charles Brother of Des Moines, Iowa, writing to the *Advocate*, states:

I have been very interested in an article in your paper of August 7, regarding the old Bath Artillery company and its famous cannon. I remember well the old company. I can remember Captain, afterwards Colonel L. C. Whiting, Captain Stocum and Lieut. Mowers: also many of the rank and file, some of whom figured in the war of the rebellion.

Not the least of them was the drum corps of Julius Smead, Miles Terrel, Merlin Graham and Ira Edwards. Ira struck the old bass drum quite as vigorously as he pounded iron on his anvil in the old blacksmith shop. They made plenty of noise, which was music to my ears as I followed them many a mile through the streets and roads in and around Bath.

I remember well the old brass cannon "Bringold" and "Bragg" but I think they were 12-pounders. I do not remember about the target practice with them on Lake Salubria. But that was not the only time that cannon balls were fired in Steuben County, for I once saw a target practice with these same guns out on the Mitchellville road. The cannon were [sic] stationed in the field across the road from Robert Lyon's farm and a little north of the driveway leading to his house, while the target was planted at a stone quarry on the hillside on Mr. Lyon's farm. I remember that the gunners used up all their caps before the other ammunition gave out, and then the guns were primed with loose powder and fired with a red-hot iron bar and sometimes with a lighted cigar.

I remember another target practice with muskets by the same old company, held in the Lyon pasture field just east of the of the old brewery. There were several prizes awarded, —the only one I can remember being a fine double barreled shotgun won by Levi Metcalf. Some years afterwards the shotgun was lost overboard from a boat on Lake Selubria.

—*Corning Journal*, Jan 31, 1873

Brother visited Bath in August, spending time with Rebecca's daughter Anna, Mrs. Casin B. Obert, who was now a widow. She moved back to Bath after Obert's death in Clinton, Iowa. Brother visited the fresh grave of his sister Rebecca, who died in June at the age of seventy-nine.

"Mr. Charles Brother of Des Moines, Iowa, and Mrs. T.C. Wellman of Bayonne, NJ., were guests of Mrs. C.B. Pratt and family last Friday and Saturday." (*Prattsburgh News*, Aug 27, 1908)

"Mrs. Casin B. Obert and her daughter, Miss Louise Obert, who spent the summer in Bath, left Monday for their home in Clinton, Iowa." (*Steuben Courier*, Sep 18, 1908)

That winter, Brother's wife traveled often for her health. Both Frank and Charley's sister Mary encouraged him to improve too and get out of Dodge.

In 1910 he headed south and became a patient at the Army Navy Hospital in Hot Springs, Arkansas. Mary spoke up about how the hot springs cured her arthritis and gave her testimonial for the newspapers. While he tried to get better, Frank left for two months at the Lake Okoboji Inn resort.

In September 1910 someone placed a want ad in the Des Moines newspaper for a girl helper to assist with housework for at their flat at the Maryland apartments: "family of two, in a light apartment." A year later they moved to the Hotel Victoria.

Charley's son Henry, age thirty-three, was now a stock and grain buyer. His daughter Esther was now fourteen years old. Henry rented his place. By 1915, Henry Brother lived in Sioux Falls, South Dakota. The 1915 State Census noted: "Arrival Year in State (estimated) 1907." Divorced.

Charley Brother's wife, living at Minnie's apartment at the Maryland Hotel, returned to Des Moines in August from a two-month stay at Lake Okoboji Inn resort.

In 1912 Brother started off the year like always, educating the children about George Washington, this time at the Cooper School. His wife Frank was sick and getting worse. Her brother and daughters rushed her to the hospital in July. While sorting things out in a crowded apartment, Charley got news that his sister Mary died. Charley and his stepdaughters were focused on trying to make things easy for Frank, perhaps not even telling her that October that her son George was arrested for vagrancy and low-life activities.

In 1913 Charley visited the Garfield School for George Washington's
birthday. But by September he was in quite a different place. Frank died
of liver cirrhosis and was sent quickly, without flowers, to be buried with
her first husband in Monticello, ending his ties to the Garlocks.

Charley Brother looked to his children: Henry lived in Sibley, Iowa,
and was doing well as a stock trader, but with his rural life and traveling,
he could not take care of his father. Mary was still in Seattle, Washington, so she could not help. Fannie was now in Indiana with her husband
and young daughter, but her house was so small. Cornelia lived close
by in Des Moines, so she was the best option for now, but her house
was tightly packed as well with young children. Fannie thought about
moving to something bigger. So the arrangement was temporary, perhaps just for the winter to blow over the way it did for Charley Brother.

Brother's pension file dated for June 26, 1914, reported his address
at 3206 First Street in Des Moines, Iowa, where Cordelia lived. The pension office told him he had to wait until he turned seventy before he
could get an increase. He was aware by then of a fire that destroyed the
motion picture studios of Thomas Edison. The Bronx company set and
costumes were destroyed for the movie that was in production: *The Battle of Mobile Bay*. (*The New York Times*, Mar 28, 1914)

CHAPTER 12

Indiana

From his August 1914 pension records, we know that Charles Brother moved to South Bend, Indiana, to live with his daughter Fannie. About this time she was moving to Ashland Avenue near the intersection of Leland Avenue. As Brother got to know the neighborhood in his walks, he smiled when this location triggered memories of his old friend and Marine, George Leland. Brother wondered, *What ever happened to him?*

Charley's pension file has a handwritten note signed Charles Brother on his birthday, August 10, 1914, notifying the Bureau of Pensions of his new address (with Fannie) as well as his seventieth birthday, which entitled him for an increase.

The next summer, Brother visited Bath. He had plans to attend the centennial celebrations of the founding of St. Thomas Episcopal Church in July. The festivities highlighted the Brother family's contributions, and his sister Cornelia and other long-time members attended.

64. St. Thomas Episcopal Church, courtesy Steuben County Historical Society

The highlight of 1915 for Charley Brother was not the stop in Bath however, but of a train ride to Boston that August, certainly arranged for his birthday treat. He went to see a Marine. His meeting was described in the local paper.

MEET AFTER FIFTY YEARS

Charles Brother, Farragut's Orderly, Has Reunion with Old Comrade

The Worcester (Mass) Telegram *of Wednesday, Aug 4, had an interesting account of a meeting between Charles Brother, of Des Moines, Iowa, and George R. Leland, of Worcester. Both fought under Farragut in the naval conflict of Mobile bay. Mr. Brother was orderly on board the flagship Hartford and carried messages from the admiral. He was never wounded but his comrade, Mr. Leland, was wounded twice.*

Mr. Brother belongs to Crocker Post GAR. After leaving the United States navy shortly after the war, he returned to his home in the West, prepared to enter business. He has been in the railway mail service for 28 years, retiring only a short time ago.

About six months before he retired from marine duty. Mr. Brother and Mr. Leland were almost inseparable, both when on duty at the barracks and while on shore. They corresponded for some time, but finally lost track of each other. About 10 years ago Mr. Brother sent an inquiry to Post 10, concerning Mr. Leland, and since then the two old comrades have written regularly to each other.

They are going to Boston today to pass a few days, and will visit the old marine barracks at Charlestown navy yard to see if any of the old landmarks remain.

Before Mr. Brother was orderly on the Hartford he served on the Vanderbilt and also on the North Carolina, which was a receiving ship for sailors at Charlestown. He grew tired of this inactive work and volunteered for sea duty.

Mr. Leland has also served on various ships. He was on the San Jacinto which chased the Confederate privateer Alabama, also on the Wachusett and the Vanderbilt before he was detailed to Brooklyn in Farragut's squadron, and took part in the two-month blockade that preceded the fight.

The two veterans, one 72 and the other 70 years of age, appeared delighted to be with each other again. "It seems a long time since the war," said Mr. Brother, "but it doesn't seem 50 years since I saw George. I am certainly glad to be here."

Mr. Leland celebrated the "reunion of Mobile bay veterans," as he called it, by fluttering the stars and stripes from the flagstaff before his home, all day yesterday.

Mr. Brother was born and spend this early life in Bath and visited relatives here within the past few weeks.

—*Steuben Courier*, Aug 13, 1915

65. Charley Brother and his sister, Cornelia Pratt

Still high from seeing Leland, Brother returned to Prattsburgh, staying at his sister Cornelia's dairy farm in September, but she also had real business at hand: the old Pratt Homestead was approaching its centennial and it was fitting that a celebration be planned.

In 1916 Brother heard about the death of William E. Howell in Bath that February. Howell never married. He was the son of the man (Old Man Howell) who had discouraged Brother from joining the Marines.

In September, Brother learned that his daughter Cornelia gave birth a boy in Des Moines and that his son Henry, now age forty, married his second wife in Sibley, Osceola, Iowa.

In 1917 Brother visited Bath and celebrated his seventy-third birthday with old friends. His sister Cornelia, now almost ninety, was doing what she could to help with the anniversary of the Joel Pratt Homestead. Invitations were sent out and a commemorative booklet was printed (a souvenir copy is now in the family archives) that noted some of the more prominent guests in attendance, which included old family and friends with surnames that appeared in Charley Brother's diary, including Mrs. Harris, the widow of Marine T.R. "Dora" Harris. Friends knew her as the former Maggie Gregg, Josiah's sister. The *Prattsburgh News* on August 8,

1918 reported that about 140 friends "took to the hill of the Pratt Homestead and dairy farm to take part in the celebration."

Judge William W. Clark gave a speech. He was an old family friend, joining the law practice of Judge Henry Valentine Pratt, Charley Brother's nephew. Standing on the land settled by Revolutionary War Patriot Joel Pratt and with the First World War on their minds, Clark told his friends: "Our security as a nation rests not in the busy marts of trade, where selfishness too often controls the actions of men, but in the homes of the countryside, where the hills and valleys furnish the inspiration for patriotism and where the influence of Christian parents points their children the way to teach and to preach and to live. We are living today in the most heroic period of the world's history and no mortal power can read the story of the future. We beheld the most enlightened nations of the world ruthlessly assailed and their property destroyed and their men and women and children wantonly slaughtered. . ."

Taking in all of these images and affections, he said goodbye to Bath.

On November 21, 1917, Charles Brother left a note for his daughter Fannie and went for a walk.

OLD MAN TAKES LIFE IN RIVER

Charles Brother, 73 Years Old, Suicides–Believed to be Slightly Demented.

Charles Brother, 815 Ashland Ave, 73 years old, was drowned shortly before 9 o'clock Wednesday morning when he jumped into the St. Joseph river, near Marion St.

Neighbors, living near the river, say they noticed the old man walking up and down the bank for some time, and when he jumped the police were notified at once. The body was taken out of the water in less than 10 minutes, but life was extinct.

Mr. Brother was slightly demented, according to his family, and left a note which mentioned something about his being kidnapped. He had left his house less than an hour before his death.

SEEKS DEATH IN RIVER

Charles Brother Jumps into Stream Because of Ill Health.

Charles Brother, 815 Ashland Avenue, committed suicide this morning at 9:05 by jumping at the foot of Marion street. Mrs. Riggs of 729 Riverside Drive, called the police and the ambulance, in charge of Officers Cutting, Pinter and Lovegrin, rushed to the scene and soon recovered the body but life was extinct. The body taken to the McGann & Coats morgue and was identified by J.W. Toyne, a son-in-law, of the deceased. According to witnesses Mr. Brother walked back and forth on the bank of the river for some time and then took off his coat and hat and leaped into the water. . .

—*South Bend Tribune*, Nov 21, 1917

The same day that Charley Brother took his life, his son Henry welcomed a baby boy. They introduced Charles Henry Brother, who grew up to serve with the U.S. Navy in World War II.

~

Fannie's husband told the coroner's office in St. Joseph County, Indiana, that her father was increasingly frantic, hallucinating that a mob was after him. Before this horrible moment, they were finally able to get him to a doctor, her husband told the coroner, after Brother considered the boys would be with him: "The reason we gave him was, I suggested that I have some of the boys call on him and assure him that there was nothing going to happen to him. He thought that a very good idea."

Charles Brother's remains were sent to Bath. A service was held at St. Thomas Episcopal Church. He left a life insurance policy with more than enough to cover the costs of these arrangements, according to a letter from the Office of John W. Toyne, Engineer, to the Department of Interior's Bureau of Pensions on February 16, 1918.

The newspapers in New York got it wrong, instructing that Charles Brother died in Indianapolis, not South Bend. Fannie told her daughter that Charley Brother died of a heart attack while taking a walk. Fannie put his diaries, letters, stamp collection, and photographs in a box.

The boys at the Des Moines GAR honored Charles Brother during their annual memorial service. Held at the Odd Fellows Hall, fifteen chairs were draped in black and held a floral wreath for their fallen comrades throughout the year. After his name was read, the roll of a muffled drum answered, followed by a white carnation placed on his empty chair. Byron C. Ward delivered the memorial address.

"Nothing so tries a man's soul as to ask him to sacrifice himself for the good of his country. To make such a sacrifice requires true heroism; and all these men were such heroes." (*Des Moines Register*, Dec 22, 1918)

Afterword

About the time of Brother's death, Fannie had a regular place in the local newspaper for her poetry, although she did not let it be known who she was. Mindful of her husband's social standing as a city engineer or her situation as a beginner, she used playful pseudonyms: "Fran Toy" and "Ima Hen."

During the Great Depression, Fannie's only child, Peg, married. As Peg introduced grandchildren, Fannie introduced poems that were published in a book called *Indiana Poets* (Henry Harrison, 1935).

Fannie was serious when she taught her granddaughters domestic skills like dressmaking and baking pies. She always had a fresh-baked pie on hand. They routinely called out for her to tell stories about the orphanage, treasuring when they were privy to events that she *could* tell, knowing when to let her change the topic and when to back off. As they pressed her, Fannie only refined her skills at coming to a certain angle of the truth, with distraction, dancing around the bad spots. Grandma had rules.

Following Indiana poet James Whitcomb Riley, Fannie crafted her rhymes and puns. The girls treasured their Raggedy Ann dolls, inspired by Riley, and they delighted to tell their friends that their grandmother had something in common with his Little Orphan Annie.

In 1962 Fannie died at the age of eighty-two. Informally she gifted to her granddaughters only her best memories and poetry. They compiled them to share among themselves, using a yellow carpeted binder.

Highlighting the popular, the lighthearted poems, Peg and the girls wrote comments alongside the margins. They flagged the clever poems, noting with exclamation points if one poem was their personal favorite, or their mother's favorite, often adding a comment or two to explain what the poem was *really* about.

66. Fannie and her daughter Peg

You can hear her granddaughters, now grown, but still knowing what silly felt like, laughing at a kitchen table, in their cheeky dimples, reading aloud in jolly meter the poem about her indulging all her cute critters, knowing that Fannie would bring to bed with her the baby chickens when it was too cold for them to be outside, or even place them in the warm oven.

One poem was about her learning how to drive with her frightened husband. There was one about her first love; they all knew that it was a true story! It was that butcher boy who delivered meat at the orphanage; all the girls would run to the window to watch and swoon. One day the boy spoke to her, he *honest-to-God* really did, saying, "Hello, kid."

There was a poem about Frances's mother: *oh, how sad!* They knew only tiny fragments. They turned to each other to find out if anyone ever had any luck getting past her brick wall. They only knew that she lost her mother when she was five or six years old.

The girls accepted their pithy inheritance, knowing they were, even after her death, still required to follow the rules, forced to treasure these moments from their cramped position, as if they were only let in back stage, forced to stand on each other's backs, knowing they would never get to see the show from any of the good seats out front. I don't blame them for giving up, maybe they thought it was what she wanted. The girls knew better than to poke her backside, especially from the grave, where she had even more power.

When the girls found the long and heavy poem, "When Ships Come In," they set it aside. Maybe they were tired by then. At this point, Fannie's poetry was work. No one knew what to make of it.

Acknowledgments

I thank Civil War Marines expert David M. Sullivan for his scholarship and for identifying men who were with Brother. I thank the family of C. Carter Smith, Jr., especially his widow Betsy, daughter-in-law of Sidney Adair Smith. This family's early work with the diary and the Mobile Historic Preservation Society kept the story alive.

Some oral history, documents, and photographs were provided by descendants of Civil War Marines: Marjorie (nee Brother) Peterson, Claudia Boggs, Troy Hillman, Griff Towle, Lewis Darling, Nancy Pence, Mary Pat Livingston, Adrienne Sache, Wesley Moody, and David MacNair.

A thank you to archivists. The following repositories, historians, curators, and librarians provided important information: Karen M. Mason, Curator with Iowa Women's Archives, University of Iowa, Iowa City (Safford); Cherry Hill, David Fraser, and Ericka Dowell of the Lilly Library at Indiana University; Deborah Gurt, interim director for the Doy Leale McCall Rare Book and Manuscript Library, University of South Alabama. In Bath I was assisted by local historian Ron Wyatt at the St. Thomas Episcopal Church; Helen K. Brink, and Kirk House with the Steuben County Historical Society; and Bath historian Eleanor R. Silliman as well as the Bieber family of Prattsburgh, New York. Retired teacher Deanna Spitz was especially generous with her time when my timing was awful. Thanks also to Donna Eschenbrenner of the History Center in Ithaca, New York, and the librarians at Cornell University Archives; Shelly Sjovold with the Siouxland Heritage Museum for research on the Esther Brother Ward papers; Bob Allen, Mobile Historic Preservation Society in Mobile, Alabama; Curt Witcher of the Genealogy Center, Allen County Public Library in Fort Wayne, Indiana; Ontario County Historical Society, New York; Daughters of the American Revolution, especially the Bloomington, Indiana Chapter; and The Daniel Guthrie Chapter of the Indiana Society of the Sons of the American Revolution.

For publication support I thank Joe Eykholt, Karen Solheim, Robert Meitus, Ryan Scheife of Mayfly Design, miracle worker and editor Marly Cornell, Kristen Weber of iLibri Book Design, Kendall Reeves of Spectrum Creative Group, Jay Wilson, David Anderson of Index Busters, Mark Law, Clay W. Stuckey, and Nate Laible of Only Company.

Sincere thanks to Peter Barratt, Craig Symonds, Ron Burkhart, Richard Dunbar, James Alexander Thom, Karen Like, Jim Timperman, Jennifer Lewis, Susan Chapman, Sonia Henderson, Charles Laughinghouse, Susan Armeny, and my wonderful siblings, parents, and in-laws. Deep appreciation goes to my two sons and my husband, whose constant support in all kinds of weather kept me plodding.

In Fannie's poem about Charles Brother, she paints an image of him in heaven, at the pearly gates, asking St. Peter to "Make me an angel," to let him smooth the way for his granddaughter, and to "help her to see what is best." Without Fannie, we would never have known what is best—what courage and strength look like. I thank her for writing poetry and for inspiring the charismatic drive in my beautiful mother, who helped me see what is best simply by watching her, the gold standard of mothers, someone who wanted me write about the family, and, in a way, iron out those wrinkles that could never be told and those things that left her own mother in a dark knot all her life. I thank Charles, for being a true companion and angel for me. I thank him for his bravery, sacrifices, and diary of course, but mostly for holding his end for as long and as nobly as he could. His life renewed my faith in obstacles, and I no longer need anything to smooth the way.

Bibliography

Aldrich, Lewis Cass, and George S. Conover. 1893. *History of Ontario County, New York*. Syracuse, NY: D. Mason & Co.

Altschuler, Glenn C., and Stuart M. Blumin. 2000. *Rude Republic: Americans and Their Politics in the Nineteenth Century*. Princeton: Princeton University Press.

Babbitt, John S., and Sue Babbitt. 2010. *Steuben County* . Charleston: Archadia Publishing.

Barnes, Robert William. 1978. *Maryland Marriages, 1778–1800*. Baltimore, MD: Genealogical Pub. Co.

Barratt, Peter. 2018. *Farragut's Captain: Percival Drayton, 1861–1865*. Lulu Publishing Services.

Beckman, E. H. n.d. *History of Grundy County, Iowa, from the earliest records up to July 4, 1876; . . . collection of. . . information upon. . . its settlement. . . anecdotes*. Grundy Center, Iowa: Atlas Print.

Benson, William Shepherd, James J. Walsh, Edward J. Hanna Hanna, and Constantine E. McGuire. 1923. *Catholic Builders of the Nation: A Symposium on the Catholic Contribution to the Civilization of the United States*. Boston, Massachusetts: Continental Press.

Bonner, John, George William Curtis, Henry Mills Alden, Samuel Stillman Conant, Montgomery Schuyler, John Foord, Richard Harding Davis, et al. 1860. "View of Broadway, Opposite Fulton Street, New York." *Harper's Weekly*. [New York], February 18.

Bowman, Fred Q. 1987. *10,000 Vital Records of Eastern New York, 1777–1834*. Baltimore, MD: Genealogical Pub. Co.

Briggs, Erasmus. 1883. *History of the Original Town of Concord: Being the Present Towns of Concord, Collins, N. Collins, and Sardinia, Erie County, New York*. Rochester, NY: Union and Advertiser Co.'s Print.

Brother, Cornelia. 1846. "Letter to Rebecca P. Brother." July 22.

Brother, Valentine. 1796. *Val. Brother's Journal from Infancy to 1796*. Frederick, MD.

Brumbaugh, Gaius Marcus. 1915. *Maryland Records, Colonial, Revolutionary, County and Church, from original sources*. Baltimore, MD: Williams & Wilkins.

Burhans Genealogy : Descendants from the First Ancestor in America, Jacob Burnhans, 1660, and his Son, Jan Burhans, 1663, to 1893. New York, NY: Samuel Burhans. http://catalog .hathitrust.org/api/volumes/oclc/14403412.html.

Callahan, Edward W. 1969. *List of Officers of the Navy of the United States and of the Marine Corps from 1775 to 1900: comprising a complete register of all present and former* commissioned, warranted, and appointed officers of the United States Navy, and of the Marine Corps. . . New York: L.R. Hamersly Co.

Carroll, Dillon Jackson, and Stephen Berry. 2016. *Scourge of War: Mental Illness and Civil War Veterans.* University of Georgia. Athens, Georgia. http://purl.galileo .usg.edu/uga_etd/carroll_dillon_j_201608_phd.

Chapman, F. W. 1864. *The Pratt family: or, The Descendants of Lieut. William Pratt, one of the First Settlers of Hartford and Say-Brook, with Genealogical Notes of John Pratt, of Hartford; Peter Pratt, of Lyme; John Pratt (Taylor) of Say-Brook.* Hartford, Conn.: Case, Lockwood and Co.

Child, Hamilton. 1867. *Gazetteer and Business Directory of Ontario County, N.Y., for 1867–8.* Syracuse, NY: Printed at the Journal Office.

Child, Hamilton. 1868. *Gazetteer and business directory of Steuben County, N.Y. for 1868–9.* Syracuse, NY: Printed at the Journal Office.

Church, Frank L., James Pickett Jones, and Edward F. Keuchel. 1975. *Civil War Marine: a Diary of the Red River Expedition, 1864.* Washington DC: History and Museums Division, Headquarters, U.S. Marine Corps.

Churchman Associates, Inc. 1908. *The Churchman 24.*

City of New York. 1865. *Manual of the Corporation of the City of New York.* New York, NY.

Clark, Will L., and J. E. Norris. 1890. *History of the Counties of Woodbury and Plymouth, Iowa, including an Extended Sketch of Sioux City, Their Early Settlement and Progress to the Present Time.* Chicago, IL: A. Warner & Co. https://archive.org/details/history ofcountie00warn.

Clayton, W. W. 1879. *History of Steuben County, New York, with Illustrations and Biographical Sketches of Some of its Prominent Men and Pioneers.* Philadelphia: Lewis, Peck & Co.

Cleveland, Stafford Canning, and Thelma E. Burton Bootes. 1873. *History and Directory of Yates County: Containing a Sketch of its Original Settlement by the Public Universal Friends, the Lessee Company and Others, with an Account of Individual Pioneers. . .* Penn Yan, NY: S.C. Cleveland.

Cooley, Thomas McIntyre, and Thomas Curtis Clarke. 1890. *The Railways of America; Their Construction, Development, Management, and Appliances.* London: J. Murray.

Corbit, Robert McClain. 1910. *History of Jones County, Iowa, Past and Present.* Chicago, IL: S.J. Clarke Publishing Co.

Crosby, Nathan. 1858. *Annual Obituary Notices of Eminent Persons Who Have Died in the United States. For 1857[-1858].* Boston, MA: Phillips, Sampson and Company.

Cutler, Deborah W., and Thomas J. Cutler. 2005. *Dictionary of Naval Terms.* Annapolis, MD: Naval Institute Press.

Cutter, William Richard. 1912. *Genealogical and Family History of Central New York: A Record of the Achievements of Her People in the Making of a Commonwealth and the Building of a Nation.* New York, NY: Lewis Historical Pub. Co.

Daughters of the American Revolution. 1911. *Directory of the National Society of the Daughters of the American Revolution.* Washington, DC: Memorial Continental Hall.

———. 1914. *Lineage Book.* Pittsburgh, PA: Press of Pierpont, Siviter & Company.

———. 1903. *Lineage Book, Vol. XXXIX.* Harrisburg, PA.

———. 1895. *Lineage book: National Society of the Daughters of the American Revolution.* Harrisburg, PA: Harrisburg Publishing Company.

_____. 1899. *Lineage Book: National Society of the Daughters of the American Revolution, Vol 8*. Harrisburg, PA: Harrisburg Publishing Company.

De Neui, Donald, and Carolyn De Neui. 1999. *Circles of Time: The Story of the Homestead of Johannes & Frauke de Neui, 1865 to 1999*. Eldora, Iowa (207 Washington St., Eldora 50627): D. and C. De Neui.

Department of the Navy. 1894–1922. *Official Records of the Union and Confederate Navies, 1861–1865, Series 1, No. 21* . Washington, DC: United States Navy.

Doty, Lockwood R. 1925. *History of the Genesee Country (western New York) Comprising the Counties of Allegany, Cattaraugus, Chautauqua, Chemung, Erie, Genesee, Livingston, Monroe, Niagara, Ontario, Orleans, Schuyler, Steuben, Wayne, Wyoming and Yates. . .* Chicago, IL: S.J. Clarke Pub. Co.

Drayton, Percival. 1906. *Naval letters from Captain Percival Drayton, 1861-1865*; printed from the original manuscripts presented to the New York Public Library by Miss Gertrude L. Hoyt. New York.

Dunham, Valgene L. 2015. *Gregory's New York Brigade: Blue-Collar Reserves in Dusty Blue Jackets*. Archway Publishing.

Duvall, J. A. 2015. *Frederick County Maryland Slave Manumissions 1748–1867*. http://mdh mapping/wp-content/uploads/2018/09/Frederick-County-Manumissions-1748 –1867.pdf.

Ellis, Franklin, and Nash, E.A. 1879. *History of Cattaraugus County, New York*. Philadelphia, PA: L.H. Everts.

Faulkner, Joseph P. 1878. *Eighteen Months on a Greenland Whaler. New York*. New York, NY: Joseph P. Faulkner.

Federal Archives and Records Center (Bayonne, N.J.), and Genealogical Society of Utah. 2000. *Index (soundex) to naturalization petitions, 1792–1906*. North Salt Lake, UT: HeritageQuest.

Federal Publishing Company. 1908. *The Union Army : A History of Military Affairs in the Loyal States, 1861-65 : Records of the Regiments in the Union Army, Cyclopedia of Battles, Memoirs of Commanders and Soldiers*. Madison, WI: Federal Pub. Co. https://catalog.hathitrust.org/api/volumes/oclc/1473658.html.

Field, Ron. 2004. *American Civil War Marines 1861–65*. Oxford, England: Osprey Publishing.

Fox, Dorus M. 1895. *History of Political Parties, National Reminiscences, and the Tippecanoe Movement*. Des Moines, IA: Iowa Print. Co. http://catalog.hathitrust.org/api/ volumes/oclc/6551346.html.

Friend, Jack. 2001. *West Wind, Flood Tide: The Battle of Mobile Bay*. Annapolis, MD: Naval Institute Press.

Furmansky, Dyana Z. 2010. *Rosalie Edge: Hawk of Mercy: The Activist Who Saved Nature from Conservationists*. Athens, Georgia: The University of Georgia Press.

Gable, Walt. 2017. "Looking Back: Crowds Turned Out for the Marquis de Lafayette," *Finger Lake Times*. June 22. www.fltimes.com.

Genealogy Trails. n.d. http://genealogytrails.com/ny/steuben/gazette_history_bath .htm.

Genoways, T., and H.H. Genoways. 2001. *A Perfect Picture of Hell: Eyewitness Accounts by Civil War Prisoners from the 12th Iowa*. Iowa City, IA: University of Iowa Press.

Gregg, Josiah. 2013. *The Diary of a Civil War Marine: Private Josiah Gregg*. Edited by Wesley Moody and Adrienne Sachse. Lanham, MD: The Rowman & Littlefield Publishing Group, Inc.

Guardianship Records 1814–1840. n.d. http://genealogytrails.com/ny/steuben/guardian shiprecords.html.

Gue, Benjamin F. 1903. *History of Iowa from the Earliest Times to the Beginning of the Twentieth Century*. New York, NY: The Century History Company.

Hakes, Hon. Harlo, and Lewis Cass Adrich. 1896. *Landmarks of Steuben County, New York*. Syracuse, NY: D. Mason & Co.

Harrison, firm, publishers. 1935. *Indiana Poets*. New York, NY: Henry Harrison.

Heitman, Francis B. 1965. *Historical Register and Dictionary of the United States Army, from its Organization, September 29, 1789 to March 2, 1903*. Urbana, IL: University of Illinois Press.

Herrmann, E. C. 1998. *Yeoman in Farragut's Fleet: The Civil War Diary of Josiah Parker Higgins*. Carmel: Guy Victor Publications.

Hillman, Troy A., and Joan Hillman-Hill. 2019. *The Diaries of George H. Bandfield Civil War Marine*. Hindale (NY): Troy Hillman and Joan Hill.

History and Business Directory of Madison County, Iowa Containing a Complete History of the County; Together with a Description of its Natural Resources, and Sketches of its Public Buildings, Schools, Churches, Prominent Citizens, &c. Des Moines. 1869. J.J. Mills & Davies & Company.

History of the Original Town of Concord: Being the Present Towns of Concord, Collins, N. Collins, and Sardinia, Erie County, New York. 1883. Rochester, NY, NY: Union and Advertiser Company.

Holdcraft, Jacob Mehrling. 1985. *Names in Stone: 75,000 Cemetery Inscriptions from Frederick County, Maryland, Vol. 1*. Baltimore: Genealogical Publishing Co., Inc.

Holley, O. L., George Roberts Perkins, and John Disturnell. 1845–6. *The New-York State Register for 1845 : Containing an Almanac for 1845-6. : With Political, Statistical, and Other Information Relating to the State of New-York and the United States. : Also, a Complete List of County Officers, Attorneys, &c. : The National Register Contains a Full List of United States Government Officers, &c*. J. Disturnell: C. Van Benthuysen and Co. http://catalog.hathitrust.org/api/volumes/oclc/80033519.html.

Hoyle, Edmond. 1830. *Hoyle's Improved Edition of the Rules for Playing Fashionable Games: Containing Copious Directions for Whist, Quadrille, Piquet . . . Together with an Analysis of the Game of Chess and an Engraved Plate for the Instruction of Beginners*. New York, NY: W.C. Borradaile. http://catalog.hathitrust.org/api/volumes/oclc/6407172.html.

Hull, Nora. 1893. *The Official Records of the Centennial Celebration, Bath, Steuben County, New York, June 4, 6, and 7, 1893*. Edited by Noral Hull. Bath: Press of the Courier Co.

Hurlbut, Henry H. 1888. *The Hurlbut Genealogy: or, Record of the Descendants of Thomas Hurlbut, of Saybrook and Wethersfield, Conn., Who Came to America as Early as the Year 1637: with Notices of Others not Identified as his Descendants*. Albany, NY: J. Munsell's Sons. http://catalog.hathitrust.org/api/volumes/oclc/7260663.html.

Hutchins, Stephen C., and Edgar A. Werner. 1879. *Civil List and Constitutional History of the Colony and State of New York*. Albany, NY: Weed, Parsons & Co.

Iowa State Agricultural Society. 1876. *Report of the Secretary of the Iowa State Agricultural Society, for the year*. Des Moines, IA: [The Society].

Jackson, Mary Smith Jackson, Edward F. 1998. *Death Notices from Steuben County, New York newspapers, 1797–1884*. Bowie, MD: Heritage Books.

Jeffrey, Julie Roy. 1991. *Converting the West: A Biography of Narcissa Whitman*. Norman, OK: University of Oklahoma Press.

Jericho, Vt. Historical Committee, and Chauncey H. Hayden. 1916. *The History of Jericho, Vermont*. Burlington, VT: Free Press Printing Co.

Jewett and Company, John P. 1859. *Annual Obituary Notices of Eminent Persons Who Have Died in the United States for 1858*. 300–301.

Johnson, Harry, and Frederick S. Lightfoot. 1980. *Maritime New York in Nineteenth-Century Photographs*. New York, NY: Dover Publications.

Johnson, William W. 1884. *Clarke-Clark Genealogy: Records of the Descendants of Thomas Clarke, Plymouth, 1623–1697*. North Greenfield, WI. http://catalog.hathitrust.org/api/volumes/oclc/10485238.html.

Johnston, Charles Ernest. 1900. *Genealogical Record of the Descendants of Peter Johnston : Who Came to America From Lockerby, Scotland, in the Year 1773, and Settled in Wilton, N.Y. Also a Short History of the Clan of Johnston, of Annandale*. Washington, DC: Mitchell. http://catalog.hathitrust.org/api/volumes/oclc/6675509.html.

Leavitt, Jonathan, et al. 1837. *The New York Annual Register for the Year of our Lord 1837: Containing an Almanac; Civil and Judicial List; with Political, Statistical, and other info. . .* New York, NY: J. Leavitt.

Levy, M. 1857. *A Topographical Map of Steuben Co., New York, from Actual Surveys*. Philadelphia: J.E. Gillette. https://lccn.loc.gov/2013593234.

Levy, M., John E. Gillette, and Robert Pearsall Smith. 1857. *A Topographical Map of Steuben Co., New York: from actual surveys*. Philadelphia, PA. https://lccn.loc.gov/2013593234.

Livingston, E. A. "Bud." 2012. *Brooklyn and The Civil War*. Charleston, SC: The History Press.

Lossing, Benson John, and Woodrow Wilson. 1912. *Harper's Encyclopedia of United States History from 458 A.D. to 1912*. New York and London: Harper Bros.

Main, William. 1899. *Charles Williamson: A Review of His Life*. Perth, Scotland: Cowan & Co. https://archive.org/details/charleswilliamso00main/page/n7

Martin, John H. 2005. "Saints, Sinners and Reformers: The Burned-Over District Re-Visited." *The Crooked Lake Review*. Fall. http://www.crookedlakereview.com/book/saints_sinners/martin4.html.

McKinley, Alexander to Samuel Francis du Pont, 1864-09-18, Item WMSS 9-16430, Winterthur Manuscripts (Accession WMSS), Hagley Museum & Library, Wilmington, DE 19807

McIlhany, Hugh Milton. 1903. *Some Virginia Families: Being Genealogies of the Kinney, Stribling, Trout, McIlhany, Milton, Rogers, Tate, Snickers, Taylor, McCormick, and Other Families of Virginia*. Staunton, VA: Stoneburner & Prufer. https://archive.org/details/somevirginiafami00mcil/page/n215/mode/2up.

McMaster, Guy H. 1853. *History of the Settlement of Steuben County, NY; Including Notices of the Old Pioneer Settlers and Their Adventures*. Bath, NY: R.S. Underhill & Co.

Melendy, Peter. 1893. *Historical Record of Cedar Falls, the Garden City of Iowa: Containing a Brief History of Iowa, of Black Hawk County, and a Full and Complete Description of*

Industrial and Picturesque Cedar Falls. Cedar Falls, IA: P. Melendy. http://catalog
.hathitrust.org/api/volumes/oclc/23874937.html.

Miller, James Alexander. 1897. The History of the Presbytery of Steuben: Including that
of all the Other Presbyteries to which the Churches of Steuben and Allegany Counties have
Belonged, Notices of Ministers, Elders, Missionaries, Sketches of the Existing Churches of
Presbytery, . . .Angelica: Allegany County Republican Press.

Milo B. Stevens & Co. 1888. The Soldiers' Manual : A Handbook of Useful and Reliable
Information, Showing Who Are Entitled to Pensions, Increase, Bounty Pay, etc. https://
collections.countway.harvard.edu/onview/items/show/6047.

Mulford, Uri. 1922. Pioneer Days and Later Times in Corning and Vicinity, 1789–1920.
Corning, NY: The author. http://catalog.hathitrust.org/api/volumes/oclc/654
7760.html.

New York (State), Adjutant General's Office. 1864. A Record of the Commissioned Officers, Non-commissioned Officers, and Privates, of the Regiments which were Organized in
the State of New York and Called into the Service of the United States to Assist in Suppress-
ing the Rebellion. . . Albany, NY: Comstock & Cassidy, Printers. https://archive.org/
details/cu31924092925167.

Noel, John V., and Edward L. Beach. 1988. Naval Terms Dictionary. Annapolis, MD:
Naval Institute Press.

Oviatt, Miles M. 1998. A Civil War Marine at Sea: The Diary of Medal of Honor Recipient
Miles M. Oviatt. Edited by Mary P. Livingston. Shippensburg: The White Mane
Publishing Company.

Paasch, Capt. Heinrich. 2014. Paasch's Illustrated Marine Dictionary. New York, NY:
Skyhorse Publishing.

Political Graveyard. n.d. www.politicalgraveyard.com.

Porter, David D. 1886. The Naval History of the Civil War by Admiral David D. Porter, U.S.
Navy. New York: Sherman Publishing Company.

Powell, William Henry, and Edward Shippen. 1892. Officers of the Army and Navy
(Regular) Who Served in the Civil War. Philadephia, PA: L.R. Hamserly & Company.
https://archive.org/details/officersofarmyna00powe/page/n4/mode/2up.

Proceedings. 1882. National Education Association of the United States.

"Railway Mail Service: A Review of the Workings of This Important Branch of the
Postal Department." 1885. Sioux City Journal. December 12.

Railway Purchasing Agent Company. 1891. Official Railway List: A Complete Directory
of the Presidents, Vice Presidents, General Mangers and Assistants of Railways in North
America. And Handbook of Useful Information for Railway Men. Railway Purchasing
Agent Company .

Reed, Avery H. 1958. Boogher Family Later Genealogy, Embracing the Lineage of 13 Boogher
children: Descendants of Nicholas Boogher and Rebecca Davis Coombs (Boogher). Charlot-
tesville, VA: A.H. Reed.

Rensselaer Polytechnic Institute. 1887. Biographical Record of the Officers and Graduates
of the Rensselaer Polytechnic Institute, 1824–1886. Edited by Henry B Nason. W.H.
Young.

S.J. Clarke Publishing Company. 1902. A Biographical Record of Calhoun County, Iowa.
New York and Chicago: S.J. Clarke Pub. Co. http://www.accessible.com/accessible/
preLog?Browse=BIA000736.

_____. 1898. *The Biographical Record of Kane County, Illinois*. Chicago, IL: S.J. Clarke. http://www.accessible.com/accessible/preLog?Browse=BIL000108.

Scharf, J. Thomas 1843-1898. Publication: Philadelphia : L.H. Everts, 1882. 1882. *History of Western Maryland: Being a History of Frederick, Montgomery, Carroll, Washington, Allegany, and Garrett Counties from the Earliest Period to the Present Day; Including Biographical Sketches of Their Representative Men, Vol. 1*. Philadelphia: L.H. Everts.

Schermerhorn, Richard, Jr. 1914. *Schermerhorn Genealogy and Family Chronicles*. New York, NY: Tobias A. Wright.

Schuyler, Hartley & Graham. 1985. *Illustrated Catalog of Civil War Military Goods: Union weapons, Insignia, Uniform Accessories, and Other Equipment*. New York, NY: Dover Publications.

Sedgwick Brothers and Stilson. 1887. *Map of Black Hawk County, Iowa*. Philadelphia, PA: E.W. Smith & Co., Map Publishers.

Seneca Presbyterian Church (Stanley, NY). 1942. *Seneca Presbyterian Church, "Old Number Nine," 135th Anniversary: 1807–1942*. Stanley, NY: Seneca Messenger.

Shaffer, Stefanie R. 1998. *Inhabitants of Frederick County, Maryland, Vol 1. 1750–1790*. Westminster, MD: Family Line Publications.

Shanks, Charles G. 1879. *The State Government for 1879: Memorial Volume of the New Capitol, Being Sketches of the Old and New Capitols, and Biographies of the State Officers and Members of the Legislature*. Albany, NY: Weed, Parsons.

Du Pont, Samuel Francis, and John D. Hayes. 1969. *Samuel Francis Du Pont: a selection from his Civil War letters*. Ithaca, N.Y.: Eleutherian Mills Historical Library.

Simmons, Rev. William, Henry McNeal Turner, and A.G. Haven. 1887. *Men of Mark: Eminent, Progressive and Rising*. Cleveland, OH: Geo M. Rewell & Company. https://archive.org/details/06293247.4682.emory.edu/page/n763/mode/2up.

Smith, C. Carter. 1964. *Two Naval Journals, 1864, at the Battle of Mobile Bay: the Journal of Mr. John C. O'Connell, CSN, on the C.S.S. Tennessee, and the Journal of Pvt. Charles Brother, USMC, on the U.S.S. Hartford*. Chicago, IL: Wyvern Press of S.F.E., Inc.

Spears, John Randolph. 1905. *David G. Farragut*. Philadelphia: G.W. Jacobs & Company.

St. Joseph Saturday Herald (St. Joseph, MI). 1886. "Obituary." May 22.

Stellwag Von Carion, Karl. 1873. *Treatise on the Disease of the Eye, Including the Anatomy of the Organ*. New York, NY: William Wood & Co. https://archive.org/details/treatise ondisea00carigoog/page/n11/mode/2up.

Steuben County Bicentennial Commission (Steuben County, NY). 1996. *Steuben County: the First 200 Years: A Pictorial History*. Virginia Beach, VA: Donning Co.

Steuben Farmers' Advocate. 1915. "Complete History of Babcock Hollow School District No. 11: From the Time of the First Settler to the Present Events, Covering a Period of Over 122 Years." December 8. http://www.fultonhistory.com.

Stout, Neil R. 1972. "Excerpts from John Howe's Smiggler's Journal." 1954. *Vermont History. [Burlington]: Vermont Historical Society*. Vermont Historical Society 40(4):262.

Sulivan, David M. 1997. *The United States Marine Corps in the Civil War–The Second Year*. Shippensburg: White Mane Publishing Company.

_____. 2019. *Marines of the Civil War: The Officers, Honors, Records, and Regulations*. Morrisville, NJ: Lulu Press, Inc.

_____. 2000. *The United States Marine Corps in the Civil War–The Final Year.* Shippensburg, PA: White Mane Books.

_____. 1997. *The United States Marine Corps in the Civil War–The First Year.* Shippensburg, PA: The White Mane Publishing Company.

_____. 1998. *The United States Marine Corps in the Civil War–The Third Year.* Shippensburg, PA: The White Mane Publishing Company.

Sullivan, James, E. Melvin Williams, Edwin P. Conklin, and Benedict Fitzpatrick. 1927. *History of New York State, 1523–1927.* New York: Lewis Historical Pub. Co.

The Baltimore Sun (Baltimore, MD). n.d.

The Gazette (Cedar Rapids, IA). n.d.

Towle, Mary Brother. n.d. "Brother Towle's Family Notebook." Clinton, IA.

Toyne, Frances. n.d. "When Ships Come In." Indiana.

Treicher, Bill. Oct, 1989. "What Manner of People Started Franklin Academy?" *The Crooked Lake Review.*

Tucker, Cynthia Grant. 1994. *Prophetic Sisterhood: Liberal Women Ministers of the Frontier, 1880–1930.* Bloomington, IN: Indiana University Press.

Turner, O. 1851. *History of the Pioneer Settlement of Phelps and Gorham's Purchase, and Morris' Reserve: Embracing the Counties of Monroe, Ontario, Livingston, Yates, Steuben, most of Wayne and Allegany, and parts of Orleans, Genesee, and Wyoming. . .* Rochester, NY: William Alling.

Union Publishing Company. 1883. *History of Butler and Bremer Counties, Iowa together with. . . . Biographies of Representative Citizens. History of Iowa.* Springfield, IL: Union Pub. Co.

United States. 1892. *Official Register of the United States, Containing a List of the Officers and Employees in the Civil, Military, and Naval Service on the First of July, 1891; Together with a List of Vessels Belonging to the United States. Volume II.* http://docs.newsbank .com/select/serialset/111C8EF058174838.html.

United States Navy, Robert L. Scheina, George K McCuistion. 1971. *Civil War Naval Chronology, 1861–1865.* Washington: Department of the Navy, United States of American.

United States. 1897. *Official Register of the United States: Containing a List of Officers and Employés in the Civil, Military, and Naval Service.* Washington, DC: G.P.O.

_____. 1885. *Official register of United States: Containing List of Officers and Employees in Civil, Military, and Naval Service.* Washington, DC: U.S. G.P.O.

Waite, Paul J. 1970. "Outstanding Iowa Storms." *Annals of Iowa* (Iowa State Historical Dept., Division of Historical Museum and Archives, etc.) 40(3): 194–209. https://ir.uiowa.edu/

Wall, Caleb A. 1896. *The Historic Boston Tea Party of December 16, 1773. Its men and objects: incidents leading to, accompanying, and following the throwing overboard of the tea. Including a short account of the Boston Massacre of March 5, 1770. With. . .* Worcester: Press of F.S. Blanchard.

Walling, Henry Francis. 1852. *Map of Ontario County, New York: from Actual Surveys.* Philadelphia:. Philadelphia, PA: John E. Gillett. https://www.loc.gov

Watson, John Crittenden. 1916. "*Farragut and Mobile Bay—personal reminiscences.*" http://catalog.hathitrust.org/api/volumes/oclc/4474543.htm.

Weaver, James B. 1912. *Past and Present of Jasper County, Iowa.* Indianapolis, Indianapolis, Ind: B.F. Bowen & Co.

Weinfeld, Daniel R. 2012. *The Jackson County War: Reconstruction and Resistance in Post-Civil War Florida.* Tuscaloosa: University of Alabama Press. http://site.ebrary.com/id/10538032.

Welles, Gideon, and Edgar Thaddeus Welles. 1911. *Diary of Gideon Welles, Secretary of the Navy under Lincoln and Johnson.* Boston, MA: Houghton Mifflin Co. https://archive.org/details/diaryofgideonwel02well.

Welsh, Robert L. 2006. *The Presbytery of Seattle, 1858–2005: The "Dream" of a Presbyterian Colony in the West.* Philadelphia: XLibris Corp.

Western Historical Co. 1879. *The History of Jones County, Iowa, Containing a History of the County, its Cities, Towns, &c., Biographical Sketches of Citizens. . . History of the Northwest, History of Iowa.* Chicago: Western Historical Company.

Whittelsey, Charles Barney, and Walter Wilcox Pratt. 1900. *The Ancestry and the Descendants of John Pratt of Hartford, Conn.* Hartford: The Case, Lockwood & Brainard Company.

Wolfe, Patrick B. 1911. *Wolfe's History of Clinton County, Iowa.* Indianapolis, IN: B.F. Bowen. http://catalog.hathitrust.org/api/volumes/oclc/3582817.html.

Yates, John R., and Thomas Yates. 2015. *The Boston Marine Barracks: A History, 1799–1974.* Jefferson, NC: McFarland & Company, Inc.

Index

About the Author

Christine Friesel has a BA from Hanover College and an MLS from Indiana University. In the second grade she won a prize for her writing, allowing her to meet an author who was giving a lecture at the public library. He told her to never stop writing. She did not. A diarist for forty-five years and a genealogist for forty, Friesel has chronicled life as a wife, mother, and reference librarian. She has dedicated her twenty-five-year career at Monroe County Public Library to running with people's tough questions, often about lost ancestors. With her conscientious attention to detail and focus on historical accuracy, Friesel enjoys researching to near exhaustion to achieve a satisfying result.

She lives with her husband in Bloomington, Indiana, where they raised two boys. She enjoys a vast landscape with a wide-angle view of the weather and her tolerant neighbors—Angus cows and those in a graveyard, where she is known to run and greet the dead.

Made in United States
North Haven, CT
27 April 2022